P9-CBI-925

A TORAH COMMENTARY FOR OUR TIMES

VOLUME I : GENESIS

HARVEY J. FIELDS

Illustrations by
GIORA CARMI

UAHC PRESS · New York, New York

For
Norman and Reva Fields
Joseph and Reva Sandler

They taught Torah diligently to their children

Library of Congress Cataloging-in-Publication Data
Fields, Harvey J.
A Torah commentary for our times / Harvey J. Fields ;
illustrations by Giora Carmi.
    p.   cm.
Includes bibliographical references.
Contents: v. 1. Genesis.
ISBN 0–8074–0308–3 (v. 1)
1. Bible. O.T. Pentateuch—Commentaries. [1. Bible. O.T.
Pentateuch.]   I. Karmi, Giora, ill.   II. Title.
BS1225.3.F46   1990
222'.1077—dc20   89–28478
                                          CIP
                                          AC

Copyright © 1990 by Harvey J. Fields
Manufactured in the United States of America
10   9   8   7   6   5   4   3   2   1

Feldman Library

THE FELDMAN LIBRARY FUND was created in 1974 through a gift from the Milton and Sally Feldman Foundation. The Feldman Library Fund, which provides for the publication by the UAHC of selected outstanding Jewish books and texts, memorializes Sally Feldman, who in her lifetime devoted herself to Jewish youth and Jewish learning. Herself an orphan and brought up in an orphanage, she dedicated her efforts to helping Jewish young people get the educational opportunities she had not enjoyed.

In loving memory of my beloved wife Sally
"She was my life, and she is gone;
She was my riches, and I am a pauper."

"Many daughters have done valiantly,
but thou excellest them all."

Milton E. Feldman

Contents

Acknowledgments vii

INTRODUCTIONS

I · Sparks, Fragments, Meanings: A Reader-Friendly Introduction 3

II · Turn It and Turn It!: Introducing the Torah Commentators 7

THE TORAH PORTIONS OF GENESIS

Parashat Bereshit 19
  God's creation is a blessing
  Humanity is responsible for the world
  Adam's and Eve's expulsion from Eden
  Human beings are responsible for one another

Parashat Noach 28
  One righteous person can save the world
  Ingredients for destroying the world
  Sources of human unhappiness and confusion

Parashat Lech-Lecha 36
  Defining "leadership"
  The importance of honesty
  How to settle disagreements
  The mitzvah of rescuing captives
  Circumcision in Jewish tradition

Parashat Vayera 44
  The art of hospitality
  Consequences of injustice
  "Loyalty" to God

Parashat Chaye Sarah 53
Jewish mourning practices
Purchasing at the full price
Defining "beauty"
The meaning of "love"

Parashat Toledot 60
Jealousy between siblings; stereotypes and prejudice
Favoritism by parents
Intermarriage

Parashat Vayetze 71
The role of angels in the Torah
Proper and improper prayer
Dealing with dishonest people

Parashat Vayishlach 80
Confronting "power"
Wrestling with ourselves
Responding to rape

Parashat Vayeshev 91
Hostility between siblings
Delivering what is promised; embarrassing others
Measuring loyalty and success

Parashat Miketz 100
Interpreting dreams
Choosing between revenge and caring
Choosing between death and survival

Parashat Vayigash 108
Speaking out for justice
Achieving reconciliation between enemies
Fearing the stranger
Economic planning and justice

Parashat Vayechi 119
Jewish burial practices
Making "honest" evaluations; more on "leadership"
Lying in the cause of peace

Glossary of Commentaries and Intepreters 127
Bibliography 133

Acknowledgments

Just over thirty years ago, I journeyed to Jerusalem in search of teachers who might open the gates of Torah and its wisdom to an inquiring student. By that time I was convinced, as I remain to this day, that the Torah and its centuries of interpretation are a fabulous treasure of the human spirit.

Appreciating that "treasure," however, requires the creativity and partnership of teachers and students. My own journey has been enriched by many with whom I have shared the joy of Torah study.

Noteworthy among them are: Dov Bin Nun, Rabbi Zev W. Gotthold, Nehama Leibowitz, Rabbi Sheldon Blank, Rabbi Samuel Sandmel, Rabbi Jakob J. Petuchowski, and Rabbi Roland B. Gittelsohn.

A host of students of all ages from four congregations have challenged and searched the Torah text with me. I am grateful to all of them from Temple Israel, Boston, Massachusetts; Anshe Emeth Memorial Temple, New Brunswick, New Jersey; and Holy Blossom Temple, Toronto, Ontario, Canada. Special thanks are due to the several junior high school, high school, and adult education classes at Wilshire Boulevard Temple, Los Angeles, California, who tested many sections of this commentary with me.

It was Aron Hirt-Manheimer who first urged me to pursue this project. His support, wisdom, and enthusiasm have all helped to make it possible. I am also deeply appreciative to Rabbi Howard I. Bogot for his critical suggestions, and to Rabbi Shelton Donnell, Rabbi Steven Z. Leder, Rachel Fields, Steven Schnur, Annette Abramson, and Dorian Kreindler for their wise advice and editing assistance, and to Stuart L. Benick for his understanding and important role in producing these volumes for Torah study.

Finally, thanks to my wife, Sybil, for her devotion, rich knowledge of Jewish tradition, and always for the gift of her love.

Harvey J. Fields

INTRODUCTIONS

·I·

SPARKS, FRAGMENTS, MEANINGS
A Reader-Friendly Introduction

What is the "Torah"?

The Torah is more than the treasure of the Jewish people, more even than the sacred scroll that bonds Jews to one another and to all the generations who have praised it with the words: "It is a tree of life to all who grasp it, and whoever holds on to it is happy; its ways are ways of pleasantness, and all its paths are peace." (Proverbs 3:17–18)

The Torah is a vast and diverse library. It contains ancient stories, science, histories, ritual practices, philosophy, and ethical standards. Its pages are filled with powerful prose and poetry about the clash of individuals and nations. Within its five books, Genesis, Exodus, Leviticus, Numbers, and Deuteronomy, we encounter the unique way in which the Jewish people views the universe, humanity, and God. No subject is excluded: birth and death, rivalries between children and parents, battles for power, lust, cheating, charity, sexual discrimination, greed, community building, responsibility for the homeless and hungry, taxation, real estate, ecology, business and medical ethics, marriage and divorce. First-century C.E. teacher Ben Bag Bag captured the truth when he told his students: "Turn the Torah, and turn it again, for everything you want to know is found within it." (*Avot* 5:25)

How can we understand the Torah?

Ben Bag Bag may have been correct, but, for many of us, reading and understanding the Torah is not easy. Often we find the language confusing and the stories or flow from one subject to another puzzling. We want to "turn it" and be enriched, even inspired by it, but we end up frustrated and bewildered. "What," we ask, "can the ancient Torah teach us today? What meaning can it have in our lives?"

A Torah Commentary for Our Times has been written with the conviction that there is not only much that we can learn from the Torah but also that studying and sharing its insights can be both inspiring and enjoyable. Our purpose is to present each *parashah*, or "weekly Torah portion," so that it is easy to understand and so that its themes are relevant and accessible.

With each *parashah* we will ask two basic questions: "What is this Torah portion about?" and "What meaning can this Torah portion have for us?"

For clarification, we will identify the most important themes of each *parashah* and then present the varying, and often clashing, opinions of Jewish interpreters throughout the ages. At times we will advocate a particular point of view, but most often we will leave final conclusions to the reader.

The art of "interpreting" Torah

While the organization and presentation of our material may be new, the method we are employing has been tested by Jews over thousands of years. We are not the first to find the contents of the Torah difficult, confusing, and challenging. As far back as the fifth century B.C.E., when Ezra and Nehemiah read the Torah in Jerusalem to Jews who had just returned from Babylonian exile, it was apparently necessary to explain its meanings. We are told that Ezra and Nehemiah gathered all the people into the city square and opened the scroll so that everyone could see it. Afterwards, they read from the Torah in Hebrew, translated it, and interpreted it so that everyone present might understand its contents. (Nehemiah 8: 4–8)

Ever since that time, and perhaps even before, Jews have found it necessary not only to "hear" the Torah in its original Hebrew but also to hear a *targum*, or "translation," and to analyze the text for its messages and wisdom. The rabbis, who were among the earliest interpreters of Torah, called that process of analysis *midrash*, which means "probing" or "searching."

Among Jews, deciphering the intent and meanings of Torah is a high form of art. For many, it is the means through which God's voice speaks to the heart and is decoded by the human mind and soul.

Times change, so do explanations

Throughout most of Jewish history, the Torah functioned as "the law" for Jews. Its commandments and the interpretation of them regulated all of Jewish personal and communal life. The calendar was set according to the festivals and sacred holy days prescribed by the Torah. Regulations concerning business transactions, public safety, diet, criminal behavior, marriage, divorce, and the rearing of children were all derived from the sacred text.

Society, however, changes and evolves. New situations, circumstances, and questions arise. For the Torah to remain "the law," it was necessary for it to be interpreted and applied to every culture, society, and age in which Jews lived.

For instance, observance of the Sabbath in Jerusalem during the time of Ezra and Nehemiah was very different from circumstances one encountered in Babylonia during the third century B.C.E. The application of commandments having to do with care for the poor while Jews were farmers in the Land of Israel during King David's time was very different from the function of such laws in the thirteenth-century C.E. city of Seville, Spain. An interpretation of laws concerning the determination of death that might have worked for Jews living in seventeenth-century Europe clearly requires updating for the high-tech civilization of today.

In order to accommodate such changing needs and circumstances, Jews created a process of interpreting Torah that continues to this day. Early rabbinic scholars initiated this tradition with two kinds of *midrash: Midrash Agadah,* or "literary/moral explanations" often in the form of sermons, and *Midrash Halachah,* or "legal explanations." Eventually, many of these interpretations were collected, organized, and expanded into the *Mishnah* and *Gemara,* which together make up the Talmud. Special collections of *midrashim* as well as many *targumim,* or "translations" of Torah, were also preserved by the scholars of Jewish tradition.

After the completion of the Talmud in the sixth century C.E., rabbis continued to evolve new interpretations of Torah to meet the conditions of Jews living throughout the world. Sa'adia Gaon in Babylonia; Bachya ibn Pakuda and Yehudah Halevi in Spain; Moses Maimonides in Egypt, Spain, and Morocco; and later Rashi, Rashbam, and Radak in France and Abraham ibn Ezra, Ramban, and Don Isaac Abravanel in Spain—all contributed to the vast literature of evolving new meanings and applications of Torah.

No generation of Jews has been without its commentators. In every age they have "turned" the Torah and produced creative insights and applications of its wisdom. Sometimes they have agreed; at other times they have clashed over whose explanation was "correct." Like the generations of critics who have studied the great Greek playwrights or the works of Shakespeare or like Supreme Court justices who interpret the United States Constitution, Jewish commentators have left us a legacy of differing views to consider.

Today the adventure of exploring the meanings of Torah continues. So do the differences of opinion. There are those who settle for what past authors have said. Others apply the new sciences of psychology or literary criticism to the ancient text. Many view the text as sacred poetry and probe it for new spiritual understandings about God's relationship to earth and to human beings. Still others—using the revolutionary discoveries of archeology, comparative religion, linguistic analysis, and even computer technology—are decoding what they argue are the authentic intentions and wisdom of the Torah. Like a fabulous gem, the Torah continues to surprise, baffle, and enrich those who study, explore, and possess it.

What's our strategy for exploring the Torah?
Our adventure with each *parashah* will employ a set of six tactics.

1. We shall begin with a brief and clarifying overview of the Torah text. It is meant for a "quick" read, the equivalent of a city map with just the major roads and highways outlined, without all the details of streets and neighborhoods. In other words, the overview is meant to tell us where we are and where we are going in the Torah text.

2. The next section we call "Our *Targum*," or our "translation." Like the ancient translations, it provides a more detailed presentation of the *parashah*. The purpose of the *targum* is to translate the Torah into our idiom, into the way we use language today. Our *targum* will be divided into numbered parts, making it easier to grasp the flow of the story. You may wish to compare our *targum* with the actual text of the Torah. If you do, you will note that sometimes the *targum* contains explanations about the names of places or people or creates connections between one part of the Torah and another. Note that the numbers of the parts of our *targum* do not refer to the numbers of the chapters and verses of the text in the Bible.

3. Each *parashah* is crammed with potential themes or subjects for discussion. No one book or set of books could possibly cover them all. Our "Themes" section will present those themes that have been chosen for exploration. Again, our purpose is clarity. We want the reader to understand where we are headed. Surprises are for the next section.

4. Our commentary on each Torah portion proceeds one *perek*, or "segment," at a time. Each segment will examine one theme, but it will present a variety of opinions by commentators from different times and places. Often the points of view will clash and remain unresolved. It is not our intention to harmonize them. Instead, we want to call attention to the rich diversity of approaches and explanations that coexist within the tradition of interpreting Torah. To that end, we have often placed side by side ancient and modern views, suspending judgment so that the readers-explorers can draw their own conclusions.

5. Within each *perek*, you will also find additional boxed comments. These are meant to enrich the reader with special insights or to amplify ideas discussed within each section.

6. Concluding each chapter are "Questions for Study and Discussion." Their purpose is to stimulate discussion about some of the significant ideas and themes raised by both the Torah text and its commentators. "What can the Torah and the insights of its interpreters teach us today?" is the guiding question of this section.

A warning and final strategy!
Jewish tradition holds that the study of Torah is of supreme importance. Yet we are warned about how that study and exploration ought to be carried out. Rabbi Joshua ben Perachyah, who was president of the Sanhedrin, the Supreme Court of seventy-one scholars, during the second century B.C.E., taught that one should study Torah with a teacher and with a friend. (*Avot* 1:6) Sharing Torah with others has two advantages. It provides us with a check on our assumptions and a means of challenging our conclusions. It also has the advantage of sharpening our understandings against other points of view.

Take Joshua ben Perachyah's advice. Find a teacher and some friends with whom to investigate the meanings of Torah.

Sparks and fragments, or studying Torah is always a surprise!
According to an ancient legend, when God gave the Torah to Moses on Mount Sinai, the people grew frightened and stood at a distance from the mountain. Thunder shook the ground. Lightning lit up the sky. Then, as each word and sentence of Torah burst forth, an ear-shattering crash was heard. Sparks and fragments flew in every direction as God spoke to the people: "As the hammer

splits the rocks into thousands of sparks and fragments, so My Torah will generate thousands of interpretations." (*Sanhedrin* 34a)

A legend, of course! But within its drama is a significant message. The teachings of Torah are splendid sparks—glowing particles providing light for the seeker of knowledge and illumination for our ethical choices. Yet the teachings of Torah are also multifaceted fragments revealing a multitude of angles, features, and surfaces. Within each face are new meanings to be explored and revealed.

Today, after thousands of years of studying and interpreting Torah, the adventure continues. It is an enterprise without end.

Go and learn!

·II·

TURN IT AND TURN IT!
Introducing the Torah Commentators

The Torah grew and evolved over many centuries out of the ancient thoughts and experiences of the Jewish people. Within it are views about the creation of the world and the first human beings, along with accounts of Abraham and Sarah, Isaac and Rebekah, Jacob, Leah, and Rachel—the founders of the people of Israel. Its pages are filled with stories about Moses liberating the people from Egypt, about their wandering for forty years in the desert. We are told how they received God's law at Mount Sinai and built their first sanctuary.

No one knows how or when the Torah, the Five Books of Moses, was written or given its final form. Perhaps it existed for many hundreds of years as a tradition, memorized by priests or teachers and passed on from one generation to the next. Perhaps some of its most important parts—the Ten Commandments, the laws concerning sacrifices, details about the festivals, and regulations having to do with property—were written down and placed in arks or other special containers where they would be preserved.

It is possible that during the period from 1200 B.C.E., when the Israelites conquered the Land of Israel, until 586 B.C.E., when they were defeated and exiled by the Babylonians, various fragments of the Torah existed, and *soferim,* or "scribes," rescued them and took them to Babylonia.

We know that when Ezra and Nehemiah, both of whom were known as priests and scribes, led Jews back from Babylonian exile between the years 465 and 359 B.C.E., they brought with them the Torah. Most scholars believe that it contained the Five Books of Moses and had been compiled and edited by *soferim* during the exile in Babylonia. It was to serve as the "constitution," the *law,* for the rebuilt Jewish nation.

When Ezra and Nehemiah gathered the people in Jerusalem to hear the Torah, they faced a difficult problem. While in Babylonia for nearly three generations, Jews had abandoned Hebrew and now spoke Aramaic, the prevailing language of Babylonian culture. How then would they understand the Torah, the sacred text and laws of their tradition? Ezra and Nehemiah responded to the challenge by adding both a *targum,* or "translation," and a commentary to the public reading of Torah. (See Nehemiah 8.)

Clearly, this early tradition of translating the Torah into the vernacular and of explaining its contents set the stage for the creative evolution of both Judaism and the Jewish people. As the Torah was read and translated, the people became familiar with its stories and laws. As it was interpreted and applied to the questions and issues facing them, it emerged as their supreme source of wisdom.

Which came first, the targum or the midrash?

As we have already noted, Ezra and Nehemiah offered both a *targum,* or "translation," and a *mid-*

rash, or "explanation," of Torah to the people. What is impossible to know is which of these two critical "tools" for understanding came first. In truth, they seem to have developed simultaneously. For that reason, we are dividing the next part of this Introduction II into two sections.

Section One: Targumim—"Translations"

During the period of the Second Temple in Jerusalem until its destruction in 70 C.E., many different Torah translations in Aramaic, Greek, Egyptian, Median, and Elamean appeared. Most of these are now lost to us, but we can assume that some of their language and views are reflected in the later Greek and Aramaic versions that have been preserved.

The most famous Greek *targum* is known as the **SEPTUAGINT.** According to one tradition, the Greek leader Ptolemy II Philadelphus (285–247 B.C.E.) invited seventy-two rabbis to Alexandria, Egypt, and ordered each to prepare a translation of Torah into Greek. When they compared notes, all of them had composed the same translation. Beyond the charming story, the Septuagint is written in the Koine, or colloquial Greek spoken during the third century B.C.E. Even more significantly, it contains elaborations of the Torah text that are meant to clarify it for the listener. As early Christianity emerged, Church leaders selected the Septuagint as their official text of Torah.

During the second century C.E., after the destruction of the Jerusalem Temple and the emergence of Christianity, leading rabbis invited a convert to Judaism, Aquila, to prepare a new Greek translation of Torah. While fragments of the text have survived, the **TARGUM AQUILA,** as it became known, combines translation with interpretation by incorporating many early rabbinic views into the text. Some scholars believe that Aquila, and those who urged him to write his translation, were anxious to create a text that differed from the Septuagint and answered early Christian challenges about the meaning of Torah.

While Aramaic translations existed during the time of Ezra and Nehemiah, the best-known and most complete text is the **TARGUM ONKELOS.** Dating from the third century C.E., it, like Targum Aquila, was the work of a convert to Judaism. Indeed, there are some scholars who believe that Aquila and Onkelos were the same person! Targum Onkelos became the most important translation within Jewish tradition and appears alongside the Torah text in nearly every "rabbinic Bible."

Onkelos presents a straightforward translation while avoiding phrases that leave the reader with the impression that God possesses human attributes or reacts with human feelings. Excuses are often cited for the faults of major biblical personalities, and often the intent of the text is clarified. For instance, Onkelos translates "You shall not boil a kid in its mother's milk" (Exodus 23:19, Exodus 34:26, and Deuteronomy 14:21) as "You shall not eat meat with milk." This combination of translation and interpretation helped to make Targum Onkelos one of the most valued texts among later Babylonian rabbis.

Two other Aramaic translations were popular in their times, but they have been lost to us. We have a few fragments of a **TARGUM OF JONATHAN BEN UZZIEL** and of another called **TARGUM YERUSHALMI.** The first of these draws heavily on the Targum Onkelos and the Yerushalmi, and some of it may date back to the second century B.C.E. during the time of the Maccabees. On the other hand, the origins of Targum Yerushalmi seem to date from the first century B.C.E. Scholars discovered pieces of the text in a Cairo, Egypt, *genizah* (a storage place above a synagogue) and also called it the "Galilean" or "Neofiti Targum." The text often provides geographical information about remote places mentioned in the Torah. Like the Targum Onkelos, it avoids describing God in human terms and contains many observations about both the stories and laws of Torah.

The best-known Arabic translation of Torah is the **TARGUM TAFSIR,** prepared by the tenth-century Babylonian philosopher and interpreter Sa'adia ben Joseph Ha-Gaon. *Tafsir* means "commentary," and Sa'adia seems to have had as his purpose the creation of a Torah text that could be read by the majority of Jews who knew no Hebrew and felt ignorant about their tradition. Born and reared in Egypt, Sa'adia moved first to the Land of Israel and then to Babylonia. There, as head of the rabbinic academy at Sura, he emerged as both a political and religious authority.

Sa'adia's *targum* reveals his deepest anxieties about the future of the Jewish people. On the one hand, they were being attacked by Moslems who wished to make converts by demonstrating the superiority of their faith and the Koran over Judaism and the Torah. On the other hand, the Jewish community was deeply divided between those, like Sa'adia, who followed the rabbinic tradition of interpreting Torah, and the Karaites who claimed that the Torah was to be read literally, without any interpretations by the rabbinic tradition.

Targum Tafsir clarifies the Torah text with rabbinic explanations, and Sa'adia's bias against portraying God as a human being is similar to the treatment Onkelos gives to his translation. The text is clear, and Sa'adia's later commentaries to the Torah remain a valuable resource for those seeking to understand the divisions between Jews living in Babylonia at his time.

From Sa'adia's era to the present, the process of translating Torah continues. Today, the Hebrew Bible has been translated into nearly every language spoken by human beings.

Section Two: Midrashim—"Explanations"

Parallel to the evolution of the many *targumim* is the development of a tradition of explaining the Torah text called *midrash*. As we have already mentioned in Introduction I, the early teachers of Jewish tradition divided their explanations into two categories: *Midrash Halachah* (legal interpretations) and *Midrash Agadah* (literary/moral interpretations). These two approaches to the Torah text were most likely used from the time of Ezra and Nehemiah as the means for understanding and justifying how the Torah should be applied to the changing circumstances of political, economic, and personal life.

During the second century B.C.E., early rabbinic scholars pioneered in creating both legal and literary (sermonic) *midrash*. They taught that God had given the people of Israel two Torahs at Mount Sinai. One was the *Torah Shebichetav,* or "Written Torah"; the other was the *Torah Shebealpeh,* or "Oral Torah," which contained all the interpretations to be uncovered by students of Torah throughout the ages.

Zugot

Among the most famous of the early rabbinic interpreters were five *zugot,* or "leadership-pairs," who also served as president and vice-president of the Sanhedrin, the Supreme Court of the Jewish people. They were Jose ben Yoezer and Yosi ben Yochanan (about 165 B.C.E.), Joshua ben Perachyah and Nittai of Arbela, Judah ben Tabbai and Simeon ben Shetach, Shemayah and Abtalyon, and Hillel and Shammai.

These early rabbis compared the Torah to a wonderful "garden," whose fruits might be extracted by using four different methods signified by the Hebrew letters of the word for "garden," *PaRDeS.* They called the first method *peshat,* the search for the straightforward, literal meaning of the text. The second was *remez,* uncovering hidden or implied meanings. The third was *derash,* finding the meaning through comparing one text with another or drawing parallels between the text and human experiences. The fourth was *sod,* investigating the text for secret, mystical, or allegorical meanings.

In his time, the famed but modest Rabbi Hillel, who taught his students "to love peace, love human beings, and bring others to the study of Torah," suggested seven principles or rules for interpreting Torah.

1. *Kal va-Chomer:* You can draw a conclusion from either a minor or major assumption.

2. *Gezerah Shavah:* You can draw a conclusion from the similarity of words or phrases in two separate biblical sentences.

3. *Binyan Av mi-Katuv Echad:* You can derive a general principle from a single biblical sentence.

4. *Binyan Av mi-Shene Ketuvim:* You can derive a general principle from two biblical sentences.

5. *Kelal u-Ferat:* All general rules that are followed by one or more particulars are then limited to those particulars.

6. *Ka-Yotze Bo be-Makom Acher:* You may draw a similar conclusion from another Torah text.

7. *Davar ha-Lamed me-Inyano:* You may uncover the meaning of obscure or ambiguous words and phrases from the context in which you find them.

Later, the first-century B.C.E. leader Ishmael, who defied the Romans by continuing to teach Torah after they had forbidden him to do so, elaborated Hillel's seven rules into thirteen. Ishmael was put to death by the Romans, but his student, Akiba, continued to derive new meanings from the Torah text. Akiba held that each word, every letter, even the crowns on the letters possessed potential messages and wisdom. Eliezer ben Yose Ha-Galili, one of Akiba's students, extended the rules for interpreting Torah from Hillel's seven and Ishmael's thirteen to thirty-two different means for extracting new ideas and legal formulations from the Torah. With each increase in the rules of interpretation, the adventure and art of finding new meanings in the ancient text became more flexible and creative.

The many rabbis who continued to evolve new understandings of Torah between the second century B.C.E. and the third century C.E. were known as *tannaim,* or "teachers." Those living between the third century C.E. and sixth century C.E. were called *amoraim,* or "speakers," "interpreters." Many of their explanations of Torah are reported in the *Mishnah* and *Gemara,* which were later combined into the Talmud. They were also collected into books of *midrash,* which include: *Genesis Rabbah, Exodus Rabbah, Leviticus Rabbah, Numbers Rabbah, Deuteronomy Rabbah, Pesikta, Tanchuma, Mechilta, Sifre,* and *Sifra.* In each case, these collections of early rabbinic explanations of Torah, like the *targumim,* were the means through which generations of Jews kept expanding Jewish knowledge and law to meet new circumstances.

Meet those who never stopped turning it

Rashi

The most famous of all commentators of Jewish history is Rabbi Shelomoh (Solomon) Itzhaki, known by his initials as **RaSHI** (1040–1105),

who was born in the city of Troyes, France. As a young man Rashi studied the talmudic scholars in Mayence (Mainz) and Worms and then returned to the expanding industrial and business center of his birth. Earning his living from his vineyard, Rashi, like many Jews of his time, was caught up in defending his faith against Christians who claimed that God had replaced Judaism and the Jewish people with Christianity and the Church. After the slaughter and destruction of the First Crusade in 1096, he played a significant role in comforting and supporting suffering Jewish communities.

Rashi's commentaries often include selections from the *Midrash.* He also made use of current French words for clarification and, today, his writings are a major source for the study of Old French. Throughout the centuries Rashi's work has remained a model of simplicity and clarity for all commentators, and his reputation as *Parshandata,* "the interpreter of the Torah," is firmly established.

Rabbi Shemuel (Samuel) ben Meir, known also by his initials, **RaSHBaM** (1085–1174), was Rashi's grandson and earned his living as a sheep farmer. Known for his piety, he defended Jewish beliefs in public disputes that had been arranged by Church leaders to demonstrate the inferiority of Judaism. Fearful of those who twisted the biblical text to suit their conclusions, Rashbam argued that the only justified meaning of the Torah text was the *peshat,* or "plain meaning." He criticized those, including his grandfather, who employed the methods of *remez, derash,* or *sod,* calling them "crooked explanations" and "nonsense."

Ibn Ezra

While Rashbam was writing his commentary in France, **ABRAHAM IBN EZRA** (1092–1167) was gaining a significant reputation as a poet, physician, philosopher, and astrologer in

Spain and Italy. The first part of ibn Ezra's life was spent in his native Spain. From about 1140 he resided for brief periods in France, England, Egypt, Ethiopia, Italy, and finally again in Spain, where he died. Many believe that his wandering began in the bewildered disappointment of his only surviving son's conversion to Islam. Ibn Ezra's interests in both science and grammar, along with his experiences as a traveler, are expressed within his commentary to the Torah. He often includes discussions of mathematics, astrology, and linguistics within his explanations.

Rabbi David Kimchi, or **RaDaK** (1160–1235), of Narbonne, France, was a popular teacher. His town was a crossroads for trade and for visiting Jewish scholars from Spain and France. Kimchi was well known as a lecturer and was often called upon to defend Judaism and the Jewish people before hostile Church leaders. Like ibn Ezra, he stressed the scientific and grammatical approach in his commentary. Concerned with Christian claims and misinterpretations of Genesis, Kimchi often engages in sharp philosophical argument and attempts to reveal the authentic intention of the Torah. His commentary makes use of the *targumim* and frequently quotes early rabbinic explanations.

Ramban (Nachmanides)

Rabbi Moses ben Nachman, known as **NACH-MANIDES,** or by his initials, **RaMBaN** (1194–1270), was born in Gerona, Spain, and given the Spanish name Bonastrug da Porta. He earned his living as a physician, but his talents in the areas of poetry, philosophy, Torah interpretation, and leadership all earned him a reputation as *ha-Rav ha-Neeman,* "the trustworthy rabbi." Throughout his lifetime, Nachmanides worked to bring peace among differing Jewish factions in his community. In 1263, he defended Judaism at a public debate held in the court of King James. Two years later,

Christian authorities requested that the pope force the king to penalize Nachmanides for what he had said during the disputation. Fleeing Spain, Nachmanides settled in the Land of Israel, where he spent the last years of his life writing his commentary to the Torah.

Unlike Rashi's terse interpretations on nearly every verse, Nachmanides deals in depth with various ideas and issues raised by the Torah text. At times he will quote Rashi, ibn Ezra, or one of the rabbis of the Midrash, agreeing or disagreeing with them. His explanations are filled with psychological insights into biblical characters and contain many of his own philosophical, political, and scientific observations.

One of the most curious and fascinating commentaries to appear in the thirteenth century is the *ZOHAR*. This mystical interpretation of Torah, which seeks to unveil the *sod* and *remez,* the "secret" and "hidden" meanings, is said to have been collected and written by **SIMEON BEN YOCHAI** (100–160 C.E.). Many scholars, however, believe that it was the work of **MOSES DE LEON** (13th century) of Granada, Spain. Whoever wrote or compiled the *Zohar* created more than a book. It is a library of differing views, fragments of interpretations, and intriguing speculations about the relationship between God and the world. In it we are given a variety of explanations about God's concern for humanity and for the people of Israel. Using mathematics, combinations of letters and words, mystical observations, and a rich imagination, the *Zohar* seeks to reveal the unseen and to surprise students with new insights into the mysteries of the universe and human life.

Abravanel

The man who pleaded with King Ferdinand and Queen Isabella of Spain to reverse their March 31, 1492 decree to expel all Jews from their land was **DON ISAAC ABRAVANEL** (1437–1508). Born in Lisbon, educated in both Jewish and classic sources, Abravanel not only served as treasurer of Portugal but as finance minister to the rulers of Spain and Italy.

Drawing upon his experience as a statesman and his knowledge of history and philosophy, Abravanel's Torah commentary is crammed with observations about politics, along with warnings against the concentration of power and authority. He questions the ethical behavior of biblical characters and defends Judaism against attacks by leaders of the Inquisition. Abravanel's study of Torah is divided into separate chapters, each beginning with a list of critical questions. For Abravanel, Torah is the ultimate source of wisdom, and the practice of its commandments strengthens the bond between the Jewish people and God.

OBADIAH SFORNO (1475–1550) lived most of his life in Bologna, Italy. In his youth he studied philosophy, mathematics, linguistics, and medicine. While practicing as a physician, he also managed a Hebrew printing business and a Jewish educational center and was an active leader of the Bologna Jewish community. As his reputation as a scholar of Jewish tradition spread, Jewish leaders from throughout Italy turned to him seeking advice. In his Torah commentary, Sforno seeks to explain the *peshat,* or "plain meaning," of the text. He employs his knowledge of contemporary science and medicine in his interpretations, but unlike Abravanel he does not provide historical observations. His outlook has been called "humanistic" by some scholars because he seldom emphasizes the difference between Jews and non-Jews, choosing instead to teach that all humanity is God's treasure. (Deuteronomy 33:3)

Mendelssohn

Between 1780 and 1783, **MOSES MENDELSSOHN** (1729–1786) published his *Biur,* or "explanation" of the Torah. Mendelssohn, who had been born in Dessau, the son of a *sofer,* or "Torah scribe," had already gained a reputation among Jews and non-Jews as a respected philosopher, literary critic, and defender of his faith.

Making his living as a merchant, Mendelssohn concluded that Jews needed to abandon Yiddish and to learn German in order to play an active role in German society.

Mendelssohn's *Biur* presents not only a commentary on the meaning of the Torah text but also a translation of the Torah into German using Hebrew characters. Actually, Mendelssohn invited his friend Solomon Dubno to write the commentary to Genesis and Naftali Herz Wessely to create the commentary to Leviticus. The *Biur* emphasizes the literary and moral beauty of the Torah. Nonetheless, it was met with a storm of protest from traditional Jewish circles objecting to Mendelssohn's bias for German. Today it is recognized as one of the significant building blocks of the *Haskalah,* or Jewish "Enlightenment" movement, which was to sweep Jews into the emerging nineteenth-century Western culture and to generate early Reform Judaism.

Meklenburg

Opposing early Reform Judaism was **JACOB ZVI MEKLENBURG** (1785–1865), author of the Torah commentary *Ha-Ketav ve-ha-Kabbalah.* Meklenburg worked as a businessman until 1831 when he became rabbi of Koenigsberg. His commentary attempts to explain the laws of Torah and to prove that the talmudic laws are based upon the authority of Torah. In part, his approach reflects his disagreements in his community with Reform Jews who were claiming that some laws of Torah were no longer applicable to society.

Malbim

Meir Lev ben Yechiel Michael, known also by his initials, **MaLBIM** (1809–1879), was born in Volochisk, Russia. He married at fourteen and divorced soon afterwards. His early life was filled with wanderings and study in many different centers of European Jewish learning. In 1858, he was appointed Chief Rabbi of Rumania, but his battles with Reform Jews ultimately led to his dismissal.

Malbim bases his Torah commentary upon the Midrash of the early rabbis. For him each word is important and filled with insights from God. While he prefers explaining the literal meaning of the text, he does not hesitate to add observations of his own. For instance, he cleverly invents discussions of Jewish law and then places them in the mouths of biblical characters.

Luzzatto

While Malbim was interpreting Torah in Eastern Europe, **SAMUEL DAVID LUZZATTO** (1800–1865) was creating his commentary in Padua, Italy. Luzzatto, also known by his initials as **ShaDal,** worked as a philosopher, historian, translator, and interpreter of Torah. His life was marked by the tragic death of his first wife and their two sons. In 1821–1822, after publishing a translation of the Jewish prayer book into Italian, Luzzatto was appointed a professor at the Padua Rabbinical College. His Torah commentary shows great respect for Rashi's views and highlights moral lessons and ethical values he believes are central to the Torah text. Luzzatto seeks to foster a love for Jewish tradition and knowledge and a loyalty to the Jewish people. His urging of young people to return to the Land of Israel marks him as an early Zionist.

Hirsch

One of the most important nineteenth-century European Jewish leaders was **SAMSON RAPHAEL HIRSCH** (1808–1888) whose Torah commentary remains a classic expression of Orthodox Jewish beliefs. Born in Hamburg, Hirsch studied Talmud with his grandfather and was deeply influenced by Rabbi Isaac Bernays, an opponent of early Reform Judaism. Hirsch worked for the emancipation of Austrian and Moravian Jewry, and in 1851 he began thirty-seven years of service as a rabbi in Frankfort. By that time his philosophical study, *Nineteen Letters on Judaism,*

published in 1836, had won him the admiration of many in the Orthodox community.

Hirsch's Torah commentary "seeks to derive the explanation of the text from the words themselves." He makes use of early rabbinic views along with those of other commentators to underscore his belief that Jewish tradition offers the highest form of human life. Hirsch vehemently opposes the notion of Reform Judaism that the Torah tradition has historically evolved through the ages. He asserts that the Torah was revealed by God at Mount Sinai, and, therefore, nothing in it can or will be changed.

Hertz

JOSEPH HERMAN HERTZ (1872–1946) follows Hirsch's philosophy and approach to the Torah, yet his Torah commentary, one of the first written in English, is more concise and offers brief essays on significant questions. While Hertz was born in Slovakia, he arrived in the United States at the age of twelve and was the first graduate of the Jewish Theological Seminary in 1894. He served as rabbi in South Africa but was deported because of his outspoken criticism of the government's policy of discrimination against aliens. In 1913 he was appointed Chief Rabbi of England. His Torah commentary, published between 1929 and 1936, takes issue with biblical critics of his day, who argued that the Torah as well as the rest of the Hebrew Bible was edited from many different documents and that it evolved into a sacred literature through many centuries. Hertz maintains the fundamental-traditional view that the whole Torah was given by God to Moses at Mount Sinai.

Benno Jacob

BENNO JACOB (1862–1941), a rabbi and biblical scholar, escaped from Germany in 1939 and settled in England. In his commentary, Jacob not only takes issue with many biblical scholars of his time but also with fundamentalists like

Hirsch and Hertz. Jacob believed that a study of the Torah text did not justify the notion that Moses had either received it at one time or that he had written all of it. The Torah, however, was to be respected as a reliable and whole document representing the early religious history of the Jewish people.

Speiser

One of the first to apply the science of archeology to Torah commentary was **EPHRAIM AVIGDOR SPEISER** (1902–1965). Trained as an archeologist in the United States, Speiser spent many years in Iraq directing surveys of ancient cities. From 1928 until his death he lectured at the University of Pennsylvania. In his commentary on Genesis, Speiser applies the knowledge accumulated by modern historians, archeologists, linguists, and students of comparative culture and religion to the stories and history of ancient Israel. He sees Judaism emerging out of both Mesopotamian and Egyptian cultures.

Morgenstern

Biblical scholar **JULIAN MORGENSTERN** (1881–1976), who served as president of the Hebrew Union College from 1922 to 1947, also believed that the Torah had evolved through the Jewish people's experience with ancient Middle Eastern cultures. Morgenstern also applied economic and social considerations to his analysis of emerging Jewish beliefs and traditions. For him, however, the chief meaning of Genesis was in its moral message.

Israeli scholar **NEHAMA LEIBOWITZ** (1905–   ) differs from Morgenstern and Speiser in her approach to explaining the meanings of Torah. Rather than seeing the Torah as limited to the history, religion, and social realities of a particular era, Leibowitz seeks meanings out of the tradition of rabbinic interpretation. By comparing and contrasting varying insights of rabbis from different periods and places, Leibowitz challenges her students to reach new understandings about the intent and purpose of the Torah text.

As a professor of Bible at Tel Aviv University, Leibowitz developed a large following of students in Israel and throughout the world with her weekly "teach-yourself" Torah study packets. Her guiding principle is that the Torah is crammed with potential meanings, and its students are invited to discover all of them.

Sarna

Professor of Bible **NAHUM M. SARNA** (1923–   ), like E. A. Speiser, seeks to uncover the message of Torah by studying it within the context of its time and culture. He compares the religious practices, mythologies, and legal procedures of ancient Near Eastern peoples with those described within the Torah. His *Understanding Genesis* and *Exploring Exodus* were written "as an aid to enhancing the message of the Bible for the highly sophisticated youngsters of our generation."

In 1981, after years of research and writing, the Union of American Hebrew Congregations published *The Torah: A Modern Commentary*. This first "official" commentary by the Reform movement was written and edited by Rabbis **W. GUNTHER PLAUT** and **BERNARD J. BAMBERGER,** with critical essays by Professor **WILLIAM W. HALLO.** Like many traditional commentaries, the UAHC Torah commentary offers a line-by-line analysis of the text. However, it also employs the accumulated knowledge of historians, archeologists, linguists, and students of comparative religion. Essays at the conclusion of each section deal with important questions raised by the text and present varying conclusions based not only upon traditional rabbinic views but also upon modern biblical study.

The turning of Torah continues

Today, scholars and students of Torah continue the process of exploring the ancient text for new insights and meanings. There are many differing views. Some see the Torah primarily as a history of the ancient Israelites; others view it as a record of early Middle Eastern religion and myth. Some believe that its worth is in its literary power; others argue that the Torah represents the primary ethical guide of Western civilization. Still others hold that the Torah evolved out of the Jewish people's relationship with God, that its interpreters in every age have continued to enlarge its meanings, and that God continues to speak each time the message of Torah is celebrated in study or ritual or in the ethical behavior of those who shape their lives with its commandments and wisdom.

The roll of Torah interpreters whose views are presented in *A Torah Commentary for Our Times* is long and distinguished. For a complete listing, see the "Glossary of Commentaries and Interpreters" at the back of the book.

The Jewish people has never ceased to "turn the Torah" and to extract from it valuable treasures. *A Torah Commentary for Our Times* invites you to participate in this great expedition. We will encounter a diversity of views and opinions, and we will sharpen our wits and sensitivities with a variety of perspectives. Yet, Torah study is more than an intellectual adventure, more than knowing what this commentator said or this scholar argues. It is a serious spiritual challenge. Its purpose is to *turn us* until we have the courage to begin transforming our lives and communities with the sacred truths of Torah. Through the study of Torah, the rabbis taught, a person makes the world worthwhile . . . and promotes peace. (*Avot* 6:1; *Sanhedrin* 99b)

So let your "turning" begin!

THE
TORAH
PORTIONS
OF
GENESIS

PARASHAT BERESHIT
Genesis 1:1–6:8

Bereshit may be translated as "In the beginning" or "At first." The Torah begins by telling us how God created the heavens and earth, human beings, and the Sabbath. It continues with the stories of Adam and Eve in the Garden of Eden and of their sons, Cain and Abel, and it concludes with the report that God regretted having created human beings because of all their wickedness. For that reason, God decided to destroy everything on earth except for Noah and his family.

OUR TARGUM

· 1 ·

In the beginning the earth was unformed, and there was only darkness. Then God commanded, "Let there be light," and saw how good it was. Then God separated between the light, which was named "Day," and the darkness, which was called "Night." That was the first day of creation.

On the second day Sky was created.

On the third day Earth and Seas were formed, along with plants and trees of every kind. And God saw how good it was.

On the fourth day the sun, moon, and stars were set in the sky to separate between day and night. And God saw how it, too, was good.

On the fifth day God brought forth birds out of the waters to fly, and creeping creatures of every kind, and swarms of fish and sea animals to swim in the seas. And God saw how good it was, and ordered them to be "fruitful and increase."

On the sixth day God created all the beasts of the earth. Seeing it was good, God then decided to create human beings. God said: "I will make Adam in My image, after My likeness." God created male and female human beings and commanded them to "rule the fish of the sea, the birds of the sky, the cattle, the whole earth." God also blessed them and told them to "be fruitful and increase." And God saw that it was very good.

When heaven and earth were finished, God rested and declared that the seventh day of each week should be set aside as a Sabbath, a day of rest. God blessed the Sabbath and called it *kodesh,* which means "holy," or "unique."

· 2 ·

God then planted a beautiful garden from which four rivers flowed. The rivers were named Pishon, Gihon, Tigris, and Euphrates. The garden was called *Gan Eden,* the "Garden of Eden," and was located in what was once known as Babylonia and afterwards called Persia and Iran.

Within the garden were colorful and fruitful trees of every kind. One special tree called the *Etz ha-Chayim,* or "Tree of Life," grew at the center of the garden. Nearby was another called the *Etz ha-Daat Tov va-Ra,* or "Tree of the Knowledge of Good and Bad."

God placed Adam, the first human being, in *Gan Eden* and warned him: "You may eat from every tree in the garden except from the Tree of Knowledge of Good and Bad. If you eat from it, you will die."

Then God brought all the creatures of earth and sky before Adam so that he might name each of them.

Afterwards, God saw that Adam was lonely and needed a partner, so God created a wife for him. And Adam called her *Chavah,* or "Eve," which comes from the word *chai* ("life") and means "mother of all the living."

One day a serpent tempted Eve by telling her that neither she nor Adam would die if they ate from the Tree of Knowledge of Good and Bad. So she tasted its fruits and then gave some to her husband. When God questioned them about what they had done, Adam blamed Eve, and she blamed the serpent. All three were punished for having disobeyed God's command. The serpent was condemned to crawl and eat dirt, and Adam and Eve were banished from the Garden of Eden.

· 3 ·

Later, Eve gave birth to Cain and then to another son named Abel. After they were grown, Cain turned on his brother in anger and killed him. When God asked him, "Where is your brother, Abel?" he answered, "I do not know. Am I my brother's keeper?" For murdering his brother, God punished Cain by sending him off to become a lonely wanderer on earth.

After creating heaven and earth, and all living creatures, God saw that human beings were wicked and constantly doing evil. So God decided to destroy humanity and all living things—but a man by the name of Noah changed God's intention.

THEMES

Parashat Bereshit contains four important themes:

1. God's creation of the heavens, earth, all living creatures, and humanity is a blessing.

2. Human beings are responsible for the survival of all that was created by God.
3. The expulsion of Adam and Eve from the Garden of Eden.
4. Human beings are responsible for one another and for the survival of humanity.

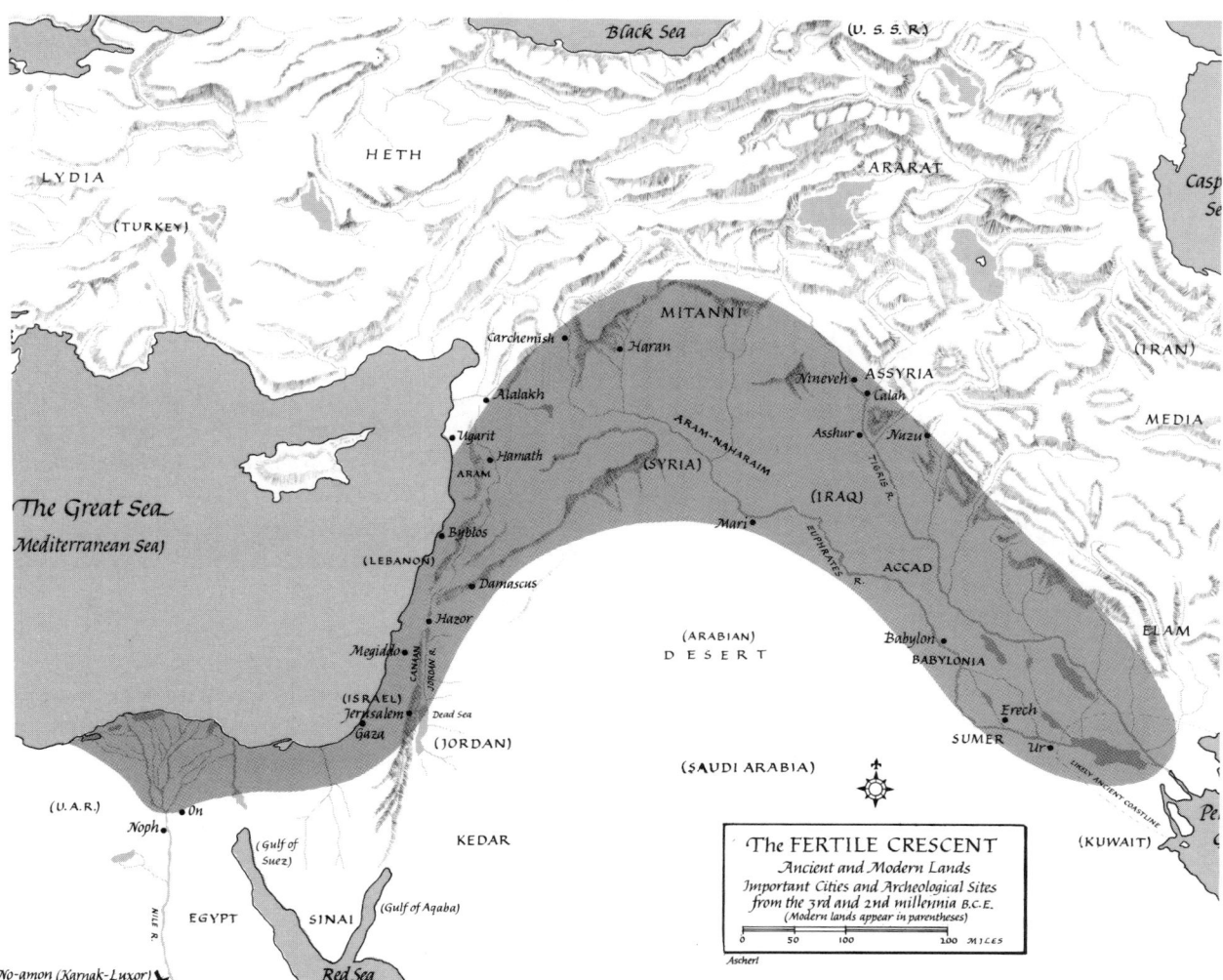

The FERTILE CRESCENT
*Ancient and Modern Lands
Important Cities and Archeological Sites
from the 3rd and 2nd millennia B.C.E.
(Modern lands appear in parentheses)*

0   50   100   100   *MILES*

PEREK ALEF: *Is There a Jewish View about "Creation"*?

There are many different views about how our planet and galaxy of stars originated. Most scientists who study the stars (they are called astrophysicists and cosmologists) believe that, between ten and twenty billion years ago, all of the matter of the universe concentrated in a single place and then exploded in a "Big Bang." About a billion years later, clusters of galaxies, composed of gas, dust, and clumps of matter, began to take shape. There were over one hundred billion of them, each with an average of one hundred billion stars. Among these was our Milky Way galaxy containing a vast ocean of four hundred billion stars.

Scientists believe that many stars, such as our own, have planets revolving around them. When a star has revolving planets, this arrangement is called a solar system. Our planet, Earth, revolves around our star, Sol, the sun. Here on Earth, with all its shimmering blue skies, oceans, forests, deserts, and green valleys is the only place in the cosmos where, to our knowledge, intelligent life has evolved.

> **At the beginning . . .**
> Scientist and writer Carl Sagan describes the "awesome transformation" that the Torah calls "creation": "At the beginning of this universe, there were no galaxies, stars, or planets, no life or civilizations, merely a uniform radiant fireball filling all space. The passage from the Chaos of the Big Bang to the Cosmos that we are beginning to know is the most awesome transformation of matter and energy that we have been privileged to glimpse. And, until we find more intelligent beings elsewhere, we are ourselves the most spectacular of all the transformations—the remote descendants of the Big Bang, dedicated to understanding and further transforming the Cosmos from which we spring." (Cosmos, Ballantine Books, New York, 1980, p. 12)

> One of the most famous of the "creation" stories is the Enuma Elish, told by early Babylonians, Assyrians, Akkadians, and Sumerians:
>
> The holy house, the house of the gods, in a holy place had not yet been made;
> No reed had sprung up, no tree had been created;
> No brick had been laid, no building had been erected. . . .
> The Deep had not been made. . . .
> Then there was a movement in the midst of the sea. . . .
> At that time Eridu was made. . . .
> And the gods, the spirits of the earth,
> Marduk made at the same time. . . .
> Marduk laid a reed on the face of the waters,
> He formed dust and poured it out beside the reed;
> That he might cause the gods to dwell in the dwelling of their hearts' desire, He formed mankind. (Excerpt from Robert Graves and Raphael Patai, Hebrew Myths: The Book of Genesis, Greenwich House, New York, 1983, p. 22)

Throughout history people have gazed into the heavens—or observed life on earth—and wondered how it all began. Nearly every culture developed an explanation. Thousands of years ago in the Middle East the ancient Sumerians, Akkadians, Assyrians, Babylonians, and Egyptians all told "creation" stories.

Most of these, like the Babylonian epic *Enuma Elish,* put forward the belief that many gods had created the heavens, earth, and human life. In most of these versions of creation, everything depended upon the whim of the gods. It was believed that they could order rain or blow away the clouds, send plagues or wipe out whole populations with floods or famine. In these ancient stories human beings were helpless. Whether they suffered or were successful and happy did not depend upon their accomplishments but rather upon the arbitrary decisions of the gods.

The Jewish people introduced a revolutionary theory about the creation of the heavens, earth, and human life. Unlike the other ancient stories, which attribute all that was created in the heavens and on earth to numerous gods, the Torah begins by teaching that one God alone created everything. It puts forward the idea that creation is "good," that the world and the galaxy of stars in which it spins are not a random accident but have a unique design and purpose.

Furthermore, the Torah teaches that human life is a result of God's will, and human beings are not "toys" of the gods. Instead, human beings are created in God's image. They have choices and can exercise freedom. They are partners with God in shaping life and preserving the world.

Echoing the Torah's "creation" story, the Psalmist not only captures the mystery of God's creation but also elaborates the role and responsibility of human beings.

O God, our God,
How majestic is Your name throughout the earth,
You who have covered the heavens with Your
splendor! . . .
When I behold Your heavens, the work of Your
fingers,
the moon and stars that You set in place:
what are human beings that You have been
mindful of them,
mortals that You have taken note of them,
that You have made them little less than divine,
and adorned them with glory and majesty;
You have made them master over Your
handiwork,
laying the world at their feet. . . .

(Psalms 8:1–7)

Jewish tradition holds that one God created the heavens and earth, but it also teaches that human beings are "masters" of the world. Their choices make a difference. The power of life or death, survival or destruction is in their hands.

But Jewish tradition goes a step further. While the first chapters of *Bereshit,* or Genesis, describe in detail what was created on each of the six days of creation, Jewish interpreters of Torah did not take that explanation as an exact report of what had happened. Instead, they offered many different opinions.

For example, some of the rabbis argued that God had created everything on the first day. Then, on each of the five following days, God introduced what had already been formed. Other rabbis disagreed. They believed that the creation of light came before everything else. Still others taught that God, like an unsatisfied artist looking for perfection, had created and destroyed many worlds before deciding that this one was acceptable. (*Genesis Rabbah* 1:15; 3:1,7; 9:2; and 12:14)

And do Jewish teachers say that the world was created in six twenty-four-hour days?

Rashi

The most famous interpreter of the Torah, Solomon ben Isaac, known best as Rashi, denied

this. He pointed out that the word *yom,* or "day," could mean "thousands of years." As proof for his argument he quoted the ancient Psalmist who had written: "For a day in Your sight is like a thousand years. . . . (Psalms 90:4) For Rashi, God's creation of the world did not happen within six twenty-four-hour days but rather over thousands of years. "The Torah," he explained to his eleventh-century students, "does not intend to teach us the order of creation." (Rashi on Genesis 1:1)

Most Torah interpreters agree with Rashi. The Torah does not offer us a "scientific" explanation of creation. It offers us something else of great importance.

Well before modern science, Jews realized that the purpose of Torah was not to tell us "how" the world was created but to help us understand "Who" created all the wonders of the heavens and earth. The "creation" story of *Bereshit* is not a lesson in evolution. It neither contradicts modern scientific theories nor requires proofs from the laboratory. The Torah's story of creation is meant to express our sense of wonder about the origins of the world in which we live. It affirms our faith that one God formed and sustains all of cosmic existence and that human beings are partners with God in preserving and advancing the precious gift of life.

PEREK BET: *We Must Care for Creation*

Modern scientists are fond of referring to our Earth as a "tiny fragile world . . . drifting in a great cosmic ocean." Certainly our contemporary studies about space confirm the vastness of the cosmos and the fact that our planet is a mere speck where, miraculously, all of the conditions that promote life happen to be present.

Scientists agree that there is a very delicate balance between all earthly life forms and the atmosphere surrounding our planet. They speak of a "cooperating system" between the five million separate species of animals and plants on Earth and its stone foundations, waters, and blue blanket of sky. Without the delicate interrelationship between all forms of life and the conditions of our atmosphere, Earth would be a lifeless planet.

As an example of our "cooperating system," British chemist and inventor James Lovelock describes how the Earth's atmosphere is amazingly shaped to fit life's needs. "With no oxygen, for instance, there would be no respiration. With just a little more oxygen, on the other hand—even 25 percent instead of 21—the whole living world would burst spontaneously into flames. . . . Similarly, without carbon dioxide, photosynthesis would fail, plants would die, and life would vanish from the Earth. With more carbon dioxide, however, so much heat would be trapped in air and sea by the greenhouse effect that the planet would descend into hell." (Jonathan Weiner, *Planet Earth,* Bantam Books, New York, 1986, p. 327)

Abravanel

Interpreters of the Torah's "creation" story also called attention to the fragile balance of conditions they observed in the heavens and on earth. For example, Don Isaac Abravanel, who lived and taught in late fifteenth-century Spain, speculated that, had the sun been larger, or placed closer to the earth, its heat would have destroyed our planet. Had it been placed a fraction farther away, our Earth would have been locked forever in a frozen winter. God, Abravanel taught, had wisely set each star in its precise position. (Abravanel on Genesis 1:1)

Other Jewish teachers went several steps beyond Abravanel. They likened the world to a "palace" brought into existence for the benefit of human beings. God, they explained, had not only created it but had furnished and filled it with opportunities for enjoyment. Then, God had presented it as a gift to human beings. From that point on, they maintained, human beings had been appointed as "caretakers" of the world. (*Sanhedrin* 38a)

> *It is up to human beings. . . .*
> *The heavens belong to God, but the earth God gave to humanity.* (Psalms 115:16)
>
> *In interpreting the phrase: "Let the earth sprout vegetation . . ." Aderet Eliyahu explains that God placed the potential for growth in the earth. It is up to human beings to sow the seeds.* (Genesis 1:11)

As "caretakers" of this "palace" called Earth, Jewish tradition teaches that human beings have important, even critical, choices to make, especially today.

The advance of industrial power and technology have brought us many blessings in this century, but they have also brought us serious "curses." For instance, we warm our homes from the cold of winter and cool them from the heat of summer by using huge quantities of energy drawn from critical resources. We are polluting the air we breathe, the water we drink, and our sources of food production. We are cutting down forests to build our homes, industrial centers, and cities and to make room for more farmlands on which to grow enough food to feed increasing numbers of human beings. One recent United Nations report warns that, because of overpopulation, by the end of the twentieth century "all accessible tropical forests will have disappeared."

And there is another frightening condition to add to our burden as "caretakers" of this "palace" we call Earth. It is the danger of nuclear destruction. Today, there are enough nuclear warheads to end all life on our planet. It is estimated that a full-scale nuclear war between the United States and the Soviet Union would not only bring death to hundreds of millions of human beings but would probably eliminate the civilizations of Europe, China, Japan, Russia, and the United States.

Jewish tradition teaches us that human beings are responsible for the earth. According to the rabbis, after Adam was created, God led him around the Garden of Eden, showing him all the beautiful flowers and trees. Then God told him: "See how beautiful everything is that I have created. It has all been made for you. Remember this, and do not corrupt or destroy My world. For, if you do, there will be no one left to save it." (*Ecclesiastes Rabbah 7:13*)

According to the Torah, God gave humanity the power to rule the world. We are its "caretakers." It is ours to enjoy, but it is also our responsibility to preserve. The choice is ours. The Torah challenges us with God's commandment: "I call heaven and earth to witness against you this day: I have put before you life and death, blessing and curse. Choose life. . . ." (Deuteronomy 30:19)

PEREK GIMEL: *Expelled from the Garden of Eden*

The Garden of Eden was a beautiful place in which to live. All of Adam's and Eve's needs were satisfied, but in the end they were expelled. What happened? What did they do to deserve such punishment?

One answer may be found in the differences between what God commanded them to do and how they reported it to each other and the serpent. Compare the following two versions found in the Torah:

God says to Adam: *"Of every tree of the garden you are free to eat; but as for the Tree of Knowledge of Good and Bad, you must not eat of it; for as soon as you eat of it, you shall die." (Genesis 2:16–17)*

Eve says to the serpent: *"We may eat of the fruit of the other trees of the garden. It is only about fruit of the tree in the middle of the garden that God said: You shall not eat of it or touch it, lest you die." (Genesis 3:2–3)*

It is clear that Adam was given one version of the commandment and that Eve reports another to the serpent. Adam is told that, if they eat from the Tree of Knowledge of Good and Bad, they will die. Eve reports that, if they either eat from the "tree in the middle of the garden" *or touch it,* they will die. She not only fails to report the name of the tree but clearly adds a new condition to God's original statement. Later interpreters of Torah reached the conclusion that her alteration of God's commandment led to misunderstanding and, ultimately, to expulsion from the Garden of Eden.

For example, Rashi believed that the serpent took advantage of Eve's misrepresentation of God's commandment to Adam. He speculated that, when Eve told the serpent that God had warned her: "You shall not eat of it *or touch it,* lest you die," the serpent pushed her until she touched the tree. Then the serpent said to her: "You see, you have not died after touching it. Nothing has happened to you. And you will not die after you eat from its fruit."

Rashi's theory is that the serpent was very clever, using Eve's misrepresentation of what God had said to Adam as a way of tricking her into eating the fruit.

On the other hand, perhaps it was Adam who misrepresented the original commandment to Eve. The Torah does not tell us what he said to her. He might only have pointed to a tree in the middle of the garden without identifying it by name. And he may have even added the warning about *touching it* in order to frighten her.

We will never know what Adam did or did not tell Eve or who was to blame, but it is clear that the first small lie about what God had said led to much trouble and, ultimately, to the expulsion of Adam and Eve from the Garden of Eden. Perhaps that explains why Jewish teachers emphasize the importance of careful communication and accurate reporting.

Be careful of your words
We are warned: *"Let your words be few,"* and *"A fool multiplies words."* (*Ecclesiastes 5:1 and 10:14; also Job 35:16 and 38:2*)

Zugot

The rabbinic teacher Abtalyon told his students: "You who are wise, be careful of your words. . . ." (Avot 1:11)

In the Book of Proverbs (30:6), we are taught: "Do not add to God's words, for you will be criticized and revealed as a liar." In other words, when we are given a message for someone else, we are expected to deliver it *exactly* as it was given. Adding to what we have been told, even if we believe that our interpretation will improve communication, may lead to distorting the truth.

That is the mistake that Eve, and perhaps Adam, made in the Garden of Eden. Then, after they had eaten the forbidden fruit and were about to be punished by God, they made things worse for themselves by blaming each other for what had happened. The Torah reports their conversation with God as follows:

> Then [God] asked . . . "Did you eat of the tree from which I had forbidden you to eat?"
> [Adam] said, "The woman You put at my side— she gave me of the tree, and I ate."
> And God said to Eve, "What is this you have done!"
> And Eve replied, "The serpent tricked me, and I ate."
>
> (Genesis 3:11–13)

Adam and Eve each offer an excuse for eating the forbidden fruit. Adam blames God for putting Eve at his side. Eve blames the serpent for tricking her. No one says: "It's my fault. I am sorry. Forgive me. I made a mistake." Neither Adam nor Eve is willing to take responsibility for what has happened.

Perhaps that is why they were expelled from the Garden of Eden. They changed the meaning of God's original commandment by not reporting it accurately. Then, after they had eaten from the fruit of the forbidden tree, they sought to place the blame on God, on the serpent, and on each other. For misrepresenting what they had been told and for refusing to accept responsibility for their actions, God expelled them from Eden.

PEREK DALET: *We Are Responsible for One Another*

The tenth-century Babylonian scholar and head of the Babylonian Academy at Sura, Sa'adia ben Joseph Ha-Gaon, commented that "the human being is the purpose of creation."

This understanding that human beings were created in "the image of God" and, therefore, represent the highest expression of God's power and love led Jewish teachers to the conclusion that every human life is sacred. And, because it is, human beings must not only care for the world in which they live but bear a special obligation to care about one another.

The life or death of the world
The Mishnah says that "Adam was created as a single person in order to teach that, if one murders another person, the Torah holds him responsible for the death of a whole world. And, if a person saves the life of one person, the Torah considers him as if he saved the whole world." (Sanhedrin 4:5)

For Jewish tradition, each human life is a precious and sacred world of possibilities. Not only does each person possess special talents, thoughts, and abilities but from each person others are born and the chain of humanity continues. "Each person is a world," the rabbis commented. Therefore individuals contain within themselves future worlds.

That is what made the murder of Abel by Cain such a serious offense. When the rabbis discussed the murder, they pointed out an unusual phrasing of God's statement to Abel. God said to him: "Behold, your brother's blood cries out to Me from the ground!" (Genesis 4:10) In the Hebrew, the words *deme [achicha] tzoakim* are plural and may be translated, "[your brother's] *bloods* cry out."

According to the rabbis the phrase "*bloods* cry out" is an indication that Cain murdered more than just Abel. He also destroyed Abel's future generations. They tell us that God said to Cain: "Not only are you responsible for murdering your brother, but you have also murdered his unborn offspring. The voice of your brother's blood, and of all his would-be descendants whom you prevented from coming into the world, cries out to Me." (*Midrash Agadah* 4,9)

In killing Abel, Cain destroyed a whole line of humanity. The great tragedy was not only the death of Abel but the loss of all the thousands of future lives cut off with his murder.

Because Jewish tradition considers every human life sacred, it holds that each human being must care for others. We are guardians or caretakers of one another. Cain murdered his brother because he failed to understand that he was his brother's "keeper," or "guardian."

The Torah tells us that, when God saw what he had done, God asked, "Where is your brother Abel?" And Cain answered, "I do not know. Am I my brother's keeper?"

The word for "keeper" in Hebrew is *shomer,* which also means "guardian," or the one who is responsible to look out for the safety and security of others. Cain failed to see himself as the *keeper* or *guardian* of his brother. He did not believe that he was responsible for protecting or caring for him. As a result, when they quarreled and became angry with each other, he struck and killed him.

We are guardians

A famed chasidic teacher, Rabbi Mendel of Kotzk (1788–1859), once warned his students: "Be sure to take care of your own soul and of another person's body, not of your own body and of another person's soul."

From the Torah's report of Cain's murder of his brother, Abel, we are taught that each human life is sacred and that we are guardians of one another. Our duty is to protect one another both physically and spiritually. We are obligated to be concerned about one another's safety, health, and welfare. Human beings are responsible for one another.

QUESTIONS FOR STUDY AND DISCUSSION

1. Why have human beings throughout the centuries created explanations about the creation of the world and human beings?

2. The nineteenth-century philosopher Friedrich Nietzsche once commented: "The world is beautiful but has a disease called humanity." How would Jewish thinkers respond to such an observation?

3. In one day American miners dig up 625 acres of land, almost one square mile; they clean up and replant about 337 acres. In one day Americans produce 1.5 million pounds of hazardous waste. In what other ways are human beings not "caring" for the world we inhabit? Why? What, according to Jewish tradition, are our obligations?

4. There is a Yiddish proverb that states: "A half-truth is a whole lie." Would you agree? Are there times when the truth should not be spoken? Why do so many of us, like Eve, have difficulty telling the truth?

5. In light of our discussion of Cain and Abel, what can we say about the scope of human destruction during World War II when eleven million men, women, and children, including six million Jews, were killed?

PARASHAT NOACH
Genesis 6:9–11:32

Parashat Noach tells the story of God's decision to destroy the earth with a flood because of the corruption and wickedness found in the world. Only a righteous man by the name of Noah, his family, and pairs of every kind of creature were to survive. Noah was told to build a large boat, an ark, and to make a place on it for every creature he was to save. After the Flood, those aboard the ark started life on earth all over again, and God promised never to send another flood. Later, human beings decided to build a city and a huge tower that would reach from earth to heaven. Seeing what they were doing, God scattered them all over the earth and gave them different languages to speak.

OUR TARGUM

· 1 ·

God looked upon the earth and saw that it was a place of evildoing. Human beings were corrupt. They made laws and then refused to obey them. People were concerned only with their own personal gain. Selfishness, cruelty, and dishonesty prevailed.

So God decided to destroy all life on earth with a flood. Noah, who was considered a "righteous" person, was ordered to build a boat, or ark, which would hold his family and a male and female of every living thing upon the earth. Noah built the ark, and, when the Flood came, everything in the ark survived.

After one hundred and fifty days of flooding, the waters subsided, and the ark came to rest in the mountains of Ararat, located in Iran. Noah sent a raven out to search for dry land. Then he sent a dove, and, when it returned with an olive branch in its beak, he knew that the floodwaters were gone.

Noah, his family, and all the living creatures left the ark, and God promised that "never again" would the world be destroyed by a flood. As a sign of that promise, God put a rainbow in the sky.

other. The city in Shinar where all this took place was named *Babel,* which means "confusion."

· 2 ·

After the Flood, human life increased on the earth. People spoke one language, and they built a city and a high tower in the land of Shinar. "Let's make a name for ourselves," they said to one another. "Let's build our tower so that it reaches high into the heavens!"

God saw what they were doing and was displeased. "If as one people with one language this is how they act, then they will be able to do anything they decide." Fearing their abuse of power, God scattered the people all over the earth and confused them so that they spoke many languages and were unable to understand one an-

· 3 ·

Afterwards, Shem, Noah's son, had a son by the name of Arpachshad, whose son was Shelah, whose son was Eber, whose son was Peleg, whose son was Reu, whose son was Serug, whose son was Nahor, whose son was Terah. Terah had three sons, Abram, Nahor, and Haran. Abram was the founder of the Jewish people, and he married Sarai. Haran was the father of Lot.

Near the end of his life, Terah took Abram, Sarai, and his grandson, Lot, and they traveled from Ur of the Chaldeans, which is located on the Euphrates River in what is today Iraq, to Haran, which is located in Syria. They settled there, and Terah died.

THEMES

Parashat Noach contains three important themes:

1. One "righteous" human being can make a difference in saving the world.
2. Corruption, dishonesty, and selfishness can destroy the world.
3. When people create or build for fame or for power over others, they bring unhappiness and confusion into the world.

PEREK ALEF: *Was Noah Really a "Righteous" Person?*

At the very beginning of this Torah portion we are told three things about Noah: he "walked with God"; he was "blameless in his generation"; and he was "a righteous man." Later we read that God said to him: "You alone have I found righteous before Me in this generation."

There are those who maintain that the Torah's description of Noah is accurate. They point out that Noah followed what God commanded him to do. When God ordered him to build the ark, he did so. When he was told to round up pairs of all living creatures and to make a place for them in the ark, he did so. He did not doubt God's commandment but faithfully carried it out. As a result, life on earth was preserved after the Flood.

Ibn Ezra   *Ramban (Nachmanides)*

In addition, according to some commentators, Noah was a totally ethical person. Rabbi Abraham ibn Ezra taught that Noah was "righteous in his deeds." Nachmanides explained that Noah was "neither a person of violence, nor a person who cheated and lied as did the guilty people of his generation . . . he did not participate in the cults of astrology, enchantment, and soothsaying, nor did he worship idols. He walked with God."

But does the fact that Noah did what God commanded him to do make him a "righteous" person? Was it enough not to engage in violence or not to become involved in the cults of his day? Are we to consider Noah a "righteous" person because he followed God's orders without asking any questions? Was it sufficient for him to save himself, his family, and pairs of all living creatures from the destructive waters of the Flood?

Some teachers of Jewish tradition have com-

pared Noah to Abraham. They point out that, when God was about to destroy the cities of Sodom and Gomorrah, Abraham argued on behalf of their citizens. Even though they were corrupt, dishonest, and violent, Abraham took their side and tried to save them and their cities.

By contrast, Noah said nothing on behalf of the people of his generation. He was indifferent to the suffering they were about to experience and expressed no regret over the pain of those who would drown in the waters of the Flood. He made no effort to defend them or to intercede with God on their behalf. Noah simply followed directions and built his ark.

Righteous but . . .

The Zohar explains that Noah was out to save himself and his family. He did not intervene or speak up for the people of his generation when he was told that they would be destroyed.

"His righteousness bore the stamp of mediocrity." (Rabbi Mordechai Yaffe, Levush ha-Ora)

Noah remained silent because he did not believe that God would really bring the Flood to destroy all life. He lacked faith. He thought that God was just going to frighten the wicked people of his generation into changing their evil and violent behavior. So he did not speak up and tell them to save themselves. (Toledot Yitzhak)

A great leader is not only a person of ideas, not only a person of personal integrity and devotion, but also a person of tenderness, a person of compassion. . . . If he is insensitive to the sorrows of people, all of his ideals and all of his personal qualities fail to confer greatness upon him. (Rabbi Morris Adler, The Voice Still Speaks, *Bloch, New York, 1969, p. 20)*

In the Talmud, Rabbi Berechia asks why Noah did not at least pray for his generation to repent and be saved. Apparently, Noah was a pious man who "walked with God," but his "piety" did not extend to a concern about the welfare of others. We have no report of his going out to warn the people around him that a terrible flood was about to destroy them. Nor are we told that he pleaded with them to change their evil ways and to save themselves. Noah, it appears, was more concerned with his own safety and survival than he was with the survival of his friends and neighbors.

The eighteenth-century chasidic master Rabbi Elimelech of Lizensk once observed that there are two kinds of "righteous" persons: one is genuinely "righteous"; the other dresses like a "righteous" person in a fur coat. Each of them faces a freezing winter in a different way: one will go out and collect wood for a fire; the other will wrap himself in his fur coat. The one who collects wood lights a fire and invites others to join him. He not only warms himself but others as well. The one who makes himself cozy in his own heavy coat is secure, but those around him will freeze. For Elimelech the genuinely "righteous" person was the one who shared warmth with others. In that sense, Noah was not truly "righteous."

The author of *Toledot Yitzhak* argues that Noah doubted what God had told him about a terrible flood that was going to destroy all life on earth. Noah couldn't believe that such a destruction would take place. Therefore, he kept the information to himself rather than sharing it with others. Instead of warning them—giving them a chance to appeal to God or to build their own arks—he said nothing.

Can we consider a person who hides such information a "righteous" person?

And what kind of leadership did Noah display? Nowhere are we told that he had any followers or any students. He built his ark all by himself. He seems to have been a loner, a "righteous" man whose influence extended only to the narrow circle of his family.

Interpreters even raise serious questions about Noah's family. Some argue that his children were saved only because of *his* "righteousness," not because of any good deeds of *their* own. Like their father, none of them spoke out on behalf of those about to be destroyed. Nor did they offer any warnings or try to talk Noah into building some extra arks in which to save more people and other forms of life. Tragically, Noah failed to have a righteous influence even upon his sons, Shem, Ham, and Japheth.

Who is "righteous"?
". . . the righteous is generous and keeps giving." (Psalms 37:21)

"*The righteous must be a lover of human beings.*" (Wisdom of Solomon *12:19; also* Kiddushin *40a*)

So there are questions to be asked about how "righteous" a person Noah really was. Was it enough for him to build an ark and save his family and all the living creatures God had commanded him to place inside? Should he have protested what God was about to do just as Abraham did when God told him that Sodom and Gomorrah were about to be destroyed? (See Genesis 18:16–33.) Can we call a person "righteous" if he does not inspire followers or if he refuses to share critical information with those whose lives may depend upon it? Was Noah really a "righteous" person?

PEREK BET: *Why Did God Send the Flood?*

When the Torah describes the creation of the world, we are told that it was "good." Yet a few chapters later in the story of Noah we are informed that God said: "I have decided to put an end to all flesh, for the earth is filled with lawlessness because of them: I am about to destroy them with the earth." (Genesis 6:13)

What had happened? How could the God who had called all that had been created "good," and even "very good," now plan to destroy everything?

The Torah uses two words to illustrate what was happening in Noah's generation and to explain why God decided to send the destructive waters of the Flood. They are *shichet*, meaning "corruption," and *chamas*, meaning "lawlessness."

What was the nature of that "corruption" and

"lawlessness"? Was it really so serious that it justified the destruction of all life?

What was their "corruption" and "lawlessness"?

The people of that generation said: "For what reason do we need God? . . . We have no need of rain. We get an abundant supply of water from other sources, from all the streams and wells of the earth." (Sanhedrin 108a)

A man would take two wives—one for childbearing, the other for pleasure. (Midrash ha-Gadol 10:5)

They exchanged wives. (Genesis Rabbah 23:3)

When a person brought a basket full of peas to the marketplace, he would be surrounded by a group of people. Each would steal an amount worth less than a pruta (so small an amount that it was not considered a punishable offense). But soon the basket would be empty. The victim would be unable to present his case to a judge because each thief had cleverly taken less than the amount that was punishable by law. (Genesis Rabbah 31:50)

They removed the landmarks of their neighbors in order to extend their borders. If someone saw an ox or a donkey in the hands of an orphan or widow, he took it away. (Midrash Tanchuma, Noach 26)

Those questions were also asked by the rabbis many centuries ago. They reasoned that Noah's generation had been blessed with "good times." Harvests were plentiful. People lived hundreds of years without sickness, pain, or fear. The weather was always pleasantly mild. No one lacked for anything.

As a result, the rabbis tell us, the people of Noah's generation began to take all the benefits of life for granted. They felt no need to give thanks to God for what they enjoyed. "Why shall we waste our time on prayers of praise to God?" they argued. "Don't we have everything we need? What more can God do for us?"

Many stopped worshiping God. Their self-interest led them to conclude that nothing was as important or "sacred" as taking care of themselves. The concerns of others were less important or of no importance at all. Since they no longer believed in God, they also no longer believed that each person was created in God's image or that every human life was sacred and must be protected.

As a result they became suspicious of one another. Trust between them broke down, and violence increased. No one cared about the poor, the sick, or the homeless. People took advantage of one another. They robbed, lied, and murdered. They bribed judges and found loopholes in the law, twisting it to suit their selfish purposes. In the end, cruelty, terror, fear, and hatred ruled their civilization.

The Torah informs us that God's decision to destroy life on earth was made because of *ra'at ha-adam*, "the evil of human beings." The people of Noah's generation, we are told, spent their days planning and devising "nothing but evil all the time." (Genesis 6:5)

Yet, was there no way to save them? If God is "good" and created such a "good" world, why was there no warning to the people of Noah's generation or any chance provided for them to change their evil ways? Perhaps they could have been rescued. Perhaps, like the people of Nineveh in Jonah's time, they might have repented and asked God to forgive their violence and cruelty. Perhaps the terrible Flood was unnecessary.

The rabbis who composed the *Midrash Tanchuma* explained that God wanted the people of Noah's generation to change their behavior. That is why God commanded Noah to build the ark. It was to serve as a warning to his generation. But no one paid attention. Here is how some of the rabbis described what happened:

God said: "If Noah starts to work on the ark, people will gather around him and say to him, 'What are you making?' He will answer, 'I am building an ark because God is about to bring a flood on the earth.'" God hoped that the ark would serve as a warning, but the people of Noah's generation paid no attention to what Noah was building.

In another version the rabbis tell us:

> Noah planted cedars, and the people of his day asked him, "What are you planting cedars for?" He told them, "God is about to bring a flood and has commanded me to build an ark for me and my family to escape in." When they heard his explanation, they all laughed and ridiculed him. Later, when he was cutting down the cedar trees and planing the wood, they asked, "What are you doing with that cedarwood?" At that point he warned them, again, about the Flood, but they paid no attention and refused to repent.
>
> (*Midrash Tanchuma, Noach*)

The rabbis make the point that God did not want to destroy all life on earth. Noah's generation was given every opportunity to prevent the Flood. But they would not change their "lawlessness" and "corrupt" ways. They continued their violence toward one another. Greed and distrust, cheating and dishonesty ruled their times.

God wanted to save them, to preserve all life, but they refused to cooperate. They could have changed the course of history, but they would not change themselves.

PEREK GIMEL: *What Went Wrong at the Tower of Babel?*

The Torah tells us that, after the Flood, people moved eastward and settled in the land of Shinar. They decided to build a city for themselves and a *migdal,* a "tower," that reached up into the heavens. "Let's make a name for ourselves," they said to one another, "or we will be scattered all over the earth."

Seeing the city and tower they were building, God decided to do what the people had feared. "If, as one people with one language for all, this is how they have begun to act," God reasoned, "then nothing that they may propose to do will be out of their reach." For that reason God scattered them throughout the world and made them speak different languages.

The city where this all took place was named *Babel,* which means "confused" or "mixed up." That seems an appropriate description of the entire episode, and it raises several questions. What was wrong with people building a *migdal,* a "tower"? Wouldn't we be better off if peoples everywhere spoke one language? Wouldn't that have improved communication and, perhaps, the chances for human cooperation and peace?"

Abravanel

Abravanel, a counselor to the kings and queens in Spain and Portugal, explained that, before they began building the tower, people had lived at peace with one another. They shared everything equally and generously. But, as soon as they began building, they started to argue bitterly with one another. They disagreed over who would bake the bricks, who would carry them, and who would place them on the tower. Each one wanted the credit for laying the first brick on a new level, for the design, for choosing the color, or for organizing the work. The project of building the tower made people jealous of one another. It caused them to hate one another. They became more interested in competing for fame than cooperating for the good of the whole human community. As a result, God destroyed the tower and scattered them throughout the world.

Benno Jacob

Rabbi Benno Jacob (1862–1945), a modern biblical scholar, suggests that those who built the tower failed because their goals were wrong. They had mastered the art of brick making, of molding and heating the clay. But, instead of using their new technology to improve living conditions in their city, to create housing for the poor, sick, and aging, they decided to use all their resources and efforts to build the highest tower in the world.

They reasoned that their high tower would bring them fame and glory. They wanted others to say, "Look what they have done!" Their terrible mistake was to use their technology for pride and vanity instead of using it to improve the quality of life in their society.

No regard for a human life

The tower was built with seven steps on the east side and seven steps on the west side, and it was seven miles high. (Some versions of the story say that it was twenty-seven miles high!) It took a person one year to climb from the bottom to the top. The bricks were carried up from one side, and the line of workers went down on the other side. If a worker fell down and died, they paid no attention to him. But, if a brick fell, they would all sit and weep. "What a loss," they would say. "Look how long it will take until we can bring another brick to take its place." (Pirke de-Rabbi Eliezer 24)

According to the ancient rabbis, the creation of the tower was a huge project. They report that, because there were no natural stones with which to construct the tower in the plain of Shinar, it was necessary to invent a special process of baking the bricks. Hundreds of people were required to run the furnaces where they were baked; hundreds of others were needed to prepare the material. Thousands were used to carry them from the location of the baking-furnaces to the base of the tower; thousands more were employed to carry them up the steep steps that reached high into the sky.

It did not take long before the "project" became more important than the health or safety of those who were involved in it. People were enslaved as laborers. Individual rights and liberties were taken away. The building of the tower and the achievement of fame for the community became justification for brutality and the end of individual freedom. Bricks became more important than individual liberties or lives.

The Italian Torah commentator, scientist, and philosopher Obadiah Sforno (1475–1550), who lived through the bitter times of the Inquisition when Jews suffered and were often put to death for their differing religious views, criticized the

generation of tower builders for another reason. Their real crime, Sforno argued, was not simply the way in which they built the tower, but it was also in what they sought to accomplish by its creation. Their goal, Sforno explained, was *one* religion for everyone, *one* point of view on the world, *one* accepted political way of doing things.

The tower builders believed that differences of opinion, controversy, and diversity of belief were dangerous and unacceptable. They opposed freedom of thought or discussion. Those who questioned their views or authority were to be crushed. According to Sforno, when God saw that the tower builders were crushing freedom of thought and discussion, it became necessary to intervene and to scatter human beings throughout the world.

As we can see, the commentators found many important explanations for God's destruction of the Tower of Babel. The project produced jealousy and mean competition, a misuse of technology, and a cruel disregard for the worth of each individual life. It fostered a false patriotism and, ultimately, threatened the loss of freedom.

Could it be that God actually saved humanity from catastrophe by destroying the tower and dispersing us, with different languages and traditions, to all corners of the earth? Perhaps the real message of the Torah's story about the building of the Tower of Babel has to do with helping us understand that our differences in language, culture, and traditions all represent significant strengths and blessings for humanity.

QUESTIONS FOR STUDY AND DISCUSSION

1. One might defend or criticize Noah by claiming that he was "just following orders." Soldiers and bureaucrats have often used this excuse to justify their action or inaction. Is this a legitimate defense in Noah's case?

2. Would you have believed Noah if he had told you that God was about to destroy the whole world? Some scientists today are warning that we are in danger of "destroying our world." Why do people refuse to listen to the "bad-

news" predictions? Why do we disbelieve our experts?

3. What is so wrong with the tower builders' plan of *one* religion, *one* accepted political point of view, *one* point of view on the world?

4. In addition to buildings, what do human beings often value more than they should? Is there a difference between living as if you are "created in the image of God" or living as if you are a god?

PARASHAT LECH-LECHA
Genesis 12:1–17:27

Parashat Lech-Lecha begins with the story of Abram leaving his birthplace in Haran. God promises the land of Canaan to Abram and his descendants. Because of a famine in the land, Abram takes his family to Egypt. While there, the pharaoh orders Abram's wife, Sarai, to live in his palace. Plagues come upon Egypt as punishment for what Pharaoh has done, and Sarai is restored to Abram. Returning to Canaan, Abram and his brother's son, Lot, divide the land in order to prevent any disagreements between them. Later, Lot is attacked and taken hostage by enemy kings. Abram rescues him and his family. Because Abram and Sarai have trouble conceiving a child, Sarai, in the custom of ancient times, invites her maidservant, Hagar, to have a child with Abram. When Hagar becomes pregnant, she begins to abuse Sarai, who responds by chasing away Hagar. An angel tells Hagar to return, and she bears a son whom Abram names Ishmael. As this Torah portion concludes, Abram is instructed to circumcise himself and Ishmael. Abram is told that the circumcision of all males at eight days of age will be a sign of God's covenant with him and his people forever.

OUR TARGUM

· 1 ·

God said to Abram, "*Lech-lecha*—go forth from your native land and from your father's house to the land that I will show you. I will make of you a great nation, and I will bless you." So Abram and his wife, Sarai, and his brother's son, Lot, set out for the land of Canaan, which today is the Land of Israel. When they reached the border of the land, God said to Abram, "I will give this land to your descendants."

· 2 ·

Because of poor crops and a shortage of food in the land of Canaan, Abram and Sarai traveled to

Egypt. Abram feared that an Egyptian might admire Sarai and want to kill him in order to take her as a wife. He therefore instructed her to say that she was his sister.

His prediction proved correct. While in Egypt, the pharaoh saw Sarai and demanded that she come to live in his palace. Shortly after she had moved in, God sent plagues upon Egypt, and Pharaoh discovered Sarai's real identity. "Why did you not tell me that she was your wife?" Pharaoh asked Abram. Then, seeking forgiveness from God, he sent Abram and Sarai away with many gifts.

· 3 ·

From Egypt, Abram, Sarai, and Lot returned through the Negev desert to Bethel, which is located today about seventeen miles north of Jerusalem. When they reached Bethel, their herdsmen began to quarrel about where their cattle would graze. So Abram suggested that they divide the land between them. Lot chose the Plain of Jordan and settled near the city of Sodom. Abram remained in the land of Canaan, settling in Hebron.

· 4 ·

Later, four foreign kings raided the cities of Sodom and Gomorrah and took Lot as a captive. Hearing that Lot was in trouble, Abram gathered a troop of fighters and set out to rescue him. When they returned victoriously, the king of Sodom offered Abram a reward for having saved Lot and his city. Abram refused the reward. He told the king: "I will take nothing that is yours. I do not want you to say, 'It was I who made Abram rich.' "

· 5 ·

Now, God had promised that Abram's descendants would inherit that land, but Abram and Sarai had no children. So Sarai asked her maidservant, an Egyptian woman named Hagar, to have a child with Abram. That was a common custom in that time for childless parents. When Hagar became pregnant, she began treating Sarai disrespectfully. Sarai blamed Abram for Hagar's attitude. When Abram told Sarai: "Deal with her as you think right," Sarai forced Hagar to flee from her house.

An angel saw what had happened and told Hagar to return to Sarai's house. The angel also promised that she would bear a son whose name would be Ishmael. Abram was then eighty-six years old.

· 6 ·

Afterwards, God told Abram: "I will establish My covenant between Me and you, and I will make you exceedingly numerous." God changed Abram's name to "Abraham" (*Avraham*), meaning "father of a multitude," and promised the "land of Canaan, as an everlasting possession." As a sign of the covenant between God and Abraham's offspring, God commanded that every Jewish male be circumcised at the age of eight days. So Abraham circumcised himself and Ishmael.

God also changed Sarai's name to "Sarah," meaning "princess," and said to Abraham: "I will give you a son by her . . . rulers of peoples shall issue from her."

THEMES

Parashat Lech-Lecha contains five important themes:

1. The demands of leadership.
2. Honesty in our dealings with others.

3. Settling disagreements.
4. Rescuing captives.
5. The Jewish covenant of circumcision.

PEREK ALEF: *What Qualified Abram for Leadership of the Jewish People?*

The Torah tells us very little about Abram's early life. We are informed that he and Sarai, along with his nephew Lot, were brought by his father, Terah, from Ur of the Chaldeans to Haran. After Terah's death, Abram was commanded by God to leave Haran and promised that he would become "a great nation."

For thousands of years students of Torah have been asking: "Why was Abram chosen for such important leadership? What had he done to be named the founder of the Jewish people?"

The rabbis who studied this Torah portion suggested that, while the Torah might not tell us much about Abram's early life or why he might have been selected for leadership, there was much to learn from the legends collected and passed from generation to generation by Jews.

According to some of those reports, Abram rebelled against the worship of idols in his home and in the palace of Nimrod, who ruled at that time. At an early age he saw some people praying to different stars and planets and others making gods out of wood and stone. He said to himself: "How is it possible for this wonderful world to have been created by a star or a planet, or by an idol that is made by human hands? How is it possible for something manufactured of wood or stone to be considered responsible for the development of our human ethical sense of right and wrong or of our desire to improve the world?"

The more questions Abram asked, the more foolish idolatry seemed to him. So he began asking questions of his father and of others who worked in Nimrod's palace. They resented his questions because they could not answer them. They accused Abram of being a troublemaker and a "revolutionary." When he persisted with his questions and public rejection of idolatry, his father reported him to Nimrod, and he was persecuted for his ideas and put into prison.

Abram's rejection of idolatry
When Abram came to his father's home, he saw his father's gods, twelve in number. . . . He hurried from the room into his father's outer courtyard, where he found his father seated with all his servants; and he came and sat down before his father and asked him: "Father, tell me, where is the God who created the heavens and the earth and created all human beings on earth?" And Terah answered Abram his son, saying: "Why, those who created all these are with us in the house!"

. . . So Abram took dishes and brought them into the chamber before his father's gods . . . and saw that not one of them was stretching out a hand to eat. . . . So he took hammers and . . . smashed all the gods of his father.

. . . When Terah saw this, he grew very angry. . . . "What have you done to all my gods?" And Abram answered his father . . . "I only brought fine dishes of food before them. But, when I offered the dishes to them to eat, all of them put out their hands to begin before the biggest of them all had started eating. When the big one saw what they did without waiting for him, he grew very angry . . . and smashed them all."

When Terah heard this, he grew exceedingly angry. . . . "You are speaking falsehood to me! Have these gods any spirit or soul or strength to do all you have told me? Why, they are wood and stone, and I made them! How can you tell me such lies?"

. . . Then Abram answered his father: "Then how can you worship these idols, who do not have the strength to do anything? Are these idols in whom you trust going to deliver you? Can they really hear your prayers when you cry unto them?" (Micha Joseph Bin Gorion, Mimekor Yisrael, Volume I, 15)

God chose Abram as the founder of the Jewish people because of his wisdom and bravery. He was not afraid to ask hard questions or to stand up for what he believed. He was willing to risk ridicule, even suffering and persecution, for his convictions. He was willing to lead the minority of those who believed that idolatry was wrong and to devote his life to teaching that one God was the creative Source of all life. Those qualities made him a gifted leader.

Abram possessed other special qualities as well. The rabbis of the Midrash tell us that the prices he quoted in his business dealings were always fair, that people came to him for advice in times of trouble, and that when he was told that someone was sick he would not just offer a prayer but would visit and make the person feel better because of his concern and interest. (*Genesis Rabbah, Lech-Lecha,* 11)

Abram's priorities
Rabbi Levi explains that, when Abram was traveling through various lands, he saw people going to drunken parties. "May I not be a part of this country!" he would say. But, when he reached the location of Tyre, near the Land of Israel, and saw people working at weeding and hoeing in the proper seasons, he said: "May my portion be in this country." (Genesis Rabbah, Lech-Lecha, 8)

Abram valued creative work. He rejected the company of those who chose to waste their energies and time with drugs or drunkenness. He respected those who planned for the future and who were willing to work hard in order to transform their ideas and hopes into reality.

For all those reasons, our Torah interpreters tell us, Abram was selected as the founder and leader of the Jewish people.

PEREK BET: *Is It Ever Right to Lie?*

Abram and Sarai find themselves in a dangerous situation within our Torah portion. They have gone to Egypt in order to escape from famine in the Land of Israel. Fearing that some Egyptian will admire Sarai and kill him, Abram tells her not to reveal that she is his wife. When the pharaoh of Egypt asks her who she is, she tells him that she is Abram's "sister."

Later, after Pharaoh discovers the truth, he confronts Abram and asks: "Why didn't you tell me that she was your wife?" The Torah does not tell us what Abram answered. We are only informed that Pharaoh sent him away with Sarai and with all the riches he had acquired in Egypt.

Should Abram have lied? Was it permissible for him to say that his wife was his "sister" in order to save himself?

A half-truth
It was not a lie for Abram to call Sarai his "sister" since Sarai was his niece, and relatives may be termed brother and sister. (Midrash ha-Gadol 12:12)

On another occasion, Abram also told Sarai to say that she was his "sister." In his explanation of what he had done he said: ". . . she is in truth my sister, my father's daughter though not my mother's; and she became my wife." (Genesis 20:12)

Ramban (Nachmanides)

Faced with the fear that he might be killed by the Egyptians, Abram may have decided to tell a "half-truth." He would say that Sarai was his "sister" which, in fact, she was, but he would not reveal that she was his wife. The commentator Nachmanides condemns Abram for his behavior. He says that Abram "committed a great sin" by not telling the truth about his wife. "He should have trusted that God would save him and his wife and all his belongings. . . ." (Genesis 12:9)

Hirsch

Other commentators disagree. Rabbi Samson Raphael Hirsch, a leading scholar who lived in

Germany from 1808 to 1888, argued that Abram's actions were honorable. He knew that the Egyptians would not deal harshly with an unmarried woman traveling with her brother but that they would kill the husband of a beautiful woman and rape her. So he acted to protect both Sarai and himself. In fact, he was really telling the truth. She was the daughter of his father and actually his "sister."

The issue remains unresolved. Was Abram justified in lying? Is using a half-truth lying? And what about Sarai? Was it her responsibility to tell the truth rather than follow Abram's instructions?

PEREK GIMEL: *Dealing with Differences*

When Abram and Lot left Egypt, they took with them many flocks and herds. They had both become rich. When they reached Bethel, the Torah tells us that their herdsmen began to quarrel with one another.

What the Torah does not reveal are the reasons for their arguments. Those are suggested by the interpreters who commented on this section of our Torah portion.

One commentator explains that Lot's herdsmen paid no attention to posted borders or signs that read Private Property. They allowed their animals to graze wherever they happened to wander. Abram's herdsman saw what they were doing and accused them of robbery.

> ***What they argued about:***
> *Rabbi Berekiah said in Rabbi Judah's name: Abram's cattle would be muzzled and then taken out so that they could not graze in land that was not permitted. On the other hand, Lot's herdsmen refused to muzzle their cattle. As a result they grazed wherever they went.*
>
> *When Abram's herdsmen asked, "Is what you are doing not robbery?" Lot's herdsmen replied, "Abram is a barren mule who cannot have children! Therefore Lot will inherit everything that belongs to him. If his cattle now graze on Abram's land, it is as if they were already grazing on what belongs to Lot! (Genesis Rabbah 41:5)*

Like many arguments, the one between Abram's and Lot's herdsmen began with a disagreement over what was considered the right thing to do and ended with Lot's people hurling public insults at Abram. "He's a barren mule who can't have children," they said. And Abram's herdsmen may have answered, "Lot has become an idolater, a dishonest unbeliever!" According to the rabbis, it was the insult that turned their disagreement into a bitter battle.

Yet there may have been another reason for the disagreement between Abram, Lot, and their herdsmen. The commentator Nachmanides explains that Abram and Lot had come back to Canaan with huge herds and that Abram opposed letting them graze together because he feared that the inhabitants of the land (the Canaanites and Perizzites), seeing how great they were, might decide to rise up and destroy them. So he ordered their herdsmen to graze their animals in different places.

Lot and his herdsmen paid no attention. They did not seem to care about making trouble with the other people of the land or about their security.

Seeing that there were considerable differences between them, Abram suggested that they go their separate ways. Furthermore, according to the Torah, he gave Lot his choice. He said to him, ". . . if you go north, I will go south; and, if you go south, I will go north." Lot agreed. He journeyed eastward, and Abram remained in the land of Canaan.

PEREK DALET: *Abram Rescues Lot*

It was not long after Lot had settled in the city of Sodom that it was attacked by Chedorlaomer, king of Elam; Tidal, king of Goiim; Amraphel, king of Shinar; and Arioch, king of Ellasar. They stormed the cities of Sodom and Gomorrah, seizing their wealth and taking Lot as a captive.

Hearing what had happened, Abram immediately organized an army to pursue them and to rescue his nephew. He defeated the kings and saved Lot. Upon Abram's victorious return, the king of Sodom praised him for his bravery and offered him a large reward. Abram refused to take anything.

Several questions come to mind: "Why, if

Abram and Lot had separated from each other, did Abram feel obligated to risk his life to rescue Lot? Why did he not take some of the spoils of the battle?"

Nachmanides suggests that, even though there had been disagreements between them, Abram remembered that Lot had been a faithful companion and friend. Another interpreter points out that Abram realized that, when a person is taken captive, others must see him as a "brother" and rush to rescue him. (*Akedat Yitzhak*)

Rescuing the captive

Pidyon shevuyin, *or "rescuing the captives," is one of the most important commandments of Judaism: Abram was ready to sacrifice his life in order to save Lot because he believed that saving a life by freeing a victim of oppression was one of the highest forms of serving God.* (Genesis Rabbah *43:2*)

Rambam (Maimonides)

Abram's rescue of Lot became an ethical model for Jews throughout the centuries. According to the great twelfth-century teacher Moses Maimonides, *pidyon shevuyim,* the "rescue of captives," is a more important mitzvah even than charity for the poor. The rabbis of the Talmud ordered that charity set aside for building a synagogue could be used to ransom Jews from their captors; they taught that whoever delays in rescuing a fellow Jew is regarded as if he had spilled his blood. During the Middle Ages, in many Jewish communities, associations were formed to collect funds for the ransoming of captive Jews. Thousands were saved from pirates, kidnapers, and hostile armies. (*Mishneh Torah, Aniyyim* 8:10, 12; *Baba Batra* 8b)

Abram's immediate and brave action to save his "brother," Lot, set the standard for fulfilling the mitzvah of *pidyon shevuyin,* the liberation of captives.

Yet, having fulfilled his obligation to rescue Lot, why did Abram refuse any reward?

The rabbis of the Midrash suggest that Abram was concerned that, if he took anything, people would say that he had gone to battle in order to increase his wealth and not to save his "brother." He wanted his purpose understood. His concern was with Lot's safety and welfare, not with acquiring more riches. (*Genesis Rabbah* 43:12)

Reward for a mitzvah

Concerning the doing of a mitzvah, Antigonos of Socho taught: "Be not like servants who work for their master only on condition that they receive payment, but be like servants who work for their master without looking for any reward; and be filled with reverence for God." And (Simeon) ben Azai commented that the "reward of doing one mitzvah is the opportunity of doing another." (Avot *1:3 and 4:2*)

While most interpreters praise Abram for his rescue of Lot and refusal to take any favors for it, Rabbi Yochanan, a famous third-century teacher in the Land of Israel, was very critical of Abram. He believed that Abram had missed an opportunity to convert Lot, and even the king of Sodom, to his new faith. Rabbi Yochanan argued that they were both in debt to him and that he should have taken advantage of them. (*Nedarim* 32b)

Most commentators disagree with Rabbi Yochanan's criticism of Abram. They praise Abram for refusing any reward for his rescue of Lot. Because he did so, his example of *pidyon shevuyin* and of doing a mitzvah without strings attached, without conditions or rewards, still stands as a powerful ethical model.

PEREK HEI: *Berit Milah—The Covenant of Circumcision*

The Torah informs us that, three years after Hagar gives birth to Ishmael, God promises to establish a *berit,* a "covenant" or "contract," with Abram. The symbol of that covenant was *berit milah,* or "circumcision." Circumcision is the removal of the foreskin from the penis of the male child. In our Torah portion God instructs Abram: "At the age of eight days, every male among you throughout the generations shall be circumcised. . . . Thus shall My *berit* be marked in your flesh as an everlasting covenant." (Genesis 17:12–13)

So Abram circumcised himself, his son Ishmael, and every other male who was a part of his community. As a part of the ritual, God changes Abram's name to *Avraham,* meaning "father of many nations," and Sarai's name to *Sarah,* meaning "princess."

The practice of circumcision was common among many ancient peoples in the Middle East. It was the custom of the Egyptians, Edomites, Ammonites, and Moabites, and later it became the practice of all Moslems. Among most ancient peoples, circumcision was performed just before marriage in hope that the "sacrifice" of the foreskin would make one a father of many children.

While the promise connected to Abraham's circumcision and change of name is that he will be the "father of many nations," the timing of the ceremony of *berit milah* was set at eight days after birth. Within the Jewish community, circumcision was not done to guarantee many children but, rather, as a way in which a male child became identified as a Jew. *Berit milah* became a ceremony of pride, an initiation of the newborn child into the faith and community of the Jewish people.

Perhaps that is why Jews have observed the *berit milah* ceremony with such care through the ages and why enemies of the Jewish people have tried to prevent its practice. Rulers who wished to destroy Jewish loyalties and put an end to Judaism very often prohibited Jews from practicing circumcision.

When, for instance, Antiochus Epiphanes (165 B.C.E.) declared war on the Jews by forbidding them to observe their Sabbaths and festivals or to practice the traditions of their Torah, he also made a special point of proclaiming that all Jewish sons should be left uncircumcised. He ordered any parent who arranged for a *berit milah* to be put to death. Those who attended such ceremonies were also threatened. The Maccabees, however, refused to follow the orders of Antiochus and declared a war of liberation against his oppressive rule.

For some Jewish teachers, circumcision represents more than a sacred sign of Jewish identity or a symbol of the covenant of the Jewish people with God. There are those interpreters who believe that circumcision is a way of teaching human beings that the world is imperfect and requires *tikun,* or "improvement." In the Midrash, the rabbis report the following:

> The Roman general Turnus Rufus once asked Rabbi Akiba: "If your God is so powerful, and wanted male children circumcised, then why isn't each child simply born with the circumcision already done?"
>
> Rabbi Akiba replied: "God gave all the commandments to the people of Israel so that they could perfect themselves by doing them. God wished that individuals would take on the responsibility of perfecting themselves and the world through the practice of the commandments. The commandment of circumcision reminds us that, just as we need to improve ourselves physically, so do we need to improve ourselves and our world spiritually.
>
> (*Midrash Tanchuma* and *Sefer ha-Hinuch* 57)

In other words, circumcision is a sacred lesson. It is a powerful symbol of Jewish identity. It serves as a reminder to Jews of their ethical tasks and responsibilities. It also teaches us that our talents and abilities require improvement. Our defects and deficiencies should be corrected and repaired. Just as the male baby requires the improvement of circumcision, so the world requires human beings to perfect it. *Berit milah* is the sign that Jews were "contracted" to God for the work of perfecting both themselves and the world.

QUESTIONS FOR STUDY AND DISCUSSION

1. What qualified Abram to become the founder of the Jewish people? How would you compare his qualities of leadership with leaders of our own times?

2. Did Abram do the right thing when he lied to Pharaoh about Sarai's identity? Is a half-truth or "white lie" permissible when it can save a life? Under what other conditions might half-truths be justified?

3. The commentators present Abram as a model for solving conflicts between competing factions. Which of his techniques, as described by the interpreters, might be applied today to international and personal disputes?

4. How can the mitzvah of *pidyon shevuyin* be carried out today? Is it still the obligation of individuals or are international matters so complex that we must leave liberation of the oppressed to the "experts"?

5. Since a Jewish male child is only eight days old when he is circumcised, the *berit milah* is hardly a demonstration of his commitment to Judaism or to the Jewish people. What, then, is the meaning of the ceremony? Might the same be asked about the naming of a baby girl?

PARASHAT VAYERA
Genesis 18:1–22:24

Parashat Vayera begins with the visit of three men to Abraham. He welcomes them with generous hospitality, and they promise that Sarah will soon bear a son. When the men depart for the city of Sodom, God appears to Abraham and tells him that the cities of Sodom and Gomorrah are about to be destroyed because of the sinful behavior of their residents. Abraham protests, asking God not to destroy innocent people along with the guilty ones. God promises that, if there are as few as even ten innocent people in the cities, they will not be destroyed. Afterwards, two men-angels arrive in Sodom and are offered hospitality by Lot. He protects them from the Sodomites, who threaten to harm them. The men-angels warn Lot to leave Sodom. He escapes the next morning as fire rains down upon the cities, but his wife looks back and is turned into a pillar of salt. Abraham travels to the Negev, where Abimelech, king of Gerar, sees Sarah and wants her for a wife. Fearing the king, Abraham claims that Sarah is his "sister." The king takes her as a wife, but God appears to him and reveals Sarah's real identity. Abimelech returns her to Abraham along with a great bounty. As the visitors to Abraham had predicted, Sarah bears a son whom they name Isaac. After a few years, Sarah persuades Abraham to send Hagar and Ishmael away, claiming that only Isaac should inherit Abraham's wealth and position. Abraham agrees when God tells him that "I will make a nation of him [Ishmael]." Several years later, God tests Abraham's faith by ordering him to sacrifice Isaac on Mount Moriah. Isaac is saved at the last moment when God praises Abraham's loyalty and tells him to sacrifice a ram in Isaac's place.

OUR TARGUM

· 1 ·

Abraham sees three men approaching his tent. He rises, runs out to greet them, and invites them to have some water and food with him. Sara prepares a meal for them. The men promise Abraham that Sarah will soon become pregnant with a son. Sarah hears what they say and laughs. She is convinced that she is too old to have children.

· 2 ·

The visitors depart and travel toward the city of Sodom, located in the Jordan Valley. God appears to Abraham and tells him that the cities of Sodom and Gomorrah will be destroyed because of the wicked behavior of their citizens. Abraham protests, arguing that, if God is just, innocent people cannot be destroyed along with evil ones. He asks: "What if there should be fifty innocent within the city; will You then wipe out the place and not forgive it for the sake of the innocent fifty who are in it?" God agrees to save the city if there are fifty innocent people. Abraham then begins to bargain. He asks God: "What if there are forty-five people?" Then, pursuing his argument, he asks about forty, then thirty, twenty, and, finally, if God will destroy the city if only ten innocent people are found. God tells him: "I will not destroy, for the sake of the ten."

· 3 ·

One evening two men-angels arrive in Sodom. Lot, who is sitting at the gate of the city, welcomes them and invites them to stay the night at his house. The wicked people of Sodom gather outside Lot's door, demanding that he turn over the visitors so that they might sexually abuse them. Fearing for the lives of his guests, Lot offers the Sodomites his daughters. The crowd becomes angry with Lot, threatening to break down the door. At that point the two visitors pull Lot into the house, and the people standing outside are struck with a blinding light.

The visitors tell Lot to gather his family and flee before Sodom is destroyed. Lot's sons-in-law refuse to believe the prediction or to follow him, and the rest of Lot's family delays. Finally, in the morning, the visitors take them by the hands and escort them outside the city. They tell them: "Flee for your life! Do not look behind you . . . lest you be swept away." As the cities are destroyed, Lot's wife looks back and is turned into a pillar of salt.

· 4 ·

Later, while Abraham and Sarah are traveling in the Negev, Abimelech, king of Gerar, sees her and wishes to have her for a wife. As he had done when Pharaoh desired Sarah (see *Parashat Lech-Lecha*), Abraham tells the king, "She is my sister." God appears to the king on the night he takes Sarah into his house and reveals that she is Abraham's wife. Fearing for his life, Abimelech returns Sarah to Abraham along with a huge treasure as payment for any wrong he might have done.

Soon Sarah conceives and gives birth to Isaac. After a few years, she demands that Abraham send away Hagar and her son, Ishmael, claiming that only Isaac is entitled to inherit Abraham's wealth and leadership. Abraham, greatly upset by Sarah's demand, agrees to do as she wishes after God

assures him that Ishmael will also become a great nation.

·5·

Some time later, God tests Abraham's loyalty by commanding him to sacrifice Isaac at the top of Mount Moriah. Abraham takes his son and travels to the place. There he builds an altar and, just as he is about to kill his son, an angel stops him, saying: "Do not raise your hand against the boy, or do anything to him. For now I know that you fear God." Abraham looks up and sees a ram caught by its horns in a bush. He takes the animal and offers it as a sacrifice in the place of Isaac. The angel tells him that he and all of his people after him will be blessed.

THEMES

Parashat Vayera contains three important themes:

1. The importance of hospitality.
2. The consequences of social injustice.
3. The meaning of "loyalty" to God.

PEREK ALEF: *The Hospitality of Abraham and Lot*

Twice in this Torah portion guests are welcomed in a home: once by Abraham at the beginning of the portion and the second time by Lot just before the cities of Sodom and Gomorrah are destroyed. In each situation, the "hospitality" offered is very different. And from each we learn something about the unique Jewish standards for welcoming people into our homes.

The importance of hospitality
"Hospitality," the Talmud says, is a "great mitzvah. It is considered more important to show hospitality than to attend classes or to greet God in prayer." (Shabbat *127a*)

"Why was the prophet Micah included among those who will live for eternity?" the rabbis asked.
    "Because he shared his bread with those who passed by his home." (Sanhedrin *103a*)

The example of Abraham's special model of hospitality is clearly described by the Torah. Every gesture was important and recorded. We are told: *"Looking up, he saw three men standing near him. As soon as he saw them, he ran from the entrance of the tent to greet them and, bowing to the ground,* he said, 'My lords, if it please you, *do not go on past your servant. Let a little water be brought; bathe your feet and recline under the tree. And let me fetch a morsel of bread that you may refresh yourselves; then go on. . . .'"*

Abraham's hospitality is not passive. He is *looking* for guests. He is alert to those who might be passing by and in need of help. Nor does he wait until the strangers have approached his tent. Instead, *as soon* as he sees them, *he runs* toward them. He does not ask them all kinds of questions about their parents or people or where they are going, but, instead, he *greets* them and shows them respect by *bowing* before them. Abraham then pleads with them: *"Do not go on past your servant."* He *comforts* them by bringing them water and then rushes to feed them.

Several commentators who have studied Abraham's welcoming of his guests point out that he was still recuperating from the pain of his circumcision. Even so, he was alert to the exhaustion and hunger of others and ran out to greet them and refresh them with food and drink. (*Akedat Yitzhak*)

Ramban (Nachmanides)

Furthermore, according to Nachmanides, Abraham thought only of the needs of his guests.

It was the middle of the day; they had been traveling and would want to rest and then continue their journey; their feet were sore; they were tired from the hot sun. So he gave them water with which to cool their feet and arranged for them to sit in the shade of a tree.

The angels can wait!

A young person once visited the famed teacher known as the Chofetz Chaim. The guest had arrived at the synagogue just as the Sabbath began, having been on the road for many hours. He was hungry and weak as they walked from the synagogue to the rabbi's home. To the surprise of the guest, the Chofetz Chaim skipped the singing of "Shalom Alechem" (a song that greets the Sabbath angels) and, after quickly reciting the Kiddush *and the* Motzi, *began to eat. "Why did you skip the singing of 'Shalom Alechem,' " the young man asked his host.*

The Chofetz Chaim replied: "You were hungry. A hungry person should be fed as soon as possible. The angels can wait to be greeted."

The Torah informs us that Abraham was not alone in offering hospitality to his guests. Sarah helped him. Many Torah interpreters explain that, as husband and wife, they shared the responsibility of preparing food for their guests. And they wasted no time. They *hurried* to care for the strangers. They also made an effort to serve their guests with bread made from *choice* flour and meat taken from a *choice* calf. Nor did they turn over the feeding of their guests to servants. Abraham and Sarah waited on the strangers, serving each an equal portion. They cared for each person according to that person's need. (See *Mesillat Yesharim* 7, *Numbers Rabbah* 10:5, and *Megillah* 12a.)

Furthermore, Abraham insisted on serving his guests at the entrance of his home.

Why?

Perhaps he wanted other strangers to know that they were welcome; perhaps he wanted to remind others that each human being is created in the "image of God" and that showing hospitality to strangers is a way of welcoming God into our lives.

And, when it came time for his guests to leave, the commentator Nachmanides comments that Abraham did not just bid them farewell at his gate, but he went with them until he saw that they were safely on their way.

Who is the stranger?

One day a group of strangers came to an inn. The innkeeper and his wife were known for their kindness and hospitality. They saw that the strangers were tired, and the innkeeper ran out to heat some water in the bathhouse. Among the strangers was a poor old man with ugly sores all over his back. The other guests refused to bathe with him or to help him wash himself. When the innkeeper's wife saw that the old man needed help, she took the brush and gently washed his back. "Thank you for your kindness," he said to her. "May all the children you bear be like me."

Some say that the poor old man was none other than Elijah the Prophet, who will someday bring an era of human understanding, kindness, and peace.

Abraham's treatment of the strangers who visited him is viewed by Jewish tradition as an outstanding model of hospitality. By contrast, Lot's reception of his guests raises troubling questions. According to the rabbis who explained our Torah portion, Lot brought visitors to his home only at night, never during the day. He also never led them directly to his house but chose a long way to get there and entered always through the back door. When they arrived, he would tell them, "Do not wash your feet. Should authorities from the city come checking on us, it must appear as though you just arrived and that I am not providing anything special for you." (*Pirke de-Rabbi Eliezer* and *Midrash ha-Gadol*; also Rashi and *Meam Loez*)

Why did Lot act in such an inhospitable manner?

Some explain that the officials of Sodom had decreed that it was against the law to show any kindness or hospitality to visitors. The punishment for anyone welcoming guests or caring for their needs was imprisonment and death. Strangers were to be taken advantage of, their possessions were to be stolen, and they were to be chased out of the town as quickly as possible. (Nachmanides and *Genesis Rabbah*)

Others point out that, unlike Sarah, Lot's wife opposed offering hospitality to strangers. She refused to cook for them or to help Lot make them comfortable. On many occasions she actually complained to her neighbors about "my husband's visitors" and even reported to the authorities when Lot was entertaining guests. (*Midrash Agadah* 19:4; *Genesis Rabbah* 50:8, 9)

While many commentators are critical of Lot, a few argue that his hospitality was heroic. They point out that, unlike Abraham, Lot lived in a city where one could be put to death for offering food, shelter, and friendship to guests. One interpreter suggests that Lot's daughter, Pelotit, had been put to death by the authorities of Sodom for giving bread to a stranger.

Others emphasize that, when the crowd gathered at his door, demanding that he turn over the strangers to them, he refused. Risking his life, he went outside, closed the door behind him, and tried to calm the mob. He bravely stood his ground and tried to convince them to leave. But they demanded that he open the door and send his visitors out to them. It was only then that Lot offered to give the mob his daughters as protection for the strangers. (*Sefer ha-Yashar* 10)

Should he have made such an offer? Was it a heroic gesture or a cruel decision? Given the circumstances, can we even compare Abraham's hospitality with Lot's?

Limits even to hospitality
Lot told the crowd: 'See, I have two daughters who have not known a man. Let me bring them out to you, and you may do to them as you please; but do not do anything to these men since they have come under the shelter of my roof." We have been taught that a person should sacrifice his own life for the sake of his wife and children. Lot was ready to hand over his daughters for abuse. Therefore, he brought shame to his life. (Midrash ha-Gadol *19:8*)

In some societies, the head of a household might be justified in turning over his wife or daughters to an angry mob in order to save innocent visitors. Jewish tradition, however, demands that a person give his own life rather than sacrifice the lives of his loved ones.

Zugot

Let your house be open
Rabbi Yosi ben Yochanan taught: "Let your house be open wide, and let the needy be treated as members of your home." (Avot *1:5*)

Judging others
Rabbi Hillel cautioned: "Do not judge another person until you have put yourself in that person's place." (Avot *2:5*)

Between Abraham and Lot we have two examples of hospitality. Yet the conditions faced by each of them were quite different. How then are we to judge between them?

PEREK BET: *Should Good People Suffer for the Evil That Bad People Do?*

The Torah informs us that, when God told Abraham that Sodom and Gomorrah were to be destroyed because of the terrible sins of their citizens, Abraham boldly asked: "Will You sweep away the innocent along with the guilty? What if there should be fifty innocent within the city; will You then wipe out the place and not forgive it for the sake of the innocent fifty who are in it? . . . Far be it from You! Shall not the Judge of all the earth deal justly?"

Abraham was concerned with justice. He did not believe that good people or innocent people should suffer for the evil actions of others. So he argued on behalf of the innocent people in Sodom. When God told him that the city would be saved for the sake of fifty people, Abraham went on to argue the case for forty-five, then for forty, then for thirty, then for twenty, and, finally, for ten.

Yet Sodom was destroyed. Why? The Torah text tells us only that "the outrage of Sodom and Gomorrah was great, and their sin was serious." That is all. We are given no details.

Later, the rabbis ask themselves the question: "What was so evil about the people of these cities that God decided to destroy them? They came up with several important reasons.

The first was the selfishness of the people of Sodom. Their land was rich with gold, silver, and precious stones. Their farmers produced an abundance of food. Every citizen had a comfortable home, a closet filled with clothing, and gardens of beautiful flowers and fruit trees.

> ### Nothing for the stranger
> *Rabbi Nathaniel commented that the people of Sodom refused to give food to the stranger or traveler, and they even constructed fences above their gardens so that no bird flying by could eat from their trees. (Pirke de-Rabbi Eliezer 25)*
>
> ### Keep it all for ourselves
> *Because of their wealth, the people of Sodom became haughty. They said to one another: "Since gold and silver flow from our land, why should we allow strangers to visit in our borders, eat our food, use our resources, and share what is ours? They will only take what we have, and there will be less for us. Let's keep them from entering, and let's drive out those who get in as soon as possible—especially the poor or the sick ones." (Tosefta to Sotah 3; Sanhedrin 109a)*

Rather than being willing to share their wealth and good fortune with others, the people of Sodom wanted to keep it all for themselves. They expelled immigrants, strangers, or travelers. They chased away the poor and the sick and allowed no one in who would be a "burden" to their city. They felt no responsibility for others.

According to the rabbis, they went a step further in their selfishness. They developed clever ways of stealing from visitors without breaking

the law. For example, when a stranger entered the gates of Sodom with grain, they would each steal only a few grains from his bags until the grain was gone. In that way no Sodomite could be taken to court for stealing. And, if the visitor took a Sodomite to court for taking his grain, the Sodomite would tell the judge, "I took nothing, just a few grains." (*Sanhedrin* 109a)

But that is not all. According to the rabbis, the Sodomites also created laws forbidding any citizen of Sodom from feeding the hungry, from offering help to the poor, or from healing the sick.

> ### The proclamation of Sodom
> *Rabbi Yehudah said: The leaders of Sodom made a proclamation in which they declared: "Anyone who gives even a loaf of bread to the poor or the needy shall be put to death by fire." (Pirke de-Rabbi Eliezer 25)*

In Sodom, "kindness to strangers" was against the law! If a citizen of Sodom happened to feel compassion for a needy person and offered him support, that citizen could be convicted of breaking the law and be put to death. According to the rabbis, that is what happened to Lot's daughter, Pelotit.

> ### Lot's daughter is punished
> *Pelotit, the daughter of Lot, saw a poor person seeking bread on the streets. Her heart was filled with compassion. So what did she do? Each day she drew water for him and gave him bread and other food to eat. When the leaders of Sodom discovered that she was helping a poor man live, they put her to death. (Pirke de-Rabbi Eliezer 25)*

The great evil of Sodom was that cruelty became public policy. The leaders made oppression and abuse of the needy the law of their city. Even the courts, the place where most societies look for justice, promoted injustice. Judges sided with the rich and treated the needy without pity or fairness.

> **Their evil courts and judges**
> *Rabbi Joshua ben Korchah commented that the leaders of Sodom appointed judges who were dishonest. They lied, they cheated, they oppressed strangers. They allowed wayfarers to enter Sodom, then convicted them of breaking the law. Afterwards, they robbed them of their possessions and expelled them from the city.* (Pirke de-Rabbi Eliezer 25)

Ibn Ezra

According to the Spanish Jewish interpreter Abraham ibn Ezra (1092–1167), not one citizen of Sodom protested the cruel treatment of strangers. Instead, they remained silent. They chose the safety of "not getting involved." They refused to serve in public office or try to change the evil laws that had been passed. Because these good people chose indifference rather than opposition to evil, they were destroyed with the rest of the city.

So why were the people of Sodom and Gomorrah destroyed? The commentators offer the following reasons:

1. They refused to share their wealth and abundant riches with others.

2. They made fun of those in need and deliberately made their lives more miserable.

3. They refused to care for the sick, aid the poor, help the needy, or offer hospitality to the immigrant or stranger in their midst.

4. Their leaders were so greedy and selfish that they made cruelty a public policy.

5. They went so far as to punish their own citizens who reached out to feed the hungry or provide shelter to the homeless.

6. Their judges practiced dishonesty and robbery, and their courts offered no fair treatment for victims of oppression or injustice.

For all these reasons, the rabbis inform us, Sodom and Gomorrah were destroyed.

But what about our original question? Even if there was one innocent, good person left in Sodom or Gomorrah, should that person have been destroyed with all the evil ones? Must good people suffer because of the bad things others do?

Unfortunately, they do.

Jewish tradition teaches us that we are free to choose between good and evil, between hurting others or helping them. That gift of freedom means that God does not interfere and cannot prevent us from doing things that not only harm us but others as well. God wants us to do the right thing, to be just, kind, loving, and generous, but God cannot force us to make the right choice. We must make our own choices, and we must live with the consequences—even the consequences of the choices that other people make.

God is like a parent who says to his children, "Go out into the world and make your own decisions, but remember that what you do will not only affect you but others as well." When the decisions are good and others benefit, the parent is happy and so is God. When the decisions are bad ones that bring pain and sorrow to innocent people, the parents weep and, perhaps, so does God. But God is not responsible for those bad decisions; human beings are. God cannot be blamed for our failings; we are responsible for them.

God did not plan the destruction of Sodom and Gomorrah. The people brought their end upon themselves and others.

> **Abusing human freedom**
> *. . . much evil is not God's fault but ours. The right to choose is a great good, but we often use it to be creatively malicious. We drive too fast and maim careful drivers and innocent pedestrians. We destroy reputations, squander resources, abuse power, and make the world the worse for our freedom. Some people even choose to be Nazis and engender a Holocaust. They were not compelled by God to do so. They did it freely. They faced their moral responsibility and rejected it, abusing human freedom worse than anything else we know in human history.* (Eugene B. Borowitz, Liberal Judaism, UAHC, New York, 1984, p. 198)

Sodom and Gomorrah were destroyed because, as we have seen, their people were guilty of "abusing human freedom." They brought on their own destruction—and the death of many innocent people—because they deliberately chose cruelty over charity, selfishness over caring, and greed over sharing.

PEREK GIMEL: *What Is Loyalty to God?*

The story of Abraham being called by God to sacrifice his son, Isaac, is a frightening one. It was also considered one of the most important events in the Torah. The rabbis, who divided and assigned portions of Torah to be read in the synagogue on Shabbat and on the holidays, titled it the *Akedah,* meaning "the binding for sacrifice," and chose it for reading on Rosh Hashanah. They believed that it was a "test" of Abraham's loyalty to God.

In the story, Abraham is told to bring Isaac to the land of Moriah and to offer him as a sacrifice on one of the high places there. Abraham follows God's orders but, just as he is about to kill his son, an angel of God stops him, telling him to sacrifice a ram instead. "For now I know," says the angel, "that you fear God, since you have not withheld your son, your favored one, from Me."

What is this strange story about?

Some say that, to test the strength of Abraham's loyalty, God ordered him to kill Isaac, his son. And, without hesitation, without asking any questions, without even consulting Sarah, Abraham followed God's orders. In doing so, he not only proved himself loyal to God, but he also showed the world what true faith is all about.

Rambam (Maimonides)

In his book *Guide for the Perplexed,* Moses Maimonides explained Abraham's test in the following way:

The purpose of all tests mentioned in the Torah is to teach human beings how they are to act. . . . Abraham is commanded to sacrifice his son. . . . And, because he feared God and loved to do what God commanded, he thought little of his beloved child, and set aside all his hopes concerning him, and agreed to kill him. . . . Therefore, the angel said to him: "For now I know that you fear God," which means that from Abraham's action . . . we can learn how far we must go in the fear of God.

Many interpreters would criticize Maimonides' description of Abraham's test as an example of "blind faith." Abraham did as he was told; he did not protest. He did not say to God, "How can You do this to Sarah and me?" Nor did he take the side of his son and argue, "But he is a child. How can a just God who was willing to save Sodom if there were ten righteous people in the city now ask for the sacrifice of a child?" Instead, Abraham seems to follow "blindly" the command to take Isaac and offer him as a sacrifice on Mount Moriah.

Is that what Jewish tradition teaches us? Are we to follow the commandments of our faith without questioning them? Are we disloyal if we express doubts about what Jewish tradition says God "commands" us to do?

There is another interpretation of the *Akedah* that is also about "loyalty to God," but it is one that makes room for serious questions.

> When God commanded Abraham, "Take your son . . ." Abraham did not set out immediately. He asked, "Which son?" God answered, "Your favored one . . ." Then Abraham said, "But I have two sons, Ishmael and Isaac. And one is favored by his mother, and the other is favored by his mother." So God answered: "Take the one whom you love . . ." And Abraham replied, "I love them both, so how can I choose?" Finally, God told him, "Take Isaac!" (Pirke de-Rabbi Eliezer *31*)

According to some interpreters, Abraham had several questions and doubts about what God had commanded him to do. He did not march off immediately toward Mount Moriah. His was not a "blind faith"—but a questioning one. Because he wanted to be sure that he understood what he was being asked to do, he asked questions and evaluated the answers. He put to work his reasoning powers and examined what it was that God was asking him to do.

After hearing God's command, he waited until the next morning before setting out to fulfill it. He was not reckless or impetuous, but, instead, he gave himself time to think about it and to analyze the consequences of what he was being asked to do. Because it was one of the most important decisions of his life, he considered it carefully.

Furthermore, as Abraham was about to act on his decision and plunge his knife into Isaac, he was capable of reconsideration. His questions continued to the very end. He was constantly reexamining his understanding of what it was that God wanted of him. And, when the angel told him, "Do not raise your hand against the boy," Abraham was able to change what he had thought to do.

Abravanel

Abraham's example of faith
This story of Abraham's faith is an example, a banner for all the peoples of the world to follow. (Don Isaac Abravanel)

Loyalty to God does not mean "blind faith." Sometimes it means asking difficult questions about what it is that we should or should not be doing. Sometimes it means being willing to take risks for what we believe is just and right. Sometimes it means delaying action until the facts are analyzed carefully. Sometimes it means being willing to reconsider opinions and to make changes when presented with new evidence or a better perspective.

The *Akedah* is a story about Abraham's struggle to understand what it means to be loyal to God. He is an example of a person who tested his faith with questions and weighed his decisions carefully. He was not afraid to face doubts or to get all the facts. If necessary, he was ready to make sacrifices for what he believed, but he was also ready to rethink his convictions and commitments.

Perhaps for all those reasons this story of Abraham is considered one of the great examples of religious faith and loyalty to God.

QUESTIONS FOR STUDY AND DISCUSSION

1. Are we, as Jews, obligated to offer hospitality to strangers? Were non-Jews justified in not opening their homes to Jews during the Holocaust? Are there situations, when loved ones might be endangered, that require us to refuse giving others hospitality?

2. Read the story of Sheba, son of Bichri, in II Samuel 20:1–26. How does it compare to our story of Lot?

3. In what ways is the story of Sodom similar to the stories of Cain and Abel, Noah, and the building of the Tower of Babel?

4. Since other people and religions in Abraham's time believed in child sacrifice, perhaps the real message of the story of Abraham's willingness to sacrifice Isaac is to demonstrate that God does not require human sacrifice. If that is so, then what are the ways in which modern society "sacrifices" children? How can we protect our children from being victimized by the evil elements of the culture that surrounds us?

PARASHAT CHAYE SARAH
Genesis 23:1–25:18

While *Chaye Sarah* may be translated as "Sarah's lifetime," this Torah portion actually tells us about Sarah's death. Abraham seeks to purchase the cave of Machpelah, in Hebron, for her burial. Ephron, the son of Zohar, owns the land, and Abraham bargains with him for the purchase. After the burial, Abraham sends a trusted servant back to his native land to find a wife for Isaac. The servant chooses Rebekah and returns with her to the Land of Israel where Isaac takes her for his wife.

OUR TARGUM

· 1 ·

Sarah, Abraham's wife and the first Mother of the people of Israel, died at the age of one hundred and twenty-seven years. She died in the town of Kiriath-arba, known today as Hebron, located nineteen miles south of Jerusalem in the Judean Hills.

Abraham was filled with sadness at her death and wanted to find an appropriate burial place for her and for his family. So he spoke to the people of Heth who owned property around Hebron and said to them: "I am a foreigner living here with you. Sell me a burial place for my dead."

They replied: "You are a very special person among us. Simply choose the place you wish, and we will be happy to give it to you."

Abraham bowed, as was the custom in such negotiations, and told the people of Heth: "If you are so willing to be helpful, please go to Ephron the Hittite, the son of Zohar, and tell him that I would like to buy the cave of Machpelah, which is at the edge of his land. Also, inform him that I am willing to pay the total amount of its worth."

Now, Ephron happened to be among the people of Heth with whom Abraham was speaking. He stepped forward and told Abraham: "In the presence of my people, I present you, for no cost at all, with the cave of Machpelah and the field around it. Go bury your dead there."

Abraham thanked him but said: "Allow me to pay the full price."

Ephron replied: "My friend, what's a piece of land worth four hundred shekels of silver between us? Take it from me and bury your dead."

Instead of taking the land for no payment, Abraham gave Ephron the full price of four hundred shekels of silver before the people of Heth. The payment gave him all rights to the cave of Machpelah and to the field and trees around it. Having made the purchase, Abraham buried Sarah.

· 2 ·

After Sarah's death, Abraham called his trusted servant to his side and asked him to take an oath that he would not allow Isaac to marry a Canaanite woman but, rather, would return to Abraham's native land and find a wife for Isaac from among his people. The servant promised he would do so and set off for Aram-naharaim, which means "Aram of the two rivers," which was also called "Haran." It is located in northern Syria.

When the servant reached the place, he rested his camels near a well and prayed to God. "O God of my master Abraham, grant me good luck today. As I wait here and the women of the city are coming out to draw water from this well, let the woman You have chosen to be Isaac's future wife answer me when I say, 'Please lower your jar that I may drink from it.' Let her tell me, 'Drink, and I will water your camels.' "

As the servant finished his prayer, Rebekah the daughter of Bethuel, who was the son of Milcah the wife of Abraham's brother Nahor, came out with a jar on her shoulder. She was very beautiful, and, when she filled her jar, the servant ran to her side and said, "Please lower your jar that I may drink from it." And she replied, "Drink, and I will also water your camels."

After she had done so, Rebekah ran home and told her brother, Laban, about the man. He came out to welcome him and to invite him to be their guest. The servant accepted their hospitality, but, before he would take any food, he insisted on telling them about his prayer and how Rebekah had answered it with generosity not only for him but for his animals. He then informed them that this was all a sign that Rebekah was the woman destined to be Isaac's wife.

Laban and Bethuel agreed and asked Rebekah if she would leave them to go with the servant back to the Land of Israel to marry Isaac. She was willing and so departed without delay.

As they reached the land, Isaac happened to be out walking in the field. Rebekah saw him and asked the servant, "Who is that man?"

"That is my master," he answered. Rebekah covered her face with her veil, which was the custom of modesty at the time.

After the servant told Isaac all that had happened to him in Aram-naharaim, Isaac took Rebekah home. They married, and he loved her and found comfort with her after the death of his mother, Sarah.

THEMES

Parashat Chaye Sarah contains four important themes:

1. Jewish attitudes and practices at the time of death.
2. Paying the full price for what we acquire.

3. Beauty.

4. The meaning of "love."

PEREK ALEF: *Mourning the Death of a Loved One*

When someone we love dies, we experience deep sorrow. We miss that person's presence and caring. We miss the support and all that we shared. At times we are angry and ask, "Why did that loved one have to die?" At other times we understand that death is something that happens to every living thing, but the pain is confusing. We find ourselves wishing to share just another day or a few hours so that we might say some things that we never found the time to say.

Death is so final. We can't turn back the clock.

That must have been the sadness Abraham felt when Sarah died. They had shared so much together. In his grief he must have remembered the close call with death they had both experienced with Abimelech or how upset Sarah had been when she could not become pregnant. He must have recalled how much she loved their son, Isaac, and how jealous she had become of Hagar and Ishmael. They had been partners for so many years. He would miss her. Little wonder that Abraham wept and mourned for Sarah.

Abraham must also have realized how helpful it was to share his grief with others who were there to comfort him. Talking and weeping with friends is healthy when we lose a loved one. Friends can support us and ease our loneliness and pain. So can the rituals and customs of Jewish tradition.

> *symbolizes the warmth, wisdom, and love that the dead person brought into the lives of the mourners.*
>
> ***Kaddish and Yizkor:*** *It is a mitzvah for the mourner to recite the* Kaddish *prayer in memory of the dead at services at home and in the synagogue and to attend* Yizkor *services in honor of those who have died.* Kaddish *and* Yizkor *are ways of giving thanks to God for the gift of life and the continuing influence upon us of those who have died.*

Jewish rituals and customs at the time of mourning are meant to help us face death realistically and to find comfort with friends. Jewish tradition helps us understand that "death is not the end" but that our loved ones continue to live in the memories and influences they leave behind.

This healthy-minded approach of Jewish teachers through the ages provided not only beautiful rituals for the expression of grief but also a warning that "if we dwell too long on our loss, we embitter our hearts and harm ourselves and those about us." In this regard, the Torah's description of Abraham's mourning for Sarah provides us with a very important model.

His grief was not endless. Abraham did not stop functioning or taking on responsibilities. While his heart was filled with sadness, he knew that he had to accept her death and get on with the task of her burial and the challenges of his life.

> ***Jewish mourning customs***
> ***Keriah*** *is the symbolic cutting of one's garment or a black ribbon at the time of the funeral. It symbolizes the "tearing" that occurs when we lose a loved one.*
> ***Comforting the mourners:*** *It is a mitzvah to visit a house of mourning to comfort those who have lost a loved one.*
> ***Shivah candle:*** *After returning from the cemetery, mourners customarily light a special candle that burns for seven days. The* shivah *candle*

> ***A time to mourn***
> *A season is set for everything, a time for every experience under heaven:*
> *A time for being born and a time for dying. . .*
> *A time for weeping and a time for laughing,*
> *A time for wailing and a time for dancing . . .*
> *(Ecclesiastes 3:1–2, 4)*
>
> *My child, let your tears fall for the dead, and as one who is deeply suffering begin your period of mourning. . . .*

> *Let your weeping be bitter and your crying genuine; observe the period of mourning according to the merit of the one you have lost, for one day, or two, to avoid criticism; then be comforted for your sorrow. For too much sorrow results in death, and sorrow of heart saps one's strength. . . .* (Ecclesiasticus *38:16–18*)

Like many people who suffer a loss, Abraham must have had moments when he felt cheated that Sarah would no longer be at his side. He must have missed her and been lonely. He may even have wondered if he could go on living without her sensitivity, love, and support. But his mourning and grieving helped overcome his loss. He was strengthened by those who cared for him and comforted by his traditions. He did not become embittered by his grief. Despite the pain of his loss, the Torah tells us that he "rose" from his sorrow and went on with his life.

PEREK BET: *Paying the Full Price*

After Sarah's death, Abraham seeks a burial place for her. He comes before the leaders of the Hittites, who then occupied the Land of Israel, and asks them if he might purchase a plot of land.

They bargain with him according to the traditions of the ancient Middle East. First they flatter him. "You're a great man," they tell him. "Please bury your dead in the best place in our burial grounds."

Abraham responds by thanking them for their offer. Then he requests that he be permitted to purchase the cave of Machpelah, owned by Ephron, son of Zohar. He says to them: "Let him sell it to me, at the full price, for a burial site in your midst."

Ephron hears his request and makes a big show by offering the cave for free to Abraham. In doing so, however, he cleverly announces to everyone listening the worth of the land. "A piece of land worth four hundred shekels of silver—what is that between you and me? Go and bury your dead."

Abraham refuses the gift. He does not want a free piece of land. Instead, he insists on paying the full price. And he does so, publicly—"in the hearing of the Hittites."

Ramban (Nachmanides)

"I will give it to you . . ."
Nachmanides points up the careful steps that Abraham took in order to establish his "legal" claim to the land. "First he paid the full price, then he took symbolic legal possession of the field and cave. In that way he established them as his possession in the presence of the people of the city, of all who sat on the council of his town, the merchants and the residents who happened to be there, and after that he buried her." (Genesis 23:11)

Malbim

In his commentary, Malbim writes: "Abraham said, 'Let me pay the price of the land; accept it from me. . . .' That, too, was wisely said. For after Ephron had given him the land . . . he might have changed his mind. . . . So Abraham said to him, 'If it were a gift, you could cancel it. For a gift is really not a legitimate possession. But, if it is purchased by an appropriate sum of money, the law is on our side. . . .' "

Most biblical scholars point out that four hundred shekels of silver was a very high price and that Ephron was taking advantage of Abraham's grief and need to find a burial place for Sarah. Despite the price, however, Abraham wanted official title to the land. He did not want a gift that might be taken back or one that might obligate him to Ephron sometime in the future.

So Abraham followed all the correct and formal

procedures of purchase. As a result, the field and cave "passed from the Hittites to Abraham"—and to the Jewish people—as the first purchased possession of the Land of Israel.

Paying for what we purchase
They tell the story of a pious Jew who entered a store to purchase some item he desired. When he asked the price, the merchant quoted a very low amount. The pious Jew understood that the merchant had recognized him and wanted to pay him special respect and honor. For that reason he had lowered the price of the item he wanted to purchase. So the pious Jew said to him, "I have come to you to buy at market value, not at a price set by the fear of God."

For the pious Jew, paying the "price set" was the just thing to do. He did not want to take advantage of the merchant's respect or to owe him any favors.

Abraham was not only willing to pay the full price, but he insisted upon it. Was he foolish? Should he have taken advantage of the Hittites' respect for him? Should he have tried to bargain with Ephron or even taken the burial place as a gift?

Most commentators argue that, by paying the full price even though Ephron's price was high, and by following the correct legal procedures of purchase, Abraham made certain that no one could later come along and raise questions about his rightful ownership of the land. Had he taken the land as a gift, or at a reduced price, he might have felt himself obligated to do favors for Ephron, or others might have questioned the right of his family to the land.

PEREK GIMEL: *Rebekah's Beauty*

The marriage of Isaac and Rebekah was arranged by Abraham's servant. After Sarah died, Abraham sent his servant back to his homeland to choose a bride for his son. The challenge for the servant was a difficult one. How do you find the most suitable marriage partner? What standards do you use? How do you judge that a person will be loving and loyal?

When the servant arrived in Aram-naharaim he met Rebekah at a well. The Torah describes her as *tovat mareh*, "very beautiful." By that description most readers would assume that the Torah is commenting on her appearance, emphasizing that Rebekah was a physically attractive woman.

That may be so. Then, again, the expression *tovat mareh* may mean much more than "good looks."

Defining Rebekah's real beauty
Rebekah deliberately planned her kindness to the servant. . . . First she provided him with water, then she ran to get water for his animals. In doing so she prevented the servant from feeling that he needed to help her. (Chaim ibn Attar, 1696–1748, Or ha-Chaim)

Meklenburg

Rebekah carefully thought about each word she spoke so as not to offend anyone. She did not repeat the same words used by the servant. She had said, "Drink, and I will also water your camels." She was sensitive about equating him with his animals, so she said, "Drink, my lord." Later on, after he had enjoyed his fill of water, she offered to give some to his animals. (Jacob Tsvi Meklenburg, 1785–1865, Ha-Ketav ve-ha-Kabbalah)

She stopped the servant from drinking too much because one must be careful not to have too much cold water after being in the heat and sun. But, in order to prevent him from thinking that she did not want him to have enough water to drink, she told him, "I will draw water for your camels until they finish drinking." In that way the servant knew that she was not selfishly holding back water from either him or his animals. (Rabbi Naphtali Zvi Judah Berlin, Ha-Emek Davar)

For the teachers of Torah, Rebekah is *tovat mareh*. She is not only physically beautiful, but she is a beautiful "person." She is kind and helpful to the servant even though he is a stranger. She is thoughtful of his feelings and careful of what she says to him. And her concern is not only about him but also about his animals.

Her beauty is not in what she is wearing. There is no description of her clothing. Nor are we told about her complexion—whether her skin was soft—or whether she was thin or plump, tall or short. The details we are given are about how she treats other people, how she speaks to them, how she offers hospitality, and how she reaches out to aid a stranger and a wanderer in her land.

Before Rebekah knows who the servant is, or that he represents Abraham and has come seeking a bride for Isaac, she demonstrates that she is a generous and giving person. That is what defines her as *tovat mareh* in the servant's eyes—and in the considered opinion of Jewish tradition.

PEREK DALET: *What Does the Torah Mean by "Love"?*

The Isaac-Rebekah romance seems to have begun with "love at first sight."

After a long journey from Aram-naharaim, Abraham's servant and Rebekah enter the Land of Israel and arrive in the area of Beer-lahai-roi in the Negev. It is near sunset and Isaac is out walking in the field. He is alone, still in sorrow over his mother's death.

Rebekah is riding on her camel and sees the lonely figure walking in the field. "Who is that man walking in the field toward us?" she asks the servant. He recognizes Isaac and tells her, "That is my master."

Rebekah and Isaac meet. The servant tells him about his journey and, afterwards, Isaac takes her to Sarah's tent. Then the Torah tells us "he took Rebekah as his wife, and Isaac loved her. . . ."

It's a strange twist for high romance. One would have thought that love came before marriage. Here, however, it seems to come afterwards.

Hirsch

Love is blind
A mere glance into the novels of true life teaches us the vast difference between love before marriage and after. . . . Such love [before] is blind, and therefore every step into the future leads to new disappointments. Jewish marriage, however, is described here as follows: He married Rebekah, and he loved her. The wedding is not the summit but only the seed of future love. (Samson Raphael Hirsch, 1808–1888, Timeless Torah, Phillip Feldheim, Inc., New York, 1957, on Genesis 24:67, pp. 53–54)

Another view about love
The meaning of the words, "he took Rebekah as his wife, and Isaac loved her . . . " are meant to indicate that he was deeply grieved by his mother's death and found no real comfort until he found love with Rebekah. It was that love that really comforted him.

In the Targum Onkelos, an early Aramaic translation of the Torah used in the synagogue, we read: "And Isaac brought her into the tent and, behold, she was like Sarah his mother." That is why the Torah mentions that Isaac "loved her." It is meant to teach us that, because of Rebekah's righteousness and the kindness of her deeds, Isaac loved her and was comforted by her. (Nachmanides on Genesis 24:67)

Those who comment on the Torah's description that Isaac first married Rebekah and then he loved her do not mean to deny that there is "love at first sight." What they are saying is that there is a significant difference between "infatuation" and the evolution of mature love.

In his book *Consecrated Unto Me*, Rabbi Roland B. Gittelsohn writes that there are four differences between *infatuation* and *love*. "The first is the test of time. . . . Except for the rare instance where infatuation leads to love, it begins more dramatically, develops far more rapidly, and expires while love may still be incubating." The second test "is to see whether the emphasis is on the self or the other person, on getting or on giving." The third test is whether the couple is "interested exclusively in themselves." Finally, "infatuation is a purely physical experience while love is both physical and spiritual."

> ### Defining love
> *Love is a consuming desire to share one's whole life both physically and spiritually with another person . . . to share that person's sorrows and pains no less than his/her pleasures and joys. In love one is at least as anxious to give as to receive. Love is a relationship in which each partner is able to develop his/her own abilities and fulfill his/her own hopes in far greater measure than either could have done alone. (Roland B. Gittelsohn,* Consecrated Unto Me, *UAHC, New York, 1965, p. 19.*

According to the biblical story, Isaac and Rebekah quite obviously began their relationship with "infatuation." They were attracted to each other. They wanted to spend time exclusively with each other. Yet, according to the commentators, their powerful attraction grew into a mature commitment and a readiness for marriage. Rebekah comforted Isaac about the loss of his mother, Sarah. He may have supported her in those moments when she longed for her family in distant Aramnaharaim. They learned how to reconcile their differences and to respect each other. Finally, through time and sharing, they came to love each other.

Jewish tradition teaches that, while our romantic meetings may be the miraculous work of God, and that we may be fortunate enough to "fall in love at first sight," the real success of our love relationships depends upon how we work at them. Love must be nurtured and negotiated each day. There are no instant and magic guarantees that love will grow and mature. It all rests on the quality of the commitment, honesty, trust, and openness both people build into their relationship.

In a time when the stress is on "romance" and immediate gratification, the Jewish wisdom that "the wedding is not the summit but only the seed of future love" is a significant warning and lesson.

QUESTIONS FOR STUDY AND DISCUSSION

1. What are some of the lessons this Torah portion teaches us about preparing for the death of a loved one and about dealing with our loss? How are the mourning customs of Jewish tradition helpful to us in times of sorrow?

2. We are all tempted "to buy at the best price." Should we take discounts and deals from friends? What are the benefits and the problems that come from accepting such bargains?

3. From what the commentators say about Rebekah, can we define a Jewish view of "beauty"? How do the views of "beauty" in Jewish tradition compare with those of our modern society?

4. Abraham's servant devised a test by which he could determine Rebekah's values and the values of her family. What are your most important values? How can you determine whether or not your partner in a possible long-term romantic relationship shares those values? What test or questions should be considered when choosing such a partner?

PARASHAT TOLEDOT
Genesis 25:19–28:9

Toledot may be translated as "generations," and "history." This Torah portion begins by describing the birth of Esau and Jacob, the twins born to Rebekah and Isaac. Esau is a rugged person of the outdoors; Jacob is a gentle person, preferring the quiet of his tent. Isaac favors Esau, and Rebekah loves Jacob. While still young, Esau sells his birthright to Jacob for a pot of stew. Later, at age forty, Esau brings pain to his parents by marrying two Hittite women. When Isaac is old and near death, Rebekah and Jacob trick him into giving Jacob the special blessing he had intended for Esau. Esau discovers what they have done and vows to kill his brother. Fearing for Jacob's life and desiring that he marry someone from her people in Paddan-aram, Rebekah persuades Isaac to send Jacob to her brother, Laban. Meanwhile, Esau took his first cousin, Mahalath the daughter of Ishmael, as his third wife.

OUR TARGUM

· 1 ·

For a time after their marriage, Isaac and Rebekah have difficulty conceiving. Finally, Rebekah becomes pregnant, but she suffers great pain. When she asks the reason for her discomfort, God tells her that she is carrying twins and that, from them, two battling nations will emerge.

When the children are born, the eldest is given the name Esau, meaning "hairy," because his body is covered with hair. The younger child is named Jacob, meaning "heel," because at birth his hand was holding onto Esau's heel.

As they grow, Esau becomes a skillful hunter while Jacob remains quietly within the camp. Isaac favors Esau because he brings him food from his hunting; Rebekah favors Jacob.

Once, while Jacob is cooking some stew, Esau returns from a hunt very hungry. "Give me some of that stuff you are cooking," he demands of Jacob. "Sell me your birthright," Jacob responds. "I'm starved. What do I care about a birthright!" Esau answers. So Jacob gives him some stew, and Esau gives up his birthright.

· 2 ·

Later, at a time of famine, Isaac visits Abimelech, king of the Philistines, in the Negev town of Gerar. As happened before with Abraham and Sarah, the men of Gerar admire Rebekah. Fearing that they will harm him, Isaac tells them that she is his "sister." When Abimelech discovers what has happened, he offers Isaac protection and, as a result, Isaac prospers greatly in the land of the Philistines.

As Isaac becomes richer, the Philistines envy him and stop up his wells. Seeing the trouble between them, Abimelech tells Isaac: "Leave our land, for you are becoming too powerful for us." Afterwards, Isaac travels to Beer-sheba, where Abimelech visits him in order to confirm a peace treaty between them.

· 3 ·

Near the time of his death, Isaac asks Esau to go out hunting and to bring him back a "tasty dish," promising that he will reward Esau with a special blessing.

Rebekah overhears their conversation and persuades Jacob to dress in Esau's clothing and to put on hairy skins so that he will fool Isaac into believing that he is Esau. "What if I appear to him as a trickster and he curses me?" Jacob asks his mother. Rebekah answers, "I will take your curse upon me."

Their disguise fools Isaac. He believes that Jacob is Esau, and he blesses him with the words: "Let peoples serve you, and nations bow to

you. . . . Cursed be they who curse you, blessed they who bless you."

When Esau returns from the field with a "tasty dish" as his father had requested, Isaac informs him that he has already given away his blessing. Esau is furious. Threatening to kill Jacob, he shouts: "First he took away my birthright, and now he has taken away my blessing!"

· 4 ·

At forty years of age, Esau married two Hittite women. The mixed marriage upset both his parents. Fearing that Jacob would also intermarry, Rebekah urged Isaac to send Jacob to her homeland in Paddan-aram where he might find a wife from the daughters of her brother, Laban. Isaac follows Rebekah's suggestion. In the meantime, Esau took his first cousin, Mahalath the daughter of Ishmael, as his third wife.

THEMES

Parashat Toledot contains three important themes:

1. Jealousy between brothers; the creation of stereotypes and prejudice.
2. Favoritism by parents.
3. Problems of intermarriage.

PEREK ALEF: *Esau and Jacob—The Bitter Struggle between Brothers*

The Torah tells us that, even before Esau and Jacob were born, Rebekah felt them battling with each other in her womb. It is natural for a pregnant mother to feel the fetus "kicking" and "punching" at the wall of her uterus. With twins the activity is doubled. Physicians identify such activity as "signs of life."

According to the Torah, however, what Rebekah felt was more than normal activity even from twins. She sensed that the babies she was carrying were to become two nations and that the older would eventually serve the younger.

The future struggle between the brothers was dramatized at their birth by the names they were given. The elder, Esau, was also called "Edom," from the Hebrew *adom* meaning "red," because he was born with a bloody red mat of hair covering his body and grew to crave reddish stew. Within the Torah, he is identified as the father of the people of Edom and of the Amalekites, who were bitter enemies of the Jews. Later, during the persecution of the Jewish people by the Romans, the rabbis often referred to the government of Rome as "Edom" or "Esau."

The second born was called Jacob, from the Hebrew *akev* meaning "heel," because, as the Torah indicates, he was holding onto Esau's heel as he emerged from Rebekah's womb. Later within our Torah story, Jacob's name is changed to Israel and becomes the historic name for the Jewish people.

From Esau to Amalek to Haman
Within the Torah we are informed: "This is the line of Esau—that is, Edom. . . . Timna was a concubine of Esau's son Eliphaz; she bore Amalek. . . ." (Genesis 36:1–12)

The Torah tells us that Amalek attacked the helpless people of Israel at Rephidim just after they had left Egypt. Because Amalek had taken advantage of the Israelites' weakness, Moses declared that God would "be at war with Amalek throughout the ages." (Exodus 17:8–16)

We are also told of a King Agag of Amalek who is connected by the author of the Book of Esther with Haman "son of Hamedatha the Agagite." Clearly, the intention here is to identify all the enemies of the Jewish people as the descendants of Esau-Edom. (I Samuel 15:8 and Esther 3:1)

Both before and after the destruction of the Temple by the Romans in 70 C.E., the rabbis used the name "Edom" as a code name for Rome. They believed that, one day, Esau-Edom-Rome would be defeated and that Jacob-Israel would be victorious. They predicted that "God will throw Edom-Rome out of heaven. . . . Edom-Rome will be slaughtered. . . . Edom-Rome will be destroyed by fire." (Pesikta de-Rav Kahana 4:9)

For many Jewish commentators, and perhaps for those who wrote the Torah, Esau and Jacob were more than just human beings. They were not only the sons of Rebekah and Isaac, but they were two different nations at war with each other. Their personalities were very different, and their descendants became enemies throughout all history. They were not only Esau and Jacob, but they became Israel and Edom, then Israel and Rome, then Israel and all who plotted the destruction of the Jewish people. Esau-Edom-Rome became a code name for all the opponents of the Jewish people.

How does it happen that names for two innocent children become labels for bitter enemies and memories? How do such stereotypes develop? Perhaps for three reasons:

1. *Historical experience:* Often our viewpoints or prejudices grow out of what history has taught us. In the case of the early Israelites, the descendants of Esau, who were Amalekites, attacked weak and helpless Jews just after their Exodus from Egypt. Later, in about 485 B.C.E., the Edomites led an alliance of nations seeking to end Jewish rule of Jerusalem. Writing at that time, the prophet Obadiah angrily declared:

Thus said my Lord God concerning Edom:
I will make you least among nations;
You shall be most despised. . . .
For the outrage to your brother Jacob,
Disgrace shall engulf you,
And you shall perish forever. . . .
And no survivor shall be left of the house of Esau.
(Obadiah 1:1, 2, 10, 18)

Obadiah's connection of Esau with Edom is similar to the link made by the biblical author of the Book of Esther between Haman and Esau-Edom and Amalek. Haman, who is identified as the son of Hamedatha the Agagite, is linked with King Agag the Amalekite.

Making the connection of Haman with the Amalekites or of Rome with Edom must have seemed very logical. After all, their goal was the same. They opposed Jewish survival. Their hands were bloody with the massacre, plunder, rape, and ruin of Jews and their communities.

For each generation it was as if the battle between the brothers, Jacob and Esau, never ended. Jews and non-Jews were still at war with one another. The old names still applied. Jacob was the persecuted Jew, and Esau-Edom the non-Jewish persecutor. Because the history of prejudice and brutality was so painful, it seemed to justify the continued use of "Esau-Edom-Rome-Haman-Hitler" as the stereotype name for all the enemies of the Jewish people.

2. *The need to depersonalize the enemy:* Bitter memories, however, are only one source of stereotypes. Special names, or labels, or numbers are invented and used because they are a way of categorizing those we fear or dislike. They make it easier to express our suspicion and hostility because they rob people of their individuality.

For example, by forcing Anne Frank to wear a yellow star, the Nazis, who took her off to be killed in a concentration camp, no longer had to deal with the fact that she was a teenager, a gifted writer, a person with hopes and dreams like many of their own children. By labeling her, they had removed her individuality and justified her death.

When Jews are called "kikes" or "sheenies," or Blacks are called "niggers," or Spanish-Americans are called "spics," or Italians are called "wops," the names are not simply insulting, but they are a means of confirming that those with different names are inferior as well. Having depersonalized people into categories, we can more easily dismiss their ideas or potential contributions. "Blacks are not fit to manage teams," a baseball executive told a news conference. "The Japanese have a talent for copying everything and creating nothing," a businessman announced to his computer company board. Labeling people allows us to turn them into objects of scorn—and sometimes into targets for violence.

3. *The need to organize against the enemy:* Slogans, stereotypes, and names also fuel our natural tendency to rally against real or perceived enemies. They not only define our opponents, but they fill us with a comfortable feeling of identity with others who share our views. They confirm our conviction that we are on the superior and correct side of the battle. We become the "good guys" while the targets of our hostility are, obviously, all the "bad guys" who are plotting against us. Having named our common adversary, we can organize for the war against "evil."

For example, by portraying Jews as "Christ-killers," non-Jews could easily organize and justify violence against them. By portraying Japanese-Americans as "dangerous aliens" during the Second World War, leaders of the United States justified placing thousands of them in concentration camps. By labeling political opponents as "enemies of the state," Joseph Stalin justified the exile and murder of millions of Soviet citizens.

Yet, prejudice also works the other way. Sometimes the victim becomes so battered and violated that he comes to see the rest of the world as "Esau-Edom," the enemy. That has been so for many Jews. Because so many suffered the bitterness of pogroms and exile—or in the twentieth century watched helplessly while the Nazis slaughtered their parents, husbands, wives, and children—many Jews still retain suspicions about the friendship of non-Jews. They still consider themselves endangered as Jacob-Israel against Esau-Edom. Such names, and the prejudices they contain, are abandoned very slowly.

Will there ever be a time when human beings will forgive and trust one another? Will Jews and non-Jews, the Jacobs and the Esaus, ever be brothers and sisters and not enemies? And what is our responsibility in creating such a time of understanding and goodwill?

In answer to our questions, the rabbis offer the following fascinating story based upon the Torah commandment "You shall not hate an Edomite, for an Edomite is your fellow human being." (Deuteronomy 23:8)

Rabbi Elazar ben Shammua was once walking by the seashore when he noticed a boat sinking at sea. A moment later he watched as a man holding onto a plank of wood floated onto shore. Other Jews were walking by. Because the man was naked, he covered himself and pleaded: "I am a son of Esau, your brother. I have lost everything. Please give me a garment to cover myself." The Jews refused and said: "Your people have treated our people with cruelty. Therefore, may all your people be stripped bare as you are today." The man then turned to Rabbi Elazar and said, "You are an honorable man; please help me." Rabbi Elazar took off a garment and gave it to him. Then he brought him to his home, fed him, and gave him money with which to begin his life again.

When the emperor died, the rescued man succeeded him. He ordered that all Jews in his state be killed. The Jews turned to Rabbi Elazar and asked him to plead for them. When the man, who was now the ruler, saw Rabbi Elazar standing before him, he said: "Does not your Torah teach 'You shall not hate an Edomite, for he is your brother'? I told your people that I was the son of Esau, and they treated me with hatred, not with kindness."

Rabbi Elazar replied: "Though they are guilty of breaking the law of the Torah, forgive them."

The king, recalling what Elazar had done for him, answered: "Because of what you did for me, I will forgive them."

(*Ecclesiastes Rabbah* 11:1)

Rabbi Elazar ben Judah taught that "the most beautiful thing a person can do is to forgive." (*Rokeach* 13C) Bearing grudges only prolongs hostility. Forgiveness and understanding are the only genuine ways to reconciliation, cooperation, and peace. Perpetuating prejudices through slogans and names only increases human suffering. Perhaps that is why the Torah warns us: "You shall not hate an Edomite, for he is your brother.

You shall not hate an Egyptian, for you were a stranger in his land." (Deuteronomy 23:8)

PEREK BET: *Parental Favoritism*

Our Torah portion not only contains the story about the beginnings of the historic struggle between Esau-Edom and Jacob-Israel, but it also takes us into the biblical home of Rebekah and Isaac. We are told that the young brothers, Esau and Jacob, have very different personalities. Esau is a hunter; he prefers being outdoors. He is also impatient, demanding, and quick to lose his temper. Jacob is described as a "mild" person, quiet, patient, clever, and calculating.

The two brothers are portrayed as jealous of each other and in constant competition for their parents' interest and affection. To complicate family matters even further, we are told that each parent has chosen a favorite son. Isaac prefers Esau "because he also had a taste for freshly killed game." Rebekah "loved Jacob." Nor do Isaac and Rebekah hide their preferences. When Isaac decides to present his sons with his parental blessing, he tells Esau, not Jacob, to hunt him some fresh game and to prepare it for him. As a reward he promises to give him the gift of his "innermost blessing."

When Rebekah overhears what her husband has promised, she tells Jacob to bring her some game and she will prepare food for his father. Afterwards, she dresses him in animal skins so that Isaac might be tricked into blessing her favorite son, Jacob, instead of Esau. Her trick is successful. Isaac is fooled into blessing Jacob, but the results are tragic. The jealousy between the brothers hardens into hatred.

Did parental favoritism cause the hostility between Jacob and Esau or is such antagonism inevitable between brothers and sisters?

Some interpreters argue that the differences between Jacob and Esau made it impossible for them to get along as brothers. Jacob, they explain, was a quiet, timid, studious person while Esau spent his time trapping animals and associating with those who knew how to use a spear, a knife, and a sword. Jacob was calm and reasonable while

Esau demanded satisfaction immediately, losing his temper if he could not have his way.

A few commentators trace the differences between the brothers to their early childhood. Once, when Esau returned from hunting in the fields, he entered the house, smelled the sweet stew Jacob was cooking, and demanded a bowl of it. "I'm starving," he said. "I want it now."

Knowing that Esau would often make foolish mistakes when pressured or upset, Jacob took advantage of him. He wanted all the privileges of being the firstborn. So he said to Esau, "Sell me your birthright, and I'll give you some stew." Impulsively, Esau agreed.

The differences between them
Rabbi Pinchus said in Rabbi Levi's name that Esau and Jacob were like a myrtle and a wild rosebush growing side by side. When they had fully grown, one produced a sweet fragrance, and the other produced thorns. For thirteen years, both Esau and Jacob studied at school. Afterwards, Jacob continued to study, and Esau became an idolator. Jacob had learned that answers to questions came slowly and through hard work. Esau wanted immediate and easy answers.
(Genesis Rabbah *63:10*)

Rabbi S. Z. Kahana, a modern commentator living in Israel, claims that Esau and Jacob represented two different philosophies of living. "Esau accepts the world as it is: all is well. But Jacob is not satisfied with the world as it is. He recognizes that a great deal remains to be done."
(Heaven on Your Head, *Research Centre of Kabbalah, New York, 1986, p. 34.*)

While most commentators agree that Esau and Jacob had very different personalities, there are some who suggest that the jealousy, distrust, and hatred that developed between them was not their fault but the fault of their parents. Commenting on the relationship between Isaac and Esau, and Rebekah and Jacob, psychologist Haim G. Ginott points out that the competition and jealousy between them "was sparked" by parental favoritism and preferential treatment.

"Why did Isaac and Rebekah show such favoritism?" That is the question.

Abravanel

Don Isaac Abravanel argues that Isaac was simply blinded to Esau's faults. "Affection," Abravanel comments, "ruins judgment." Others suggest that Isaac was aloof, withdrawn, and out of touch with his sons. He spent no time with them. Therefore, he was not aware of their strengths or weaknesses.

Another explanation for Isaac's favoring of Esau is found in *Genesis Rabbah,* an ancient collection of interpretations by the rabbis. There it is suggested that Isaac never recovered from the terror he experienced when his father, Abraham, nearly offered him as a sacrifice on Mount Moriah. He remained fearful all his life and had trouble making decisions. He remained weak and frightened, always leaning on others who displayed strength. For that reason he favored Esau over Jacob.

David Kimchi disagrees. He holds that Isaac was neither weak nor incapable of making clear decisions. Isaac favored Esau because he realized that Esau was weak not strong and, therefore, required more support, more help, more direction, and care if he was to mature as a responsible adult. Isaac considered Esau the weaker son because he saw that Esau was "wild," irresponsible, undisciplined, and uncaring about others. Isaac believed that Esau would change if he gave him gifts and favored him with special attentions and blessings.

As for Rebekah, the commentators nearly all claim that she forced Jacob into dressing up like Esau and into lying about who he was in order to steal the blessing from his brother. One interpreter tells us that Jacob "acted out of duress"; another claims that he pleaded in tears with Rebekah that she not force him to deceive his father. (*Genesis Rabbah;* also *Ha-Ketav ve-ha-Kabbalah* on Genesis 18:2)

Why did Rebekah show such partiality to Jacob?

One view is that she, more than Isaac or anyone else, had a "mother's intuition" that Jacob was especially endowed with powers of wisdom to inherit the leadership of the Jewish people. Before the twins were born, God had told her: "Two nations are in your womb. . . . One people shall be mightier than the other, and the older shall serve the younger." She simply was following her inner voice, favoring the younger child she sensed was to be the "leader." (*Midrash ha-Gadol* 27:13)

Grandfather Abraham also favored Jacob
One tradition of interpretation claims that Abraham also favored Jacob over Esau. He praised his intellectual qualities and disapproved of Esau's wild behavior. Rebekah noted Grandfather Abraham's opinion and was influenced by it. (*Louis Ginzberg,* Legends of the Jews, *Vol. I, Jewish Publication Society, Philadelphia, 1968, p. 316*)

Esau was treated unjustly
Author Eli Wiesel writes the following about Rebekah's treatment of Esau. "His own mother seemed to resent him. She pushed him aside. Why didn't she love him? Because he preferred games to study? Because his hair was long and red? Because he always walked around armed? Because he was constantly hungry? She was hostile to him, that seems clear. And unjust." (Messengers of God, *Random House, New York, 1976, p. 117*)

Steinsaltz

Rabbi Adin Steinsaltz makes a different argument. He explains that, because Rebekah had grown up in the "wheeling and dealing" corrupt world of her brother Laban, "she had learned the meaning of cheating, of hypocrisy." She was a realist where Isaac was an "easy victim of duplicity; he was neither suspicious nor afraid because there was no dishonesty in his own heart."

For those reasons, Isaac did not notice Esau's weaknesses but only that he seemed well behaved and did what his father requested of him. On the other hand, Steinsaltz explains that Rebekah "was an expert in such matters. She knew that someone like Esau could have another, less pleasant aspect, an aspect that reminded her of her own brother Laban. She recognized her own family in Esau, and she knew his shortcomings and his weak points." As a result of this understanding, "she manipulated Isaac into blessing Jacob instead of Esau out of her love for Isaac, in an attempt to shield and protect him from the emotional shock of his own error." (Adin Steinsaltz, *Biblical Images,* Basic Books, New York, 1984, pp. 46–47)

In other words, Rebekah favored Jacob, not only because she knew that Esau possessed shortcomings like her brother Laban, but also because she wished to protect her husband, Isaac, from making a mistake by giving Esau and not Jacob his blessing. Rebekah's favoritism was a form of saving Isaac from his own stupidity and foolish decisions.

Parents and sibling rivalry
Psychologist Haim G. Ginott comments about how parents handle jealousy between their children. "Some parents are so angered by sibling rivalry that they punish any overt sign of it. Other parents bend backward almost acrobatically to avoid giving cause for jealousy. They try to convince their children that all of them are loved equally and therefore have no reason to be jealous. . . .

Those who want to be superfair to each child often end up being furious with all their children. Nothing is so self-defeating as measured fairness. When a mother cannot give a bigger apple or a stronger hug to one child for fear of antagonizing the other, life becomes unbearable. . . .

Children do not yearn for equal shares of love: they need to be loved uniquely, not uniformly. The emphasis is on quality, not equality. We do not love all our children the same way, and there is no need to pretend that we do. We love each child uniquely, and we do not have to labor so hard to cover it up." (Between Parent and Child, *Macmillan, New York, 1965, pp. 127–132*)

Love them equally
Love equally all your children. Sometimes the favored disappoint, and the neglected make you happy. (Berekiah Ha-Nakdan, *Mishle Shualim, 1260* C.E.)

No favoritism
Play no favoritism: Because Joseph got a multicolored coat, the brothers "hated him." (*Rabbi Eleazar ben Azariah,* Genesis Rabbah 84:8)

Each child is unique
Each child carries its own blessing into the world. (Yiddish Proverb)

Interpreters of our Torah portion all seem to agree that the jealousy and bitterness between Jacob and Esau was not simply a matter of misunderstandings between them. Their troubled relationship grew, not only out of the differences in their personalities, but also from the way in which they were treated by their grandparents and parents. Isaac's and Rebekah's strengths and weaknesses, their backgrounds and judgments, the ways in which they rewarded and manipulated Esau and Jacob clearly contributed to the sibling rivalry between the brothers.

Tragically, that rivalry ultimately developed into a distrust and hatred that drove them apart. It poisoned their relationship forever. While later the brothers would meet and make peace, they would then go their separate ways without ever achieving genuine brotherly love.

PEREK GIMEL: *The Issue of Intermarriage*

The subject of marriage is raised twice in our Torah portion.

We are told that when Esau was forty years old he married two Hittite women and that the marriages were "a source of bitterness to Isaac and Rebekah." (Genesis 26:34)

Then, near the end of the Torah portion, it is reported that Rebekah tells Isaac that she is worried that Jacob, like Esau, will marry a woman from among the Canaanites rather than someone from their ancestral home in Paddan-aram. Isaac agrees with her. He sends for Jacob and instructs him to go to Paddan-aram to find a bride among the daughters of Laban, Rebekah's brother. He also blesses Jacob, telling him that God will give him and his children rights to the Land of Israel as was promised to Abraham, his grandfather.

When Esau hears that his father has instructed Jacob not to marry a Canaanite woman, has sent him off to Paddan-aram, and has given him an additional blessing, he is hurt and angry. Perhaps to find favor with his parents, he marries his first cousin Mahalath, the daughter of Ishmael. He does not, however, divorce his Hittite wives.

As the Torah portion indicates, the subject of intermarriage between Jews and non-Jews has been a concern since the beginnings of Jewish history. We are not told what it is that "displeases" Isaac and Rebekah about Esau's Hittite wives nor that they had forbidden him to marry them. Yet it is clear that they are troubled by what Esau has done and, therefore, warn Jacob not to marry from among the Canaanites. They tell him to find a wife from among his "tribal family."

Speiser

Most modern biblical scholars are agreed that the two mentions of intermarriage in our Torah portion were written by authors who believed that religion and nationality could only be preserved through marriages within the tribal group. For instance, E. A. Speiser comments that whoever wrote these two passages was interested in "purity of lineage." (*The Anchor Bible: Genesis*, p. 216)

> ### Separate for a holy purpose
> *But there was another factor in Israel that tended to lift what might have been only a fierce instinctive separatism to a higher level of emotion. That was the passionate conviction that Israel was meant to be not only a nation but a theocracy (rule of state by God, and by God's priests). To maintain its racial integrity therefore was to maintain the religious institution of covenant and law and holy faith.* (Interpreter's Bible, *Genesis, p. 678*)

The Christian scholarly commentary, *Interpreter's Bible*, agrees with E. A. Speiser that the authors of this part of our Torah portion were xenophobic. They feared strangers. They were concerned that strangers would marry their children and remove them from their community. As a result, they would not survive as a distinct people. For them, "to marry outside the clan was to mix its blood and to break its solidarity." Fear of others and their foreign ways and beliefs was the primary motivation for the opposition of Isaac and Rebekah to intermarriage. That is the reason they were grieved.

But that was not the only reason. It was not just fear but also a positive conviction of faith. The authors of the *Interpreter's Bible* also point out that those who created the story of the opposition of Isaac and Rebekah to intermarriage did so for a more important reason. They believed in the special covenant or *berit* between the Jewish people and God and that the best way to preserve it was to permit marriages only between Jews. Mixing with other peoples meant abandoning their relationship with God and their responsibility to live as a "holy" or "separate" people dedicated to God's service.

> ### The way to idolatry
> *Twice more the Torah warns about intermarriage. In Exodus 34:16 the Israelites are told:*

> *"And when you take wives from among their daughters for your sons, their daughters will lust after their gods and will cause your sons to lust after their gods."*
>
> *In Deuteronomy 7:3–4 the Israelites are commanded: "You shall not intermarry with them: do not give your daughters to their sons or take their daughters for your sons; for they will turn your children away from Me to worship other gods. . . ."*

Not only do we find other warnings against intermarriage in the Torah, but we are also told that, because King Solomon, in his old age, married non-Jewish wives who "turned away Solomon's heart after other gods," his sons were not eligible to inherit his throne. (I Kings 11:1–13) The opposition to intermarriage within the Torah seems to have been based on the belief that it led to idol worship and to disloyalty to the faith and covenant of the Jewish people with God.

Rashi

Rashi seems to agree with that argument. In commenting upon the "bitterness" of Isaac and Rebekah at Esau's marriage to the Hittite women, Rashi explains that it derived from the smell of the idolatrous offerings that the wives burned each day. He suggests that both Isaac and Rebekah realized that the wives' loyalty to their traditions would, eventually, influence Esau away from his faith and, ultimately, endanger the survival of Jewish tradition and the Jewish people.

> ### Opposition to intermarriage
> *"From the very beginning . . . Jewish opposition to mixed marriage was based not on any notion of racial superiority but rather on realistic recognition of the fact that such matches posed an ominous threat to the survival of the Jewish people and its faith."* (Roland B. Gittelsohn, Consecrated Unto Me, *p. 193*)

> ### Group identity
> *"Jewish group identity is generally defined in terms of both religion and ethnic background. . . . Children of conversionary marriages were more than three times as likely to identify as Jews than were children of mixed marriages. The overwhelming majority of the children of conversionary marriages were identified as Jewish at birth, and virtually all continued to identify themselves as Jewish. . . ."* (*Egon Mayer*, Love and Tradition: Marriage between Jews and Christians, *Plenum Publishing Corp., 1985, p. 253*)

Other commentators trace Isaac's blindness to the stress and unhappiness he suffered over Esau's intermarriages. They argue that God blinded him in order to relieve the pain he felt each time he saw his son or the smoke of idolatry rising from his home. (*Midrash Tanchuma, Toledot 7*)

Hirsch

Some Jewish interpreters, however, take the matter one step further. Rabbi Samson Raphael Hirsch argues that "with this marriage with two Hittite women Esau set the seal on his complete unfitness to be the one who was to carry on the mission of Abraham. In a home where even two daughters of Heth ruled, the Abrahamitic principle was just buried." By intermarrying, Hirsch contends, Esau became a house divided between Abraham's belief in one spiritual God and the many idol-gods of his wives. This disqualified him from inheriting the leadership of the Jewish people from Abraham. Hirsch reasons that a home where two religious traditions are practiced or where there is not a joint commitment to a single faith by both parents is often the cause of confusion, misunderstanding, and trouble between parents and children. Children may wonder which tradition they should follow. Sometimes, without being aware of it, a parent will signal that "if you love me, you will do it my way." Grandparents

may reward children for showing a preference for their faith. Instead of providing them with a common tradition to practice and to share, religious tradition may become a source of arguments and bitter family division.

> ### The role of religion
> Ritual *"serves as a bridge from the past—across the present—to the future. It reminds us of the imponderables, the spiritual values by which our actions should be guided. We Jews are especially fortunate because our faith provides us with a rich treasury of beautiful ritual. The most important moments and emotions in life—birth, growth, adolescence, love, marriage, and death—are enhanced by rituals that grow out of our people's past and express our hopes for the future. The sharing of rituals—precisely because they are poetic symbols appealing to the emotions—can do more to bring husband and wife together than any intellectual sharing."* (*Gittelsohn,* Consecrated Unto Me, *p. 214*)

For the teachers of Jewish tradition, sharing a single religious tradition in the home is meant to unite husband, wife, and children. It is meant to provide a common identity and a rich resource of rituals and traditions for emotional and intellectual enrichment. Through sharing a historic faith, family members are bonded to one another and also to the Jewish community beyond their home. For all these reasons, Jews today continue to promote marriages where bride and groom strengthen their love and commitment to each other by sharing the joy and meaning of building a Jewish home.

QUESTIONS FOR STUDY AND DISCUSSION

1. How, according to the discussion of this Torah portion, do stereotypes and histories of hatred develop? Are there acts or words spoken by others for which there can be no forgiveness? Are there some strategies we might develop

for promoting forgiveness and the end to cycles of suspicion and hatred?

2. List the reasons given by the commentators for Rebekah's favoring of Jacob and for Isaac's favoring of Esau. Are these common factors in families you know? In your own? What can be done about such bias in relationships?

3. The Torah presents two statements critical of intermarriage: Exodus 34:16 and Deuteronomy 7:3–4. Compare these to what our commentators say about the subject in Perek Gimel. Are these observations still justified? Should we oppose interdating? How shall Jews preserve their tradition and their community in a free and open society?

PARASHAT VAYETZE
Genesis 28:10–32:3

Vayetze means "and he went out" and relates the story of Jacob's departure from Beer-sheba for distant Haran, Rebekah's birthplace. The first night of his journey, he dreams of a stairway reaching from earth to heaven and is told by God that his descendants will be blessed and that they will inherit the land already promised to Abraham and Isaac. After a long journey, Jacob arrives in Haran where he is welcomed by Rebekah's brother Laban and his two daughters, Leah and Rachel. Laban promises to allow Rachel to marry Jacob if he will work seven years for him. When it comes time for the marriage, Laban deceives Jacob by sending Leah to his tent. When Jacob protests, Laban tells him that, if he will serve another seven years, then he will also give him Rachel. Jacob agrees. With his two wives and their maidservants, Bilhah and Zilpah, he has twelve children: Reuben, Simeon, Levi, Judah, Issachar, Zebulun, and Dinah with Leah; Dan and Naphtali with Bilhah; Gad and Asher with Zilpah; and Joseph with Rachel. After working many years for Laban, Jacob decides to return to his homeland. He works out an agreement with Laban for payment of his wages. They will divide the herd. Jacob will be given all the spotted and speckled sheep and goats; Laban will keep the rest. Laban agrees, but, when Jacob's herd increases in numbers, Laban's sons accuse Jacob of cheating them. Fearing trouble, Jacob decides to leave secretly with all his family and cattle. Laban pursues him, but, when he overtakes him, they share their grievances and reconcile their differences. Afterwards, Jacob and his family continue on their way.

OUR TARGUM

· 1 ·

On the eve of his departure from Beersheba, Jacob makes a pillow with some stones and goes to sleep. He dreams of a stairway reaching from earth to heaven. On it, angels are going up and down, and God tells him that his descendants will be many, that they will spread out in all directions, that all peoples will be blessed by them, and that ultimately God will bring him back to his homeland. In the morning, Jacob names the place Bethel, meaning "House of God." He also promises that, if God will protect him on his long journey and return him to his homeland, he will worship God and set aside a tithe, ten percent, of his wealth for God.

· 2 ·

Jacob continues his journey and arrives in Haran. He asks some shepherds if they know his uncle, Laban, and they point to Rachel, Laban's daughter, who is bringing her flocks to a well. Jacob waters the flock and tells Rachel who he is. She runs to inform her father. Laban warmly greets Jacob as "my bone and flesh."

After a month, Laban says to Jacob, "You should not work for me without wages. How much shall I pay you?" Jacob, who has fallen in love with Rachel, answers, "I will serve you seven years if you will give me Rachel for a wife." Laban agrees, but after the seven years he tricks Jacob on the night of the wedding and sends his older daughter, Leah, into Jacob's tent.

The next morning Jacob complains to Laban. "Why have you deceived me?" Laban tells him that "it is not the practice in our land to marry off the younger before the older," but Laban promises to allow him to marry Rachel if he will serve him another seven years. Jacob agrees.

· 3 ·

Leah gives birth to Reuben, Simeon, Levi, and Judah. Rachel is jealous and upset that she cannot have children. So she sends her maidservant, Bilhah, to Jacob to have children for her. Bilhah bears Dan and Naphtali. Leah also instructs her maidservant, Zilpah, to bear children with Jacob, and Zilpah gives birth to Gad and Asher. Afterwards, Leah bears Issachar, Zebulun, and a daughter, Dinah. Finally, Rachel conceives and bears Joseph.

· 4 ·

After Joseph's birth, Jacob approaches his father-in-law, Laban, and says, "Allow me and my family to leave and to return to my homeland."

Laban, knowing that his riches have increased greatly over the fourteen years of Jacob's service, tells him: "I have been blessed because of you. What shall I pay you?"

Jacob answers: "Pay me nothing, but do me a favor. Let me pass through your flocks and take all of those that are speckled and spotted, or dark-colored. They will be my wages." Laban agrees but secretly instructs his sons to remove all of the speckled and spotted or dark-colored sheep from the flock, taking them a distance of three days away from where Jacob is caring for his flock.

While pasturing Laban's flock, Jacob uses a form of magical rod, causing them to give birth, not only to speckled and spotted animals, but to stronger ones. As a result, Jacob becomes very prosperous. His household includes many maidservants, menservants, camels, and asses.

Seeing Jacob's wealth, Laban's sons become

jealous. They accuse Jacob of stealing from their father. Even Laban's attitude toward Jacob changes to suspicion.

Jacob is told by God to return to his homeland. He discusses the matter with Leah and Rachel, and they agree. So he gathers his family and possessions and sets out for the land of Canaan. As they depart, Rachel enters Laban's tent and steals one of his idols.

When Laban learns that they have gone without informing him, he pursues them. Overtaking them, he asks Jacob: "Why did you flee in secrecy and mislead me and not tell me? I would have sent you off with festive music . . . [and] why did you steal my gods?"

Jacob answers that he was afraid to reveal his plans but that he has not taken anything belonging to Laban. After searching the tents of both Leah and Rachel, Laban finds nothing since Rachel has cleverly hidden the idol she had taken under the camel cushions on which she is sitting.

Jacob turns to Laban and asks, "What is my crime, what is my guilt that you should pursue me?" Laban responds by claiming that "the daughters are my daughters, the children are my children, and the flocks are my flocks," but then he suggests that he and Jacob make peace with each other. The Torah portion concludes with their setting up a pillar of stones between them, promising that they will not cross the mound against each other with hostile intent.

THEMES

Parashat Vayetze contains three important themes:

1. The meaning of angels in the Torah.
2. The difference between proper and improper prayer.
3. Dealing with dishonest people.

PEREK ALEF: *Who and What Are Angels?*

When Jacob flees from Beer-sheba, he camps the first night on the desert. Gathering some stones for a pillow, he goes to sleep and dreams of a stairway reaching from the ground to the sky. On it "angels of God were going up and down." Later in our Torah portion (Genesis 31:10–13), Jacob tells Leah and Rachel that he has dreamed of an angel who explained to him how the streaked and speckled flocks were increasing to his advantage and that he should return to his homeland.

Who and what are these angels appearing to Jacob?

Actually, the Torah contains many mentions of angels: When Hagar, Sarah's maidservant, flees to the desert, an angel comforts and counsels her. (Genesis 16:7–12) Two angels visit Lot in Sodom and urge him to escape from the city with his family. (Genesis 19) Just as Abraham is about to sacrifice Isaac, an angel appears and tells him, "Do not raise your hand against the boy. . . ." (Gen-

esis 22:11) An angel speaks to Moses out of a burning bush and commands him to return to Egypt to free the Israelites from bondage. (Exodus 3:2–10)

Most scholars would define the angels mentioned in the Torah as "messengers of God." The Hebrew word for angel is *malach*, meaning "one who carries a message."

Belief in angels was quite common among peoples in the ancient Middle East. It was assumed that angels could fly, that they often had wings, that they could walk, talk, appear, and disappear, and that they were the designated agents of the gods. Within Jewish tradition, angels were believed to be slightly superior to human beings and to work as God's agents.

The Psalmist on angels
O God, our God,
How majestic is Your name throughout the earth!

> *You who have covered the heavens with Your*
> *splendor. . . .*
> *When I behold Your heavens, the work of*
> *Your fingers,*
> *the moon and stars that You have set in*
> *place:*
> *What is man that You have been mindful of*
> *him,*
> *mortal man that You have taken note of*
> *him,*
> *that You have made him little lower than the*
> *angels. . . . (Psalms·8:2, 4–6)*

Jews during the talmudic period also believed in angels. Some rabbis taught that God had actually consulted with angels before creating heaven, earth, and human beings. Others point out that angels have a life span of only one day. They are created in the morning, praise God throughout the day, and die in the evening. It was also believed that angels accompany Jews at the beginning of their observance of Shabbat and that they protect those who are faithful in carrying out God's commandments.

Talmudic teachers on angels
Rabbi Helbo taught that God creates a new choir of angels each day. They sing God's praises and then depart. (Genesis Rabbah *78:1*)

Great is peace, for God has given no more beautiful gift to the righteous. When a righteous person dies, angels accompany him to heaven and say: "He shall enter in peace"; "He shall rest in peace"; and "He walked uprightly." (Numbers Rabbah, Naso, *11:7*)

If one does a mitzvah, a commandment, one is given one angel. If one does two commandments, one is given two, and, if one does all the commandments, one is given many angels. And who are these angels? They guard people against bad things happening . . . they make peace for them. (Tanchuma, Mishpatim, *19*)

Rambam (Maimonides)

For the medieval philosopher Moses Maimonides, angels were *forms* of intelligence through which God "ruled the world." The human mind was such a *form* or "angel." Maimonides taught that, if God wished to send a message to a human being, it was sent through the person's mind or intelligence. For him, human minds were containers for God's signals or signs. That is why he called them angels. Angels were a wonderful way in which God spoke to human beings and inspired them with new ideas and visions. (*Guide for the Perplexed,* Part II, Chapters VI–VII)

Most modern Jewish philosophers and teachers no longer believe in the existence of angels, special nonhuman messengers of God. How, then, do they interpret the mention of angels in our Torah text?

Some simply explain that ancient authors accepted the existence of angels. They believed that, like human beings, they could speak, think, and see and that they could and did influence all aspects of human life. For the ancients, who wrote and edited the Torah text, angels were as real as people are for us.

Other modern teachers argue that ancient authors used angels as a dramatic way of expressing the inner thoughts of the characters they were describing. In our Torah portion, the author may have wished to portray Jacob's fear of leaving his homeland for a distant unknown place. His dream about the stairway stretching from earth to heaven, with angels going up and down on it, may depict his anxiety about his future. Would his fortunes go up or down? Would he be a success or failure? And would God help him and protect him from evil?

In reading and interpreting the role of angels in the Torah, both approaches prove helpful. At times an angel will simply appear as a messenger; at other times as a form of intelligence, a sign of the future; and sometimes as an insight into the fears and hopes of biblical characters. Clearly, angels add excitement, dimension, and color to the Torah tradition.

PEREK BET: *Jacob's Prayer—Can You Bargain with God?*

The Torah tells us that, just after he awoke from his dream of the stairway reaching to the heavens, Jacob made a vow—a promise in the form of a prayer.

The word for vow in Hebrew is *neder*. On Yom Kippur evening, Jews recite the prayer *Kol Nidre*, "all these vows," requesting forgiveness from God for any promises made but not kept from one Yom Kippur to the next.

Within Jewish tradition a *neder*, or vow, is defined as a promise made to God to carry out some action ("God, I will give ten percent of what I earn to charity") or a commitment not to do something otherwise permitted ("God, I will not smoke").

Vows were considered so important within Jewish tradition that the rabbis devoted an entire section of the Talmud to the subject. They called the section *Nedarim*, "Vows," and it is one of the largest in the Talmud.

The Talmud on vows
The person who makes a vow places a burden around his neck. (Jerusalem Talmud, Nedarim 9:1)

It is better to do a good deed without making a vow to do it. (Nedarim 77b)

A man came to Rabbi Judah ben Shalom, asking him to void a vow that he had made. The rabbi asked him: "What did you vow not to do?" The man answered, "I vowed to make no profit."

"How can a person in his right mind vow such a thing? asked the rabbi.

"What I meant," explained the man, "was that I would no longer make profits by gambling."

Rabbi Judah refused to void the man's vow.
(Jerusalem Talmud, Nedarim 5)

Jacob's vow has raised serious questions for biblical commentators through the centuries. After he had piled up stones to mark the place where he had slept and dreamed, he named it Bethel, "House of God." Then he made a vow: "If God remains with me, if God protects me on this journey that I am making and gives me bread to eat and clothing to wear, and if I return safe to my father's house—the Lord shall be my God . . . and of all that You give me, I will always set aside a tithe for You."

What has bothered interpreters is that Jacob seems to be bargaining with God. Rather than promising what he will or will not do, which is the accepted form for a vow, Jacob laces his commitment with conditions. Over and over again, he uses the qualifying *if* in his statement to God. He says: "*If* God remains with me . . . *if* God protects me . . . gives me bread . . . clothing . . . and *if* I return safe . . ." *then* "the Lord shall be my God" and "I will always set aside a tithe. . . ."

Abravanel

Don Isaac Abravanel, in his commentary on our Torah portion, asks: "How could Jacob act like those who serve upon the condition of receiving a reward? Is it possible that Jacob meant to say that, if God did not do all these things for him, Jacob would not believe in God and would not set aside charity?"

Clearly, Abravanel is bothered by the "deal" Jacob offers God in his vow. He considers it inappropriate to make a conditional promise. As a matter of fact, Abravanel's criticism of Jacob is stated quite bluntly. He compares Jacob with his grandfather, Abraham, and notes that "Abraham never made such vows, and he was tested many times."

Others have also questioned how Jacob could have made such a vow. Did he really mean to condition his devotion to God on whether or not God met his demands? Did he doubt God's power to bring him back to his homeland? Does the Torah mean to teach us that, if our prayers are not answered, God does not care about us?

Rabbi Jacob ben Isaac Ashkenazi, author and editor of the collection of Torah interpretation called *Tze'enah u-Re'enah,* was also bothered by such questions about Jacob's vow. Rather than criticizing Jacob, however, he suggests that Jacob did not mean to indicate that his belief in God was conditional at all. What Jacob meant when he used the conditional phrase ("if . . .") had to do with the place where he was making the vow, not with the vow itself.

In other words, we should understand what Jacob said in the following way: "If God helps and protects me, I will worship God on this very spot; if God does not, I will of course still worship God but not necessarily in this place." (Comment on Genesis 28:16)

Jacob, the deal maker
*Rabbi Reuven Bulka explains that Jacob was not one of these "stock market" people who thank God when things are good and question or reject God when life turns sad and disappointing. Jacob's vow was a way of proving what God had promised. If God would return him to the place where he had experienced his dream of the ladder, then Jacob would know that God had chosen him "for special responsibility." (*Torah Therapy, Ktav, New York, 1983, p. 20*)*

Some would label Rabbi Jacob ben Isaac's explanation a "clever excuse" for Jacob. Others, like the modern Israeli biblical commentator Nehama Leibowitz, would disagree. While she is also troubled by the appearance that Jacob was making a "commercial deal" with God through his vow, she writes that this is not what the Torah intended. Leibowitz explains that ". . . no deal is involved." What Jacob meant was that "if God would not grant him to return to his father's house, how would he be able to erect a temple on the spot? All that Jacob's vow implied was: 'Give me the possibility of serving you.' " (*Studies in Bereshit,* World Zionist Organization, Jerusalem, 1980, p. 307)

It is clear that most commentators were troubled by Jacob's vow. Either they criticize him for trying to "strike a deal" with God, or they try to find an excuse for all the conditions that he attached to his prayer. They consider a person's promises or vows as a sign of his integrity and character.

Perhaps that explains why Jewish teachers paid so much attention to the subject of vows and promises. Prayers that, like Jacob's, were filled with conditions ("God, if you will do this for me, I will take on responsibilities for you") were forbidden. The rabbis taught: "Be not like servants who work for their master only on condition that they receive payment, but be like servants who work for their master without looking for any reward—and be filled with reverence for God." (*Avot* 1:3)

Vows were to be made without any conditions attached. A promise was to stand without any excuses. One's integrity was measured by the fulfillment of one's vows. It was forbidden to mislead others or oneself. The teacher Ben Sirach warned that "before you make a vow or a promise, think well. Do not mislead yourself." (*Tanchuma, Vayishlach* 8)

Jewish tradition counsels us to make our promises and vows with care. Our prayers and actions in the service of God are to be made without conditions attached. God does not want our "deals" but our deeds of kindness, justice, charity, and love. "The joy of the mitzvah, of the good deed, is its own reward."

PEREK GIMEL: *Dealing with Dishonesty*

Twice in our Torah portion, Jacob must deal with the dishonesty of Laban, the father of Leah and Rachel. In the first incident, Laban promises to give Jacob his daughter Rachel as a wife. Instead, he deceives him and sends Leah in Rachel's place. In the second incident, Laban offers to pay Jacob for all his work by giving him his choice of animals from his herd. Then, he deliberately cheats him by sending away with his sons the animals that Jacob has chosen.

These two incidents point up Laban's dishonesty. He was willing to take advantage of Jacob when it came to marrying his daughters and also when it came to paying him fair wages for all his work. Laban did not hesitate to lie when it suited his purpose nor to steal when he believed he could get away with it.

The question many interpreters ask is how Jacob should have dealt with Laban. How should you treat a person who is dishonest and may even be stealing from you? How shall we handle deceit?

Defining deceit

What is deceit? It is creating a false impression. (Hullin *94a*)

A person who practices dishonesty shall not dwell in My house. (Psalms *101:2*)

It is forbidden to deceive anyone, Jew or non-Jew. (Hullin *94a*)

To deceive with words or abuse with the tongue is a greater offense than to cheat in matters of money. (Baba Metzia *58a*)

Jacob's first response to Laban's trickery was to confront him with a series of questions: "What is this that you have done to me? Was it not for Rachel that I have been in your service? Why did you deceive me?"

One impression we get from the questions Jacob asks is that he is conducting an investigation. He is trying to sort out Laban's motives and also seeking to test his own memory of their agreement. While his questions are clear and direct and reveal his disappointment, they are not asked in an angry or even hostile manner.

When Laban explains that "it is not the custom in our place to marry off the younger before the older," Jacob seems to accept the reasoning without protest. Could it be that Jacob, the younger son, felt guilty at that moment for the trick he had played on his own father in stealing the blessing from his older brother, Esau? Some commentators believe that is the reason why Jacob

agreed, without loud complaints, to Laban's explanation. (*Midrash Tanchuma*)

How is it possible that Jacob mistook Leah for Rachel?

A great chasidic rabbi, Levi Isaac of Berdichev (1740–1809), known for his defense of Jews and his forgiving attitude to all human beings, once explained that, when Rachel learned that Laban planned to trick Jacob by giving him Leah as a bride instead of herself, she decided to do all that she could to save her sister from shame. So she taught Leah all of the secret signs of love between herself and Jacob. In this way Rachel was sure that Jacob would take Leah as his wife and not reject her. Rachel was willing to sacrifice her own happiness for the sake of her sister. When Jacob learned of Rachel's sensitivity toward her sister and her concern about her being humiliated, his love for Rachel increased. In this case, deceit committed for a "righteous" not a selfish purpose brought reward.

Is a tzadik, *a "righteous person," allowed to cheat?"*

If the person with whom he is dealing is dishonest, one is permitted to outwit him. (Megillah *13b*)

Others point out that Jacob was naive and believed Laban because Laban was his mother's brother. He trusted him, but, after Laban broke his agreement and removed all the streaked and spotted animals from his flocks, Jacob was enraged. When Jacob finally confronted him, he angrily accused Laban of cheating him out of his wages and flocks. Torah interpreter Nehama Leibowitz writes that "the Torah here teaches us an instructive lesson in human conduct and self-control. Anger . . . should be deferred till the last possible moment, till there is no other alternative—only as a last resort." (*Studies in Bereshit*, p. 341)

Leibowitz also calls attention to the fact that Jacob's response to Laban's dishonesty was "controlled" anger. It was not a wild outburst. It was carefully constructed and thought out.

When Laban pursued Jacob after he had departed with his family and herds, Jacob did not go to war with him. Nor did he become belligerent when they met and Laban confronted him with the questions: "What did you mean by keeping me in the dark and carrying off my daughters like captives of the sword? Why did you flee in secrecy and mislead me and not tell me?" Rather than losing his temper at Laban, Jacob calmly reminded Laban that he had worked faithfully for him for twenty years, often suffering hardships while caring for his property. He pointed out that he had earned everything he had taken.

Leibowitz praises Jacob's cool management of his emotions in what might have been an angry confrontation. He kept his dignity. He neither attacked Laban nor lost control of his anger. Leibowitz claims that Jacob is a model for handling those who cheat us.

Dealing with dishonesty: advice to parents
Our policy toward lying is clear: On the one hand, we should not play District Attorney or ask for confessions or make a federal case out of a tall story. On the other hand, we should not hesitate to call a spade a spade. When we find that the child's library book is overdue, we should not ask, "Have you returned the book to the library? Are you sure? How come it's still on your desk?"

Instead, we state, "I see your library book is overdue. . . ."

In short, we do not provoke the child into defensive lying nor do we intentionally set up opportunities for lying. When a child does lie, our reaction should be not hysterical and moralistic but factual and realistic. We want our child to learn that there is no need to lie to us. (H. G. Ginott, Between Parent and Child, pp. 60–61)

One other way of handling cheaters and liars is to expose them publicly. Confrontation in front of an audience not only brings satisfaction to the party that has been harmed but also warns others about those who practice deceit.

It is clear from the Torah text that Jacob shares Laban's dishonesty with both Leah and Rachel. He tells them: "Your father has cheated me, changing my wages time and again." Yet his complaint is not a public one. It is kept within the family, and, while Leah and Rachel agree that their father has treated Jacob unjustly—and even cheated them—they do not expose him in the marketplace or to his friends.

In discussing what to do about a dishonest person, Rabbi Israel Meir Ha-Cohen, who lived for nearly a century (1838–1933) in Lithuania, and whose book, *Hafetz Chaim,* became one of the most popular treatments of Jewish ethics, suggested a very careful approach. He taught that exposing a cheating or deceitful person was permitted if it would help the injured party and might protect others. But, said the rabbi, seven conditions must be met: (1) You must have hard evidence not rumors. (2) You must be absolutely certain that it was deceit and must think it over before announcing it to others. (3) You must confront dishonest persons privately seeking to change their behavior. If those people will not change, then you can speak publicly. (4) You must not exaggerate the facts. (5) You must examine your motives, making sure that you are not exposing the person for your own selfish reasons. (6) You must try all other ways to solve the situation without using slander. (7) You must not bring more harm to the dishonest person than a court might bring if the person was found guilty.

Confronting the dishonesty of others is very difficult and distasteful. No one wants to be taken advantage of or cheated. Like Jacob, we want to be given honest wages and to enjoy trusting relationships with others. Unfortunately, we do not always have our way. Sometimes we find ourselves selfishly twisting the truth to our advantage; at other times we find ourselves face to face with those who are cheating us.

Our choices are similar to Jacob's with Laban. Shall we react in anger or rush to condemn publicly the person cheating us? Do we say nothing, wait, and give the person a second chance? Shall we see it as our fault or admit, "I once cheated X. Now it's my turn to be taken advantage of"? Do we make excuses for the liar? Do we act with calm and reasonable concern or with hostility?

The choice is ours. Our examination of how Jacob chose to react to Laban reveals the growth and development of his character. He enters Haran as a trickster and cheater, and as he departs he has matured into a man of strength, reason, and integrity.

QUESTIONS FOR STUDY AND DISCUSSION

1. We know from research done by scientists that dreams often reveal our subconscious fears and longings. In that sense, they are "messengers." Do you agree with the interpretations of Jacob's dream in our text? What other interpretations would you give to his dream?

2. According to the Torah and its commentaries, what special function and roles do angels play within Jewish tradition? Why do some modern authors continue to use mystical characters or angels in their fiction?

3. Why do the rabbis consider a vow a "burden around the neck"? Why were conditional vows forbidden in Jewish tradition?

4. Given what the commentators have to say about dealing with dishonesty, would you agree with H. G. Ginott's "policy toward lying"?

PARASHAT VAYISHLACH
Genesis 32:4–36:43

Vayishlach means "and he sent" and refers to Jacob sending messengers to his brother Esau before their meeting after twenty years of separation. We are told of Jacob's fears, of his division of his community into two camps, and of his wrestling with a man-angel who changes Jacob's name to Israel. Following that struggle, Jacob and Esau meet and part peacefully, each going his separate way. After Jacob and his community settle in Shechem, Dinah, the daughter of Leah and Jacob, is raped by Shechem son of Hamor the Hivite. Jacob's sons take revenge by murdering all the males of Shechem and plundering the city. Jacob is critical of his sons for what they have done. Rachel dies giving birth to Benjamin and is buried near Bethlehem. Isaac dies and is buried in Hebron near Abraham and Sarah. The Torah portion concludes with the genealogy of Jacob and Esau.

OUR TARGUM

· 1 ·

Having journeyed from Haran, Jacob now approaches Seir, the country of Edom, located in the green forested area in the mountains east of the Dead Sea. Jacob fears meeting Esau. Though twenty years have passed, he remembers that Esau had sworn to kill him.

So Jacob sends messengers ahead to Esau, hoping they will return with a message of peace from him. When the messengers return, they tell him that Esau is coming to meet Jacob with four hundred men. Jacob is terrified and immediately divides his community into two camps. He reasons that, if Esau attacks one camp, the other will escape.

Jacob spends the night in prayer, and in the morning he selects gifts of goats, rams, camels, cows, and asses for his servants to take to Esau. He hopes that Esau will like the gifts and, therefore, be kind and peaceful in his dealings with him. That night Jacob takes his family to a safe place across the river Jabbok, and then he wanders off alone.

Throughout that night a man-angel wrestles with Jacob. Near dawn, the man-angel says to him, "Let me go!" Jacob tells him that he will not let him go unless he gives him a blessing. The man-angel asks, "What is your name?" Jacob tells him his name, and the man-angel says: "Your name shall no longer be Jacob, but Israel, for you have wrestled with divine and human beings and have triumphed."

Jacob names the place "Peniel," which means "face of God," explaining, "I have seen a divine being face to face, yet my life has been preserved." At dawn, Jacob limps away from the place, injured by the man-angel who had wrenched his hip at the socket.

· 2 ·

That day Jacob sees Esau and his company of four hundred men approaching his camp. He lines up his wives and children and then goes out to greet Esau. Esau embraces and kisses him. "Who are these people?" he asks Jacob, pointing to Leah, Rachel, and the children. Jacob introduces his wives and children to his brother and offers Esau gifts. "To see your face," Jacob tells him, "is like seeing the face of God, and you have received me favorably."

Esau offers to accompany Jacob and his family to Canaan, but Jacob informs him that it is not necessary. Esau then returns to Seir, and Jacob travels to Succoth in the Jordan Valley, where he builds a home for his family. We are also told that he purchases a plot of land outside the city of Shechem, which is near the site of Nablus, thirty-two miles north of Jerusalem.

· 3 ·

While out visiting other young women, Dinah, the daughter of Jacob and Leah, is raped by Shechem, the son of Hamor the Hivite, chief of the country. Shechem declares his love for Dinah and asks his father to arrange their marriage.

Jacob hears that his daughter has been raped, but he takes no immediate action against Shechem because his sons are out in the field tending to the herds. When the brothers hear what has happened, they are enraged and return home.

Meanwhile, Shechem's father, Hamor, approaches Jacob and tells him that his son is in love with Dinah. "Please give her to him in marriage," he says. "Intermarry with us . . . and the land will be open before you." Shechem adds his own words to those of his father. "Ask of me a bride price ever so high, and I will pay what you tell me; only give me the maiden for a wife."

Angry over what has happened to Dinah, Jacob and his sons indicate that they cannot permit their women to marry uncircumcised men. "Circumcise yourselves," they tell them, "and we will give you our daughters, and we will become like one family."

Hamor and Shechem agree, and they go before all the people of their city and announce: "These people are our friends; let them settle in the land and move about in it, for the land is large enough for them; we will take their daughters to ourselves as wives and give our daughters to them. . . . Would not their cattle and substance and all their beasts be ours?" The people agree, and all the males circumcise themselves.

Three days afterwards, while all the males are in pain from their circumcision, two of Jacob's sons, Simeon and Levi, enter the city and murder all the males, including Hamor and Shechem. Their other brothers join them, and they plunder the city, taking flocks and herds as booty and children and wives as captives. When Jacob hears what they have done, he says to them: "You have brought trouble on me. Other peoples will not trust me. We are few in numbers, and we will be destroyed."

Simeon and Levi answered their father with a question: "Are we to allow our sister to be treated as a whore?"

· 4 ·

Afterwards God instructs Jacob to return to Bethel, where he had built an altar at the time he was fleeing from Esau. Jacob tells all in his household to give him their idols and earrings. He buries them near Shechem, and they set out for Bethel.

At Bethel, God says to Jacob: "I am El Shaddai [God Almighty]; be fertile and increase; a nation, many nations will descend from you. . . . The land that I gave to Abraham and Isaac I will give to you; and to your offspring to come will I give the land."

After leaving Bethel, Jacob and the community with him travel toward Ephrath, now called Bethlehem. On the way Rachel, who is pregnant, becomes ill and dies in childbirth. Jacob names his new son Benjamin and buries Rachel near the road. Over her grave he builds a pillar of stones.

Jacob returns to the area of Hebron where Isaac, his father, dwells. At one hundred and eighty years of age, Isaac dies, and Esau and Jacob bury him in the cave of Machpelah with Abraham, Sarah, and Rebekah.

THEMES

Parashat Vayishlach contains three important themes:

1. Dealing with powerful people and nations.
2. Wrestling with angels and ourselves.
3. The appropriate response to the violence of rape.

PEREK ALEF: *Jacob's Reunion with Esau—Dealing with Power*

Rabbi Yochanan, who lived in the second century during the bitter persecutions of Jews by Roman authorities, taught that "whoever wishes to deal with a king or powerful authority . . . should study this Torah portion about the reunion of Jacob and Esau." (*Genesis Rabbah 78:6*) Rabbi Yochanan was famous for his clearheaded thinking and good advice. Why did he believe our Torah portion contained such wisdom about the tactics of dealing with powerful people and governments?

Several details should be noted about the reunion of Jacob and Esau. Jacob sends messengers to his brother. He instructs them to demonstrate his humility by referring to Esau as "my lord Esau" and to himself as "your servant Jacob." Tell him, Jacob says to the messengers, that "I send this message to my lord in hope of gaining your favor."

When the messengers return and announce to Jacob that Esau is on his way to meet him and that he is bringing four hundred men with him, Jacob is frightened. But he does not panic. Instead, he divides his community into two camps, cal-culating that, if Esau destroys one camp, the other will escape. Then he prays, asking God to save him from his brother. Afterwards, he selects choice animals from his herds of goats, rams, camels, cows, bulls, and asses and sends them as gifts to Esau. He reasons to himself, "If I appease his anger with presents in advance, and then face him, perhaps he will show me favor."

Jacob's strategy (sending a delegation to represent him, humility, practicality in dividing his community, prayer, and gifts to reduce the hostility of the enemy) was greatly praised by many biblical interpreters.

Compare the reed to the cedar
The rabbis of the Talmud commented that there is a lesson to be learned by comparing the reed to the cedar. "The reed, which is a humble plant, grows in the water, replenishing its roots which are many. No matter how hard the wind blows, or from which direction, the reed is not blown from its place. It simply bends away from the wind." By comparison, "the cedar, which is a high and prideful tree, stands tall against all

the winds of the world except for the south wind. When that wind blows, it can uproot the cedar and turn it upside down." (Ta'anit 20a)

Zugot

Beware of those in power
Shemayah and Abtalyon, who lived in the Land of Israel during the first-century persecution of Jews by the Romans, taught: "Do not seek to be close with governmental authorities." (Avot 1:10)

Be careful in your relations with those in power, for they draw people near for their own interests. They appear as friends when it is to their advantage and will not defend a person in time of trouble. (Avot 2:3)

Rabbi Bechaye commented that, because Jacob remembered that Esau loved to hunt, he sent him a falcon, which noblemen carry when they go hunting in the woods. He hoped that his gift would make a friend instead of an enemy of Esau. Another interpreter writes that Jacob instructed the messengers to make sure that Esau understood that the animals Jacob was sending to him were a gift meant to ease any angry memories Esau might have of him. (*Tze'enah u-Re'enah, Vayishlach,* p. 165)

Obadiah Sforno, who lived in Italy (1475–1550), pointed out that Jacob's tactic of humility with Esau was successful. Jacob saved his life and possessions because he was ready to appease Esau. Realizing that Esau had the power to destroy him, Jacob humbled himself like a "reed bending against the wind," rather than standing tall like a "cedar" and taking the chance of being overturned and destroyed.

By comparison Sforno recalls the reaction of Jews to Roman persecution during the first cen-

tury. At that time Roman authorities heavily taxed the community, cruelly oppressed men, women, and children, and threatened to destroy places of Jewish learning. Sforno heaps criticism upon those Jews who refused to appease the Roman authorities. He quotes Rabbi Yochanan ben Zakkai, a leader during those troubled times, who argued that, had Jews cooperated and not followed the bad advice of those who organized protests and burned the marketplaces of Jerusalem, "our Temple would not have been destroyed." (*Gittin* 56b) They should have "bent like a reed," Sforno writes, instead of trying "to stand tall like a cedar."

Other interpreters disagree.

Rabbi Judah ben Simon, who lived in the Land of Israel during the fourth century, called the attention of his students to the lesson in the biblical Book of Proverbs that teaches: "A righteous person who humbles himself before a wicked person is like a muddied spring or a ruined fountain." (25:26) A righteous person like Jacob, Rabbi Judah argued, should not have humbled himself before Esau. It was the wrong thing to do.

In another comment, the rabbis point out that Jacob humbled himself eight times by calling himself Esau's "servant" or by referring to Esau as "my lord." God, the rabbis teach, was displeased with Jacob and told him that, because he had disgraced himself, God was appointing eight kings to rule over the Jewish people.

Clearly, the rabbis were critical of Jacob for his display of humility before the power of Esau. They also point out that his tactics were bad. Jacob should never have sent messengers to Esau. He should have moved his family through the land quietly, and Esau might not even have noticed them. It was like waking a robber or a bully who was sleeping, these commentators explain. Had Jacob moved quietly by, he would not have needed to confront Esau.

Rabbi Huna, who headed the great school of Jewish learning in Sura, Babylonia, during the third century, agrees with the criticism of Jacob. He should not have become involved with Esau or paid any attention to him, Huna explains, quoting the teaching from Proverbs 26:17: "A person who passes by and gets involved with other people's disagreements is like one who takes a dog by the ears."

Goats and wolves

The Talmud teaches: "A person who acts like a goat will be eaten up by the wolves."

"I'm just a servant"

Rabbi Judah Ha-Nasi ("the Prince"), who edited the Mishnah and lived during the Roman persecutions, once said to his secretary, Rabbi Aphes: "Write a letter to Emperor Antoninus." So Aphes wrote the letter, addressing it, "From Rabbi Judah Ha-Nasi to His Majesty the Emperor Antoninus." Rabbi Judah took the letter, read it, and tore it up. Afterwards he said to Aphes: "Address it as 'From your servant Judah to His Majesty the Emperor Antoninus." Aphes asked: "Why do you humiliate yourself?" Judah replied: "Am I better than my forefather Jacob? Did he not say to Esau, "Your servant, Jacob"? (Genesis Rabbah, Vayishlach, 78:6)

Peli

"Buttering up"

The rabbis chastise Jacob, not only for "buttering up" Esau by introducing himself as "your servant" and offering him lavish gifts, but also for the very fact of Jacob's seeking Esau's approval for resettling the land that he was forced to flee earlier. . . . (Pinchas Peli, Torah Today, B'nai B'rith Books, Washington, D.C., 1987, p. 34)

Ramban (Nachmanides)

Unlike the commentator Sforno, Nachmanides disapproves of Jacob's "buttering up" of Esau. He should have acted with strength not weakness. He should not have bent in the wind or appeased him. Nachmanides argues that, had the Jews during the Roman persecutions not given in to the Romans and not fooled themselves into believing that they could make allies out of their enemies,

the Temple and Jewish life in the Land of Israel would not have been destroyed.

Nehama Leibowitz agrees. In her commentary, she claims that the reason Jews have been persecuted and battered through the ages is that they acted with humility before power rather than meeting power with power and pride. "With our own hands we sealed our own fate by lowering ourselves, allowing others to lord it over us. As the prophet Jeremiah (13:21) words it: 'You have taught them to be captains and chief over you.'"

At least one interpreter suggests that Jacob did not humiliate himself before Esau but instead met him and said to him: "If you want peace, I am with you. If you want war, then I am ready for you. I have strong men for battle, and God answers my prayers." (*Genesis Rabbah, Vayishlach, 75:11*)

In other words, Jacob retained his pride and dignity. He took matters into his own hands. First he divided his camp so that, if Esau came for battle, half of his community might escape. Then he went out to meet Esau face to face. He did not appear afraid, nor did he seek mercy from him. He refused to bend before Esau. He met power with power. He let Esau know that he was ready to make peace or to engage in battle. From a position of strength he offered to negotiate peace between them.

Rabbi Yochanan once said that, if "one wants to know how to deal with powerful kings or governors, he should study closely the Torah portion about the meeting between Jacob and Esau." (*Genesis Rabbah, Vayishlach, 78:6*) The varieties of opinions about how to treat powerful people, groups, and nations, even their conflicting opinions, are still important considerations for us today.

PEREK BET: *Wrestling with Angels and Ourselves*

After being told that Esau is approaching with four hundred men, Jacob divides his community and his possessions into two camps on either side of the Jabbok stream. By evening they are settled, and he is left alone. That night, the Torah (Genesis 32:25) informs us, "And a man wrestled with him until the break of dawn." The man wrenches his hip and says to Jacob, "Let me go, for dawn is breaking." Jacob refuses, demanding that the man bless him. The man asks his name, and, when Jacob tells him what it is, the man says, "Your name shall no longer be Jacob, but Israel, for you have wrestled with beings divine and human, and have prevailed."

When Jacob, now Israel, asks the man to identify himself, the man answers, "You must not ask my name," and then disappears. Jacob names the place where this strange wrestling match occurred *Peniel,* meaning "face of God." At dawn he limps away, saying, "I have seen a divine being face to face, yet my life has been preserved."

What is this strange "wrestling match" all about? Who is this "man"—or "divine being"—Jacob encounters? What is the meaning of Jacob's change of name to Israel? And why does he walk away from this strange night experience injured, limping?

The first interpreters of this strange story were the ancient rabbis. Some of them believed that the "man" was an angel who appeared in the form of a robber. His intention was to frighten Jacob, but Jacob was strong and unafraid. "You cannot scare me," he told the angel-robber. And, because he was brave and refused to run away from his attacker, Jacob was victorious and blessed with a new name—Israel.

> ### Religious persecution
> *Nachmanides suggests that the "man" Jacob wrestled with was Esau and that their battle "refers to the generation of religious persecution" during the time of Emperor Hadrian (117–138 C.E.) when Rome ruled in the Middle East. "What did the Romans do in that generation?" They would bring iron balls, heat them in fire, and then place them under the arms of Jewish leaders, causing their death. And there have been other generations when they have done such things to us and even worse, but in the end we have survived," just as Jacob prevailed over Esau.*

> ### The hollow of Jacob's thigh
> *We are told that the man wrestling with Jacob injured him by touching the hollow of his thigh. By "hollow of his thigh" is meant the place of his circumcision. Here, too, we have an indication of how the enemies of the Jewish people persecuted them and sought to destroy them. They would forbid Jews from practicing the ritual of circumcision through which a Jewish boy enters the covenant of Abraham.* (Lekach Tov)

As we have already noted in our discussion of this Torah portion, the rabbis often portrayed Jacob and Esau as much more than competing brothers. They also thought of them as two competing national forces—as Israel and other nations, or as Israel and Rome. For some interpreters, the wrestling match between Jacob and the angel was a match between Jacob and Esau. Esau was the angel, and the battle between them symbolized the bitter war for survival between the Jewish people and those nations that sought to destroy them. Jacob's night battle, they taught, was a preview of the future. Jacob-Israel would be attacked by Esau-Rome. They would fight throughout a long night of terror in which Israel would suffer. But, at the end of the night, Israel would emerge secure, strong, and victorious against all its enemies.

Rashi

The commentator Rashi suggests a very different approach. He argues that the "man" with whom Jacob wrestled was "Esau's angel." Rashi points out that Jacob was worried because Esau was coming with four hundred men to kill him and to destroy his community, still bearing a grudge against him for stealing his blessing from their father, Isaac. Rashi explains that, when Jacob discovered that he was wrestling with Esau's angel, he realized that he might be able to force Esau into forgiving him for taking the blessing. If he succeeded, Jacob thought, then his community would be saved. So Jacob fought on, refusing to give up until Esau's angel cried out, "Let me go."

Rabbi Abraham Chill, a modern interpreter, agrees with Rashi that the "man" was "Esau's angel," but his explanation is different. Chill believes that the night battle between Jacob and Esau's angel was between two opposing views of how human beings ought to live. Jacob's view represented compassion, kindness, and mercy; Esau represents self-centeredness, crudeness, and destruction. What we have here, Chill argues, is "a combat of values." Because Jacob remained faithful to his high standards, the only thing Esau's angel could do was to injure him physically. In the end, however, Jacob and his principles prevailed.

Jacob wanted to run away

Actually, Jacob was frightened of meeting his brother. Fearing what Esau might do to him and his community, Jacob was about to flee. God saw this and sent the angel to prevent Jacob from running away. He injured the hollow of his thigh because he wanted Jacob to know that he should have shown greater faith and that no one can flee from God. (Rabbi Samuel ben Meir, Rashbam, 1085–1174)

Jacob's real enemies

". . . the greatest enemy of Jacob is not Esau; the greatest enemy of Jacob resides within himself. It is the enemy that makes him an idol worshiper, a pagan, serving false values and going after false ideas; it is the pride of learning, of knowledge that destroys the capacity of the mind to learn the truth. And, lastly, the enemy is the hostility, the hatred, the resentment that have become deeply embedded either in our conscious or our subconscious." (Rabbi Morris Adler, The Voice Still Speaks, *p. 92)*

Other commentators point out that the battle between Jacob and the angel took place inside Jacob's mind, and it represented a major turning point in his life. He could not meet his brother, Esau, without wrestling with the guilt that he felt about stealing both his birthright and blessing. All his successes were tarnished by his feelings of having taken what did not belong to him. He could not go on. He had to struggle with what he had done, and he had to repent. He needed to admit that Esau had been cheated. He had to become a different person, a person who cared about his brother. The battle was with himself. Jacob struggled to become a better, more honest, fair, and just human being. It was only after Jacob became Israel that he was ready to reconcile with his brother. (W. Gunther Plaut, editor, *The Torah: A Modern Commentary,* UAHC, New York, 1981, Genesis, p. 221)

The modern writer Elie Wiesel enlarges this view. Wiesel writes that "at Peniel . . . two Jacobs came together."

There was the Jacob who had doubts about himself, fears about his future, and regrets about how he had stolen the blessing from his brother. This side of him said: "I deserve nothing, I am less than nothing, I am unworthy of celestial blessing, unworthy of my ancestors as much as of my descendants, unworthy to transmit God's message. . . ."

And there was the other Jacob who was the "heroic dreamer," the brave, experienced, and future-looking Jacob. That voice reminded him of how he had worked to create his family and his fortune and how he had stood up to Laban and his sons when they had plotted against him. That voice reminded him that he was the son of Isaac and that through him the Jewish people was to survive.

That night, the two sides of Jacob fought with each other. He wrestled with the most serious questions of his life. Who was he? What was really important to him? What were his responsibilities to himself and to those he loved? As dawn broke, he knew that he would never be the same. He was a changed person. He would limp away from his night battle with himself, but he would have a new name. He would no longer be *Ya'akov,* "the one who holds on to his brother's heel" or "the one who steals his brother's blessing." Now he would be *Yisrael,* "the one who had wrestled with himself and was now ready to wrestle with the world."

Wiesel writes that "it was a turning point for Jacob. He had a choice: to die before dying or to take hold of himself and fight. And win. And win he did. . . . Such, then, is the prime meaning of this episode: Israel's history teaches us that man's true victory is the one he achieves over himself." (*Messengers of God*, pp. 122–129)

So who was this "man-angel" with whom Jacob wrestled? Perhaps a figment of his imagination. Perhaps it was Esau or Esau's angel in a dream. Perhaps it was meant to represent all the enemies who would arise to destroy the people of Jacob-Israel. Perhaps the man-angel was Jacob, and the battle was between two sides of Jacob's character.

At times the intent of the Torah is unclear. Great literature and art allow for many differing opinions and interpretations. Each person, and often each generation, uncovers new meanings. That, now, is our challenge with Jacob's mysterious night battle.

PEREK GIMEL: *The Rape of Dinah*

Hertz

In his commentary on the Torah, British rabbi and scholar Joseph H. Hertz (1872–1946) called the story of Dinah "a tale of dishonor, wild revenge, and indiscriminate slaughter." It is also a story that raises important ethical questions.

Dinah, who is the daughter of Leah and Jacob, goes out to socialize with other young women and is raped by Shechem, the son of Hamor who is the chief of the country. Afterwards, Shechem tells his father that he is in love with Dinah and wants to marry her. He asks his father to arrange the marriage with Jacob.

Jacob hears that Dinah has been raped, but he remains silent until his sons return home from the fields. When they hear what has happened they are furious.

When Hamor asks that Shechem be allowed to marry Dinah, her brothers refuse. Already plotting their revenge, they tell Shechem that only if all the males of his community are circumcised will they allow such a marriage. They also promise friendship. "We will marry one another," they say. "We will dwell among you and become as one kindred."

Shechem and Hamor convince their townsmen to circumcise themselves. "These people are our friends," they tell them. Pointing out the material gain, they declare, "Will not their cattle and substance and all their beasts be ours?" Convinced, all the males are circumcised.

Three days later, Dinah's brothers, Simeon and Levi, enter the town and murder all the males, including Hamor and Shechem. The other brothers follow and plunder the town. They seize all the wealth and take the women and children as captives.

When Jacob hears what they have done, he says to Simeon and Levi: "You have made trouble for me by giving me a bad reputation among the people of the land. I am few in number, and if attacked my house will be destroyed." The brothers respond: "Should our sister be treated like a whore?"

The question posed by Simeon and Levi takes us to the heart of the matter. What should they have done? Should they have allowed Shechem to rape Dinah, their sister, without taking some revenge? Given the fact that they were fewer and weaker than Hamor's powerful fighting men, were Simeon and Levi justified in tricking them into circumcising themselves so that Dinah's brothers could take advantage of their weakness, easily killing them and plundering their town? Finally, who was really responsible for this incident—Dinah, who went out socializing without a chaperon, or Shechem, who forced himself upon her?

Defining "rape"
Laws defining rape usually indicate that the crime must involve sexual intercourse by force and against the will of the woman.

The penalty for rape
Within the Torah the penalty for rape is compensation to the family for the disgrace and mar-

> *riage to the victim without the opportunity for divorce.* (Deuteronomy 22:29) *Later, the rabbis added the payment of compensation for "pain inflicted on the woman" during the rape.*
>
> ### Who was to blame?
> *A woman should not show herself in the street wearing conspicuous jewelry. Jewelry was given to the woman for the purpose of adorning herself in her own house for her husband. It would be wrong to set a stumbling block even before a righteous man and certainly before people who are on the lookout for an opportunity to sin.* (Tanchuma, Vayishlach 5)

Rape is an act of violence whose cause has been debated over the centuries. Some interpreters of our Torah portion blame Dinah, not Shechem, for what happened to her. They point out that, had she stayed at home rather than putting on fancy jewelry, dressing in clothing that attracted attention, and running about to parties, she would not have fallen into trouble. Other commentators blame her mother, Leah. It was Leah's fault, they say, because she was constantly "running about and socializing." She set a bad example for her daughter, and that's why Dinah got into trouble. (*Genesis Rabbah, Vayishlach,* 80:1–5 and *Tze'enah u-Re'enah, Vayishlach,* 34:1)

Blaming the victim of rape, or her family, for the violence she has suffered happens frequently. "She must have done something to deserve such treatment," is a common statement. Yet, it is as logical and misleading a judgment as blaming the victims of Nazi brutality for the agony and death they suffered. In our Torah portion, Dinah was not at fault; she was the victim of Shechem's violent passions.

The question faced by Jacob and his sons was how to deal with such violence? Were they to sit by idly and do nothing? Were they to take revenge, answer the violence of Shechem's act with a massacre of his community?

Some interpreters argue that Simeon and Levi were justified in their revenge. Their sister had been treated "as public property." Shechem used her with no regard for her feelings, her rights, or her dignity. He forced himself upon her, and she would live with the terrible memories throughout her life. (*Genesis Rabbah* 80:2)

Rabbi Bechaye comments that the people of Shechem were among the world's greatest thieves and liars. No one could trust them. Although they promised to live at peace with Jacob and his sons, actually, as soon as they healed from their circumcisions, they planned to kill all of them. What Simeon and Levi did, Rabbi Bechaye says, was an act of self-defense, not of revenge. (*Tze'enah u-Re'enah, Vayishlach,* p. 171)

Rabbi Moshe Weissman, in his commentary *The Midrash Says,* writes that "Simeon and Levi acted in accordance with *halachah* (Jewish law) when they planned to kill the inhabitants of Shechem because the people of Shechem were all deserving of capital punishment according to the Seven Laws of Noah. Shechem himself was liable to capital punishment for having kidnapped Dinah (the transgression of robbery). His fellow townspeople were also guilty since they knew of his deed but did not bring him to justice. According to the Seven Laws of Noah, they were obligated to administer justice. Since they refused to do so, Weissman argues, they deserved death.

> ### The Seven Laws of Noah
> *The Seven Laws of Noah were considered by rabbinic tradition as the essential "moral laws" for all human beings. The rabbis believed that anyone who practiced them was "a righteous person." The laws prohibited idolatry, blasphemy, bloodshed, sexual sins, theft, and eating from a live animal; and they called for the setting up of a legal system of justice.* (Sanhedrin 56–60)

Rambam (Maimonides)

Weissman's opinion is close to the views of both Moses Maimonides and Joseph ben Abba Mari Caspi. They also call attention to the failure of the inhabitants of the city of Shechem who knew that Shechem raped Dinah but refused to arrest and convict him for his evil deed. They believe that it was right for Simeon and Levi to take revenge since no one in Shechem had raised a protest on Dinah's behalf. Caspi writes, "They saw and knew and did not punish him." In other words, the people of Shechem were as guilty as Shechem because they stood by and did nothing to arrest and prosecute him. Consequently, they deserved the massacre inflicted by Simeon and Levi.

> **Like a troop of murdering bandits**
> *The rabbis of the Midrash taught: "As bandits sit in the road, murder people, and seize their wealth, so did Simeon and Levi act in Shechem."* (Genesis Rabbah *80:2*)

Hirsch

Samson Raphael Hirsch offers another point of view in support of Simeon and Levi. He points out that Jacob and his sons realized that they were a small, weak group by comparison with the strength of the people of Shechem. Any protest was futile. Any appeal to "human rights" or "justice" would not be heard. Shechem attacked an innocent, weak "Jewish woman" whose people were also weak. Now he was holding her captive in his city. It was an act of brute force, and the only response was brute force. Simeon and Levi are to be praised for seeking to rescue her and for seeking revenge against Shechem and Hamor.

Rabbi Hirsch, however, adds the following: "Had (Simeon and Levi) killed Shechem and Hamor there would be scarcely anything to say against it. But they did not spare the unarmed men who were at their mercy . . . and went further and looted (and) made the inhabitants pay for the crime of the landowner. For that there was no justification." Simeon and Levi, Hirsch explains, may have thought that they would teach all their enemies a lesson. They would show that, if others used force against their women, they would have to pay with their lives. "But they went too far," Hirsch concludes. "They took revenge on innocent people for the wrongs that their powerful leaders (Shechem and Hamor) had done." (*The Pentateuch,* Vol. I, L. Honig and Sons Ltd., London, England, 1959, pp. 517–524)

In his commentary, Nachmanides also condemns Simeon and Levi for their massacre of the people of Shechem. He disagrees with Maimonides. He argues that the failure of the people of Shechem to prosecute Shechem for raping Dinah is no justification for the brutality of Simeon and Levi. Nachmanides declares: "It was not the responsibility of Jacob and his sons to bring them to justice."

Furthermore, Nachmanides speculates that, had Simeon and Levi not taken the law into their own hands, the people of Shechem, including Hamor and Shechem, might have lived alongside them as friends and as devoted followers of the one God. After all, they had willingly circumcised themselves. "They would have chosen to believe in God . . . thus Simeon and Levi killed them without cause for the people had done them no evil at all." (*Commentary to Genesis,* pp. 419–421)

Rabbi Joseph H. Hertz agrees. He comments that "the sons of Jacob certainly acted in a treacherous and godless manner, and Jacob "did not forgive [them] to his dying day." Hertz reminds us that, in the blessing that Jacob gave on his deathbed to Simeon and Levi, he said: "Simeon and Levi are a pair;/ Their weapons are tools of lawlessness./ Let not my person be included in their council,/ Let not my being be counted in their assembly./ For when angry they slay men,/ And when pleased they maim oxen./ Cursed be their anger so fierce,/ And their wrath so relentless." (Genesis 49:5–7)

Jacob's condemnation of Simeon and Levi for taking the law into their own hands, even to revenge the rape of their sister, seems clear enough. The answer to brute force, to violence, is not more violence, not the massacre of innocents. It is the pursuit of justice within the courts of society.

QUESTIONS FOR STUDY AND DISCUSSION

1. Apply the talmudic statement, "A person who acts like a goat will be eaten up by wolves," to Jacob and to Jewish history. Is that a fair assessment of what happened to Jews in Europe during Hitler's rise to power?

2. Does each individual need to "wrestle" with the meaning of life? What are the benefits of such a struggle?

3. Why was Jacob so upset with his sons when they took revenge against the people of Shechem for the rape of Dinah? Was it a matter, once again, of being a reed rather than a cedar or were there more significant issues involved in his decision?

PARASHAT VAYESHEV
Genesis 37:1–40:23

Vayeshev, which means "and he settled," contains the story of Jacob and his sons, who have settled in the land of Canaan. There is jealousy between the other brothers and Joseph, who dreams of ruling them. They plot Joseph's death, but Judah persuades them to sell him to a caravan of Ishmaelites heading for Egypt. Afterwards, they report to Jacob that Joseph was killed by a wild animal. Later, Judah's son Er dies, leaving his wife, Tamar, as a widow. Judah promises that his young son Shelah will marry Tamar, but Judah fails to keep his word. Therefore, Tamar disguises herself and tricks Judah into sleeping with her. When Judah is told that Tamar has "played the harlot" and is pregnant, he orders that she be put to death. Defending herself, Tamar reveals to Judah that he is the father of the child she is carrying. Realizing that he has not treated Tamar fairly, Judah declares: "She is more in the right than I, since I did not give her to my son Shelah." The Torah portion continues with the adventures of Joseph in Egypt, where he is sold to Pharaoh's chief steward, Potiphar, and quickly rises from being a slave to becoming manager of his master's house. Potiphar's wife is attracted to Joseph and tries to seduce him. Angry because Joseph refuses her advances, she reports to Potiphar that Joseph tried to force himself upon her. Potiphar has Joseph thrown into prison. There he meets Pharaoh's chief cupbearer and chief baker. They tell him of their dreams, and Joseph interprets them. (Later, as Joseph has predicted, the cupbearer is returned to Pharaoh's service, but the chief baker is put to death.)

OUR TARGUM

· 1 ·

Joseph, who is seventeen years old, helps his older brothers take care of their father's herds. Seeing that sometimes they are careless about their responsibilities, Joseph criticizes them to Jacob. Jacob favors Joseph and gives him a gift of an ornamented coat of many colors. Seeing that their father loves Joseph more than he loves them, the brothers resent Joseph.

One night, Joseph dreams that he and his brothers are binding sheaves in a field. His sheaf stands up and their sheaves all bow down to his. The next day he tells his brothers about the dream. "Do you mean to rule over us?" they ask him, hating him more because of his dreams.

Another night, Joseph dreams that the sun, the moon, and eleven stars are all bowing to him. He tells Jacob and his brothers about the dream. His father scolds him, "What do you mean by such a dream? Are we all to bow down to you?"

Later, Jacob sends Joseph out to bring him a report on how his brothers are caring for the herds. When his brothers see him coming, they plot to kill him. Reuben suggests that they throw Joseph into a pit rather than kill him, hoping that afterwards he might rescue Joseph.

The brothers strip Joseph of his colorful coat and throw him into a pit. As they sit down to eat, they see a caravan of Ishmaelites heading toward Egypt. Judah suggests that they sell Joseph. "What do we gain by killing him?" he asks his brothers. They agree and sell Joseph into slavery.

Reuben returns to find Joseph gone. He tears his clothes as a sign of mourning and says to his brothers, "The boy is gone! Now, what am I to do?" The brothers tear Joseph's coat, dip it in goat's blood, and take it to their father. They tell Jacob that Joseph has been killed by a wild beast. He weeps and tears his garments in mourning. Though his children try to comfort him, Jacob continues to cry over the loss of Joseph.

·2·

Soon afterwards, Judah marries Shua, a Canaanite woman. They have three sons, Er, Onan, and Shelah. Er marries Tamar but dies leaving no son. According to the tradition of the time, Judah asks Onan to marry Tamar and to continue his brother's line by having children with her. Although Onan marries Tamar, he refuses to father children. God punishes Onan for this by taking his life. So Judah now promises Tamar that, when Shelah matures, he will make sure that Shelah marries her and continues Er's line.

As the years pass, however, Judah does not keep his word. Since she is growing older and is still without children, Tamar decides to trick Judah. She dresses as a prostitute and sits by a road where she knows Judah will pass. When he sees her, Judah promises her a goat if she will sleep with him. When Tamar demands a guarantee until the goat is delivered, Judah gives her his seal, cord, and staff. Not knowing she is Tamar, Judah sleeps with her, and she becomes pregnant.

Three months later, Judah is informed that Tamar pretended to be a prostitute and is pregnant. He orders that she be put to death. Hearing this, Tamar sends Judah his seal, cord, and staff, telling him: "I am pregnant by the man to whom these belong."

Judah is shocked and realizes that he has wronged her. He declares: "She is more in the right than I, since I did not give her to my son Shelah."

·3·

Meanwhile, Joseph has been taken to Egypt where Potiphar, Pharaoh's chief steward, purchases him from the Ishmaelites. Seeing that Joseph is a talented manager, Potiphar appoints him to run his entire household. As a result, Potiphar's riches increase.

Potiphar's wife is attracted to Joseph and says to him: "Lie with me." When he refuses, she spitefully tells Potiphar that Joseph has tried to take sexual advantage of her. Furious, Potiphar has Joseph thrown into prison.

While in prison, Joseph impresses the warden with his abilities and is put in charge of all the prisoners. He meets Pharaoh's cupbearer and baker who are in prison for angering the king. Both of them have dreams and tell them to Joseph. He interprets them, predicting death for the baker and a second chance at court for the cupbearer. "Don't forget me," Joseph tells the cupbearer, hoping that he will one day be free.

The Torah portion ends with Pharaoh's cupbearer restored to his position at court, but forgetting all about Joseph.

THEMES

Parashat Vayeshev contains three important themes:

1. Suspicion and hostility among children.
2. Assuming responsibility for what we promise; refusing to demean or embarrass others.
3. Measuring loyalty and success.

PEREK ALEF: *What Went Wrong between Joseph and His Brothers?*

We have already seen the results of jealousy and hatred between Cain and Abel, and Jacob and Esau. Now, once again, the Torah returns to the theme of hostility between brothers. Clearly, problems of parental favoritism and sibling rivalry occur in every family and in each generation. By returning to these themes, the Torah emphasizes the need to deal directly and honestly with all their troubling aspects. We see something of ourselves and our own families in the story of Joseph and his brothers. Many questions emerge: What went wrong between Joseph and his brothers? Why did they feel such anger toward him? What did he do to make them want to kill him or sell him into slavery? What role did Jacob play in this grim drama?

Joseph's character
Elie Wiesel comments on Joseph's character: "Jacob refused him nothing. He owned the most beautiful clothes, for he liked to be regarded as graceful and elegant. He craved attention. He knew he was the favorite and often boasted of it. Moreover, he was given to whims and frequently was impertinent. Arrogant, vain, insensitive to other people's feelings, he said freely whatever was on his mind. We know the consequences: he was hated, mistreated, and finally sold by his brothers, who in truth were ready to kill him." (Messengers of God, *pp. 145–146*)

Joseph loved himself
Maurice Samuel in conversation with Mark Van Doren:

Samuel: *Do you ever think of Joseph as a loving person?*

Van Doren: *No, he's a person who loved to be loved. He assumed that people loved him.* (In the Beginning . . . . Love, *John Day Co., New York, 1973, p. 104*)

Some biblical interpreters claim that Joseph was "spoiled" by Jacob. He was given whatever he wanted, including a beautiful coat of many colors. Because his father favored him, Joseph believed that he was superior to his brothers and, eventually, that he was even more important than his father.

Other commentators emphasize Joseph's immaturity. He was just seventeen, still a very self-centered young boy. He was concerned with how he looked to others. He used special brushes and pencils to color around his eyes. He curled his hair. He put high heels on his shoes so that he would appear taller and, perhaps, older than his age. (*Genesis Rabbah,* 84:7)

Furthermore, according to the rabbis, Joseph made up stories about his brothers and then told them to his father. He lied about his brothers in order to make himself look good. For example, he told his father that his brothers were eating meat that was not kosher and that they were insulting to one another. (*Genesis Rabbah* 84:7)

Rashi

Rashi claims that Joseph took advantage of every opportunity to gossip about his brothers to his father. Though he knew the truth about what they were doing, he deliberately misinterpreted whatever they said or did to his own selfish advantage. He slandered their intentions as well as their accomplishments. For these reasons, Rashi concludes, they mistrusted and hated him.

It is clear that most Jewish interpreters evaluate Joseph as an immature, self-centered gossip. Some even blame Jacob for spoiling him. Why, they ask, did Jacob single out Joseph for such special treatment and affection?

Rabbi Judah believed that Jacob favored Joseph because they looked alike. Rabbi Nehemiah thought that Jacob loved Joseph because Jacob spent more time teaching Joseph the fundamentals of his tradition than any of his other sons. Could that explain Jacob's preference for Joseph? Might this also explain why the brothers were jealous of him? (*Genesis Rabbah* 84:8)

Do not favor one child over another
Resh Lakish, quoting Rabbi Eleazar ben Azariah, said: "A person should not favor one child over another, for Joseph's brothers hated him because their father made him a coat of many colors." (Genesis Rabbah *84:8*)

Morgenstern

Partiality is injustice
Jacob was at fault for manifesting greater love for Joseph than for his other sons and for spoiling him as he did. Partiality is always a form of injustice, and injustice is always wrong and

causes evil. We have seen this already in Isaac's greater love for Esau and in Rebekah's greater love for Jacob. (Julian Morgenstern, The Book of Genesis, *Schocken Books, New York, 1965, pp. 264–265)*

one who spreads lies or evil gossip is like one who shoots arrows."

Another brother said: "His tongue is like a poisonous snake. Let's throw him into a pit filled with snakes." (Genesis Rabbah *84:13*)

Other interpreters express sympathy for Joseph, blaming his brothers for the hostility between them. Writer Elie Wiesel comments: "They should have felt sorry for their small orphaned brother, whose mother had died tragically; instead they pounded on him, harassed him. They should have tried to console him; instead they made him feel unwanted, an outsider. Their father favored him above all others, and why not? Jacob loved him best because he was unhappy. But they refused to understand and treated him as an intruder. He spoke to them, but they did not answer, says the Midrash. They turned their backs on him. They ignored him; they denied him. To them he was a stranger to be driven away." (*Messengers of God,* p. 153)

Wiesel's interpretation does not excuse Joseph's bad behavior, but it does explain Joseph's feelings. He lied to his father about his brothers because he felt rejected by them. By putting them down, he hoped that his father would love him more. Perhaps, had his brothers been concerned about him, Joseph would have been loyal to them.

Instead, he spied on them and spread evil reports about what they were doing. Joseph's brothers hated him for criticizing and ridiculing them. After he told them his dreams of how they would bow down to and be ruled by him, their hostility hardened into cruelty. They decided to kill him.

So what went wrong between Joseph and his brothers? Our interpreters offer several considerations: (1) Joseph's arrogance, his vanity, his self-centeredness, his lies about his brothers, his foolish declarations of superiority over his family; (2) Jacob's favoritism of one son over another; and (3) the brothers' isolation of Joseph, their insensitive treatment of a fearful and lonely young boy. Could it be that all these factors combined to spell tragedy for Jacob and his sons?

PEREK BET: *Judah and Tamar— Models of Moral Action*

Speiser

E. A. Speiser, the modern biblical scholar, calls the story of Judah and Tamar "a completely independent unit." It does not seem connected in any way to the story of Joseph and his brothers. In fact, it seems to interrupt the story. Once Joseph is sold as a slave, we are anxious to know what happens to him. Instead, we are given a story about Judah and his daughter-in-law, Tamar. Why? What is its message?

The Torah tells us that Judah and his wife, Shua, had three sons: Er, Onan, and Shelah. Er married Tamar but died before they had a son. According to Deuteronomy 25:5–10, if a man died leaving no male heirs, his brother was obligated to marry his widow and continue his line. The marriage was called a "levirate" marriage. In Latin, *levir* means "husband's brother."

Ancient peoples were concerned about producing children and assuring the future of their families and tribes. We see emphasis upon each marriage being "fruitful" in the first chapters of Genesis when God commands Adam and Eve:

His dreams fanned their hatred
When he related his dreams, their hatred for him was fanned even more. This is the nature of hatred. Once a new motive for it is found, additional hostility is felt. (Gur Aryeh)

They decided to kill him
They saw Joseph coming, and one brother said to the other: "Let's shoot him with arrows, for

"Be fertile and increase, fill the earth and master it. . . ." (Genesis 1:28) The rule of the "levirate marriage" was of great importance. To ignore it was to *deny* a future for your brother's name and line.

In this story about Tamar and Judah, God brings death to Onan because he refuses to impregnate Tamar, his dead brother's childless wife. Furthermore, when Judah does not give his surviving son, Shelah, to Tamar in marriage, he is not carrying out the responsibility he owes to his dead son Er and to the widow, Tamar.

Does that, however, justify the trick Tamar plays on Judah? Was Tamar "right" in disguising herself as a prostitute and allowing Judah to impregnate her? Do the ends justify the means here?

According to Rashi, "Tamar acted out of pure motives." She wanted to fulfill the commandment to have children for the sake of her first husband. Rashi also points out that she acted in a way that protected Judah from public shame. Instead of publicly revealing that he had fathered the child she was carrying, Tamar sent him a private message. Rather than declaring what Judah had done, she hired a messenger to deliver his seal, cord, and staff and to inform him that she was pregnant by the person who owned them. Although Judah declared publicly that Tamar should be put to death for prostitution, she chose not to embarrass him. Instead, she revealed the truth quietly and discreetly.

Rashi concludes that we learn an important lesson from Tamar's behavior. It is "far better for a person to risk death—as Tamar did—than to shame another person publicly." (*Sotah* 10b) Tamar's reward, Rashi suggests, was that future kings of Israel, among them King David, would be born from her line.

Ramban (*Nachmanides*)

Nachmanides agrees with Rashi's interpretation. He explains that, in her case, the ends justified the means. She was desperate. Judah was not fulfilling his responsibility and promise to her. Even he realized how wrong he had been when he admitted publicly: "She is more in the right than I. . . ." By that statement, Nachmanides explains

that Judah meant to say: "She acted righteously, and I am the one who sinned against her by not giving her my son Shelah."

Judah's use of power

Tamar, in her righteousness, does not accuse Judah of being the father but sends him a quiet, dignified message saying that the father is the one who is also the owner of the seal, cord, and staff. When Judah sees this, he has the option of carrying through with the cover-up by throwing away the symbols and letting Tamar be burned. Instead, however, he publicly acknowledges his mistake. . . . Judah shows that the proper exercise of power involves the capacity to admit when one is wrong and to act accordingly. (Reuven P. Bulka, Torah Therapy, *pp. 24–25)*

Commenting on the dramatic events surrounding Judah's admission that Tamar was justified—and that he had wronged her—the fourteenth-century Aramaic translation of the Torah, called *Targum Yerushalmi*, claims that Judah was one of the judges before whom Tamar appeared when she was accused of being a prostitute. The *targum* imagines Judah, rather than remaining silent or condemning Tamar, rising to his feet and declaring:

> With your permission, my brothers, I proclaim here and now that each human being is treated measure for measure, be it for good or for bad, and happy is the person who recognizes his sin. It is because I dipped Joseph's coat in the blood of a goat and brought it to my father, saying: "Please identify it. Is it your son's shirt or not?" that I must now identify before this tribunal to whom the seal, cord, and staff belong. . . . So, I acknowledge that Tamar is innocent. She is pregnant from me not because she yielded to any illicit passion but because I did not give her to my son Shelah."

This passage from the *Targum Yerushalmi* not only portrays Tamar as justified in what she did, but it also depicts Judah as courageously admitting that he has wronged Tamar and denied his son's rights.

Yet, as the *targum* claims, Judah also admits that he is guilty for having wronged his father, Jacob. In telling his father about Joseph, he misrepresented the facts. By lying, he abused his trust and power as a son. Now, in the case of Tamar, Judah uses his power and position as a judge to condemn his behavior with Tamar by attesting to her innocence.

This explanation of *Targum Yerushalmi* may help solve the question of why this story of Judah and Tamar is placed in the midst of the tale about Joseph.

Judah lied to his father. He told him that Joseph had been killed, not sold into slavery. As a result, he brought great sorrow upon Jacob. Now, in the case of Tamar, he was again deceptive. He lied to her, promising her a marriage to Shelah, which he failed to arrange. This time, however, when Judah is confronted with the truth about what he did to Tamar, he refuses to lie. Instead, he bravely takes the blame and saves Tamar from death.

This story of Judah and Tamar, coming as it does in the midst of the tale of Joseph, contains a significant lesson about how human beings can change and grow toward honesty. Judah is portrayed as a liar who fails to make good on his promises. But he is also a person who matures. He learns from his mistakes. When Tamar confronts him with the truth, he neither makes excuses for his behavior nor continues to call for her death. Instead, he courageously admits before all his townspeople that he is wrong. And Tamar, who has been treated unjustly, forgives him rather than publicly denouncing and demeaning him.

Both Judah and Tamar emerge as models of moral integrity and behavior.

PEREK GIMEL: *How Do You Measure Loyalty and Success?*

In the story of Tamar and Judah, Tamar acts like a prostitute and easily seduces Judah. By contrast, Potiphar's wife seeks to seduce Joseph but fails. In her disappointment and anger, she accuses Joseph of raping her, and Potiphar throws Joseph into jail.

Why did Joseph resist the flirtations of Potiphar's wife? No one was at home. Potiphar's wife is reported to have been beautiful and very much attracted to Joseph. So why did he turn her down? Why did he risk making her hostile and losing all that he had achieved?

According to an explanation in the *Sifre*, a commentary on Numbers and Deuteronomy, edited in the fourth century C.E., Joseph would not let his strong sexual desires get the best of him. He remained in control of himself. "As a righteous person, he told himself not to give in to the temptations Potiphar's wife was putting before him." (Deuteronomy 3:33)

In another interpretation, the *Tanchuma* explains that Joseph resisted her because he took an oath never to approach his master's wife. Putting words in Joseph's mouth, the author of the *Tanchuma* writes that Joseph said to himself: "How can I do such an evil thing as to sin against God by breaking my oath?"

A great hero
Is there among the virtuous a greater hero than a young seventeen year old surrounded by loose women who manages to keep himself from them? Because he did so, Joseph was rewarded when, much later, his children were blessed with the words of his father, Jacob. (Zohar, *Genesis 48:19;* also Pesachim *113a–b*)

Steinsaltz

Joseph was a tzadik—a righteous man
The chief argument in favor of his being called a tzadik *is drawn from the climax of the story of the wife of Potiphar, whose temptations he firmly resisted.* (Adin Steinsaltz, Biblical Images, *p. 63*)

Other interpreters, however, do not view Joseph in such a positive way. They raise serious questions about his behavior. Rashi says that, as soon as Joseph was appointed by Potiphar to a position of importance, he began to eat and drink excessively like all the rest of the Egyptian ruling class. He curled his hair and lived lavishly. He forgot all about being a slave and assimilated into idolatry and the loose sexual practices of Egyptian society.

Modern writer Elie Wiesel raises a serious question about Joseph's character when he comments: "One does not provoke a woman unless one wants to. One does not love a woman—or a man—against one's will. Every relationship is a two-way affair." (*Messengers of God*, p. 148)

Adding to the suspicions about Joseph's behavior with Potiphar's wife, Rav Samuel says that Joseph "deliberately entered the house in order to be seduced by her." And Rabbi Abin says that "she chased him from room to room and from chamber to chamber until she brought him to her bed." It was only when they reached her bed, according to several interpreters, that Joseph began to question the morality of what he was about to do.

According to one version taught by the rabbis, Joseph is portrayed as saying to Potiphar's wife, "I am afraid that your husband will discover our affair." She answered him, "Then I will murder him." Joseph was shocked and answered, "Then I will not only be an adulterer but also the accomplice to a murder." (*Sotah* 36b and *Genesis Rabbah* 87:5)

Elsewhere, the rabbis say that Joseph looked up from the bed where he and Potiphar's wife were embracing and saw that she had placed a sheet over the head of an idol hanging on the wall. Suddenly he realized what a mistake he was making. "You have placed a sheet over the idol because you are ashamed of what we are about to do," he said to her. "How much more should I be ashamed before God, whose eyes are everywhere in the world?" To this version, Rabbi Huna commented that Joseph also declared: "By God, I will not do this wicked thing." (*Genesis Rabbah* 87:5)

Rabbi Huna taught that it was not an idol that Joseph had seen but rather the face of his father, Jacob. In that moment of temptation, just before he was about to sin and commit adultery, "Jacob appeared to him, and Joseph's passion immediately cooled." (*Genesis Rabbah* 87:7) Some interpreters speculate that Jacob said to him: "Do you want to be called an associate of prostitutes?" (*Tosafot* to *Sotah* 36b)

Joseph's moral victory

The vision of Joseph's venerable father appeared to him just as the will of the young man weakened, just as he was about to sin. Potiphar's wife believed she had at last charmed and seduced him. It was then that the sudden vision gave him the strength to control himself, to triumph over his moment of weakness, and to conquer his nature. . . . When a child's training and upbringing are such that even if he has long been separated from the family home and even if he is lost in the midst of licentious surroundings in a faraway country, his father's influence still guides him toward moral victory; then this training is the ideal Jewish upbringing." (Sefat Emet, *based on* Sotah 36a)

Do as Joseph did

When someone tries to talk you into sinning, the first thing you must do is refuse without going into details or engaging in debate on the reasons for your refusal. Only after having made it clear that you refuse to sin may you recite reasons for refusing. Do as Joseph did. He told her no, then he gave her the reasons: "Look, with me here, my master gives no thought to anything in this house, and all that he owns he has placed in my hands. He wields no more authority in this house than I, and he has withheld nothing from me except yourself since you are his wife. How then could I do this most wicked thing and sin before God?" (Sefat Emet)

Most of our commentators, it seems, conclude that Joseph came to his "moral senses" at the very last moment. Potiphar's wife offered powerful temptations. She was beautiful, alone, and anxious to make love to him. He was flattered, perhaps infatuated, by her. He nearly gave in to her flirtations and propositions. Yet, just as he was about to sleep with her, his *loyalty* to Potiphar, to the moral traditions that his father, Jacob, had taught him, and to God—all convinced Joseph to tell her: "How could I do this most wicked thing and sin before God?"

Like Judah his brother, Joseph grows and matures in his ethical sensitivity and ability to act justly. From the spoiled youngest son who lies about his brothers to win the attentions and affections of his father, Joseph becomes a person of loyalty and praiseworthy, ethical behavior.

For his decision, Joseph is called a *tzadik*—a "righteous person." It is a title he earns. He is not born to it. He becomes a "righteous person" through his struggle with temptations, with greed, and with selfishness. His achievement marks a turning point in his life.

Although Potiphar throws him into jail, Joseph's loyalty and morality are ultimately rewarded. First, he is given special privileges by the warden. Later, Pharaoh appoints him as the most powerful prince in Egypt.

QUESTIONS FOR STUDY AND DISCUSSION

1. Can parents be expected to treat their children equally? How can parents treat each child as an individual without showing favoritism?

2. What are some of the problems caused by teachers, counselors, judges, and bosses who show favoritism?

3. Levirate marriage seems to imply that the purpose of marriage is having children. Should marriage be more than that? What? How?

4. Do you agree with Elie Wiesel that "every relationship is a two-way affair"?

5. Some commentators argue that Joseph was weak and nearly seduced by Potiphar's wife. Others say that he was perfectly righteous in his responses to her. Which commentators have the most convincing case?

6. What role does guilt play in the transformation of both Judah's and Joseph's character? Is feeling guilty ever a good thing?

PARASHAT MIKETZ
Genesis 41:1–44:17

Miketz, which means "at the end of . . ." continues Joseph's adventure in Egypt. Pharaoh has two dreams that none of his advisors can interpret. The cupbearer remembers Joseph and tells Pharaoh about him. Joseph is brought from jail and interprets Pharaoh's dreams to mean that Egypt will have seven years of plenty and seven years of famine. Pharaoh puts Joseph in charge of his land. When the famine strikes, Jacob sends his sons, except for Benjamin, to Egypt. When they arrive, Joseph recognizes his brothers and accuses them of coming to spy in his land. They tell him that they have come for food and that they have an elderly father and one younger brother. Joseph seizes Simeon and tells the brothers that he will not go free until they return with their youngest brother. He takes their money and sends them off with sacks of food. Later, they discover that each of their sacks contains the money they had previously given to Joseph. As the famine worsens, Jacob tells his sons to return to Egypt. They remind Jacob that they cannot return without Benjamin. Judah pledges that Benjamin will be safe. When his brothers return to Egypt, Joseph frees Simeon and invites the brothers to his house for a banquet. He has yet to reveal his identity. When the banquet concludes, he orders that the brothers' bags be filled with food and that his wine cup be secretly placed in Benjamin's bag. After the brothers depart, Joseph sends his steward to pursue and arrest them for stealing his wine cup. They reply that they have taken nothing. When the wine cup is found in Benjamin's bag, the brothers are brought back to Joseph's house. He informs them that he will keep Benjamin as a slave but release the rest of them.

OUR TARGUM

· 1 ·

Two years after Joseph interprets the cupbearer's dream and is restored to Pharaoh's service, Pharaoh has a dream. He is standing by the Nile River when out come seven large cows. They are followed by seven thin cows that eat up the seven fat ones. Then he dreams of seven ears of solid grain growing on one sturdy stalk and of seven scorched ears that swallow the sturdy ones.

When Pharaoh's magicians and advisors cannot interpret his dreams, the cupbearer tells him about Joseph.

Pharaoh sends for Joseph and tells him about his dreams. After listening, Joseph explains that both dreams carry the same message. They forecast seven years of plenty to be followed by seven years of famine. Joseph counsels the Egyptian ruler to appoint "a man of discernment and wisdom" who can manage Egypt's resources wisely.

Pharaoh asks Joseph to assume the responsibilities and presents him with his signet ring of authority, a house, a gold chain, a chariot, and a wife. Joseph organizes storage cities for Egypt's grain and carefully plans for the future. He fathers two sons. The first he calls *Manasseh,* meaning "God has made me forget completely my hardship and my parental home," and the second is named *Ephraim,* meaning "God has made me fertile in the land of my affliction."

· 2 ·

When famine sets in, Jacob instructs his sons to go down to Egypt to purchase food. When they arrive, Joseph recognizes them but acts like a stranger. They bow before him, and he recalls his dreams.

He speaks harshly to them, accusing them of coming to spy in his land. They tell him that they are ten brothers, sons of an old man, that they were once twelve but that their youngest brother has remained with their father, and that one brother "is no more."

Once again, Joseph calls them "spies." He puts them in jail for three days. Realizing that they are being punished for what they had done to Joseph,

Reuben tells them: "Did I not tell you, 'Do no wrong to the boy'? But you paid no attention. Now comes the reckoning for his blood."

Joseph overhears them but pretends not to understand their language. He orders Simeon seized and tells them to return to their land and not to come back without their youngest brother. Secretly, he instructs his servants to fill their sacks with grain and replace the money they have paid to him in each of their bags.

· 3 ·

The brothers return to Jacob and tell him about "the man" they met in Egypt, about Simeon, and about the money returned to them. They also share "the man's" demand to see Benjamin, but, fearing the loss of his youngest son, Jacob refuses. "My son must not go down with you," he says to them, "for his brother is dead and he alone is left."

As the famine becomes more severe, however, the brothers approach Jacob again. Judah promises to look after Benjamin, and Jacob finally agrees. Taking gifts and money with them, they return to Egypt. Joseph welcomes them and tells his steward to prepare a meal for them in his house. He returns Simeon to them and, greeting Benjamin, inquires about the health of their father. However, he does not reveal his identity to his brothers.

After the meal, he tells his steward to fill their bags with food and to return their money. Cleverly laying a trap for Benjamin, he instructs the steward: "Put my silver goblet in the mouth of the bag of the youngest one." When his brothers leave, he has them followed, stopped, and searched. They protest, declaring that they have taken nothing from Joseph. When the goblet is found in Benjamin's bag, the brothers are brought back to Joseph's house.

Fearing that returning without Benjamin will kill Jacob, Judah pleads with Joseph. He tells Joseph to take all of them as slaves, arguing that they are as guilty "as he in whose possession the goblet was found." Joseph refuses, telling them that he will take only Benjamin and that the rest of them can return to their father.

THEMES

Parashat Miketz contains three important themes:

1. Knowing what to do with dreams.
2. The choice between revenge and caring.
3. The choice between death and survival.

PEREK ALEF: *Joseph Knew What to Do with Dreams*

We have already encountered Joseph the dreamer. At seventeen he dreams about his brothers' sheaves bowing down to his and about the sun, moon, and eleven stars—his parents and brothers—also bowing to him. These dreams, as we have seen, anger his brothers and make Jacob suspicious about Joseph.

Some years later, while he is in prison, Joseph the dreamer becomes Joseph the interpreter of dreams. He accurately predicts the future for Pharaoh's former baker and cupbearer. The baker will die, and the cupbearer, he forecasts, will be restored to his position in Pharaoh's court.

Now, in our Torah portion, Pharaoh's cupbearer recalls Joseph's interpretive powers. Pharaoh has dreamed dreams that neither his advisors nor magicians can explain. The cupbearer informs his ruler about "the Hebrew youth" who understood his dream and predicted the future. Pharaoh is impressed. He frees Joseph and brings him to his court so that he can tell Joseph about his own dreams.

Hirsch

Joseph listened
Rabbi Samson Raphael Hirsch explained that Pharaoh said to Joseph: "I have heard of you that you listen to a dream in such a manner that you solve its meaning from its very contents." It all depends on listening to it correctly. Of ten people who listen to a speech or a story, often hearing it differently, only one hears it correctly. (The Pentateuch, on Genesis 41:15)

Listening
Human beings were endowed with two ears and one tongue that they might listen more than speak. (Abraham Hasdai, 13th century, translator and philosopher, Barcelona)

Listen and you will learn. (Solomon ibn Gabirol)

When two students listen patiently to each other in a discussion of Torah, God also listens to them.

And, if they do not, they cause God to depart from them. (Simeon ben Lakish, Shabbat 63b)

When Joseph arrives at court, Pharaoh greets him and says: "I have heard it said of you that for you to hear a dream is to tell its meaning." The Hebrew verb "hear" is *tishema*. It derives from the root *shema,* meaning not only "hear" but also "comprehend" or "understand."

Apparently, Joseph's success at interpreting the dreams that Pharaoh's wise men and magicians could not decipher had to do with his special listening skills. Some commentators speculate that Pharaoh's servants probably heard the king's description and then rushed off to consult their books on dreams. Instead of paying careful attention to Pharaoh's unique experience, they looked for an already accepted theory and explanation. As a result, they concluded that the dreams were two separate predictions of disaster. (*Genesis Rabbah* 89:60)

Joseph's approach was very different. He was ready to experiment with various original explanations. So he listened carefully to the dreams and to the varying shades and tones of Pharaoh's description in order to comprehend the emotion inside the words and to understand the subtle distinctions of each object Pharaoh mentioned and of every gesture made by the Egyptian ruler.

Because of his careful listening and openness to original insights, Joseph concludes that Pharaoh's two dreams are actually "one and the same." His ability to "hear" makes all the difference in his successful interpretation of Pharaoh's dreams.

But Joseph does more than offer interpretations. Psychologist Dr. Dorothy F. Zeligs, in her study of Joseph's personality, calls attention to the fact that he also presents Pharaoh with "a plan for dealing with the situation." Grain is to be stored throughout the land during the period of plentiful harvest in order to provide for years of famine. "Again," Zeligs writes, "Joseph the dreamer shows himself to be also a man of action. . . . Again he uses his very real abilities and his capacity for hard work to consolidate his position. His achievements therefore cannot be said to be based on fortuitous circumstances alone. For the rest of his life, Joseph remains in Pharaoh's favor. This

is no small accomplishment when one considers how fickle were the moods of those mighty potentates."(*Psychoanalysis and the Bible*, Bloch, New York, 1974, pp. 77–78)

Rabbi Mordechai Ha-Kohen, who lived in Safed during the seventeenth century, points out that Joseph did not delegate the responsibilities for distributing food to subordinate officials. Instead, he supervised all the storage and sales, personally making sure that no one was cheated. By the example of his own hard work and his compassion for the hungry and needy, he set a model of behavior for others. (*Siftei Kohen* on *Miketz*)

Dreamers and Dreams
Do not mock the words of our dreamers. Their words become the seeds of freedom. (Heinrich Heine)

If you will it, it is not a dream. (Theodor Herzl)

You see things; and you say, "Why?" But I dream things that never were; and I say, "Why not?" (George Bernard Shaw)

Other interpreters also emphasize that Joseph was not just an interpreter of dreams but a person of action as well. He established a careful plan for dealing with the seven years of plenty and the seven years of famine. Rather than procrastinating, he developed solutions to the problems facing Egypt. Nor did he lose time in implementing his design for saving the country from disaster. He planned and built storage cities, organizing an original system for collecting one-fifth of Egypt's produce during the years of plenty by storing it in silos.

Steinsaltz

"From being a dreamer of dreams," commentator Adin Steinsaltz observes, "Joseph became the person of the dream . . . a man who experienced the dream . . . as a burden and a responsibility and a course of action from which there could be no digression." (*Biblical Images,* p. 70)

Joseph's greatness, according to our interpreters, was not only that he developed a "sensitive ear," an ability to listen to what others were saying, but that he was also ready to assume responsibility for transforming dreams into reality. Pharaoh obviously sensed Joseph's leadership qualities and, therefore, immediately told him: "You shall be in charge of my court, and by your command shall all my people be directed. . . ."

It was a wise decision, for Joseph was a person who got things done. He was not a dreamer who shirked responsibilities. He was a hard worker who willingly used his skills for turning Pharaoh's dreams into a strategy for survival.

PEREK BET: *The Choice between Revenge and Caring*

Abravanel

In his commentary to our Torah portion, Isaac Abravanel asks: "Why did Joseph denounce his brothers? Certainly it was wrong of him to take revenge and bear a grudge against them. After all, while their intent had been evil, God turned it to good. It is true that he had suffered years in jail, but he had also emerged as one of the most important and powerful leaders of Egypt. None of his good fortune would have occurred had his brothers not sold him into slavery. So what justification did Joseph have for taking revenge after twenty years? Why did he not have compassion for them or at least show more concern for the feelings of his aged father?"

Bearing a grudge

"*You shall not take vengeance or bear a grudge. . . .*" (*Leviticus 19:19*)

Do not say, "I will do to him as he has done to me." (*Proverbs 24:29*)

Do not say, "Since I have been humiliated, let my neighbor be humiliated. Know that, when you humiliate another person, you are humiliating the image of God." (*Ben Azai,* Tanchuma, Genesis Rabbah 24:7)

If you refuse assistance to a neighbor because he had been unkind to you, you are guilty of revenge; if you grant him his request for aid and remind him of his unkindness, you are guilty of bearing a grudge. (Sifra *to Leviticus 19:18*)

Author Maurice Samuel is also bothered by Joseph's treatment of his brothers and father. He accuses Joseph of "cruelty" and "revenge." He calls Joseph "the brilliant failure" because of his success in reaching the pinnacle of power in Egypt and because of his insensitivity toward his brothers and father. Samuel writes:

He accused them of being spies. He watched their consternation, and he toyed with it while they, poor devils, stammered their protests at this unbelievable turn of events and argued with him, to no effect of course. It was like arguing with a lunatic—an omnipotent lunatic. They thought of their families at home, their wives and their little ones and old Jacob—very old by now—waiting for bread. And here was this mad governor of Egypt. . . . If you have forgotten some details of the story, if you think that Joseph is now satisfied, that, having had his innocent little revenge, he calls the shocking comedy off, then you do not know your man. The actor has an insatiable appetite for encores. . . . This wantonness of Joseph's, this frivolity, this cruelty, is particularly embarrassing.
(*Certain People of the Book,* Knopf, New York, 1955, pp. 312–326)

Ramban (Nachmanides)

Nachmanides disagrees with both Abravanel's and Maurice Samuel's criticism of Joseph. He maintains that Joseph is not guilty of cruel revenge but is simply carrying out the predictions forecast in his youthful dreams. He dreamed that "all the sheaves," and "the sun, moon, and eleven stars" would bow to him.

Joseph, Nachmanides argues, now recalled those dreams and believed that it was his duty to fulfill them. Therefore, he hid his identity from his brothers so that they would be forced to bring Benjamin and, ultimately, Jacob down to Egypt where they would all bow before him. "Joseph," Nachmanides writes, "carried out everything in the appropriate manner in order to fulfill his youthful dreams."

Rabbi Isaac Arama is shocked at Nachmanides' explanation and justification of Joseph's behavior. Not hiding his surprise, he comments, "I am astonished at Nachmanides' explanation that Joseph did what he did in order to make his dreams come true. What did such behavior benefit him? And, even if he benefited, he should not have sinned against his father with such cruel treatment of him." (*Akedat Yitzhak*)

Elie Wiesel agrees. Condemning Joseph's desire for revenge, he writes: "Later, when his brothers were brought before him, he sought only to ridicule them, to take his vengeance. Instead of inquiring about his father and his younger brother, he demanded hostages; instead of feeding them, he made them tremble with fear. Weeks and weeks went by before he deigned to reassure them. Ten times he heard his brothers refer to their father as *your servant Jacob* and, unmoved, neither protested nor betrayed himself." (*Messengers of God,* p. 160)

Hirsch

Clearly, many commentators criticize Joseph for mistreating his father and brothers. Like Nachmanides, however, Rabbi Samson Raphael Hirsch believes that Joseph acted neither out of revenge nor out of selfishness by seeking to fulfill the predictions of his youthful dreams. Instead, Hirsch argues, Joseph put his brothers to the test in order to determine two important matters: *First,* he wanted to know if they would do to Benjamin

what they had done to him. If so, then he could neither forgive nor trust them. *Second,* he needed to test how they would react when, and if, he, as a ruler of Egypt, revealed himself as their brother. Would they trust him? Would they be loyal to him? Would they love him?

Hirsch calls Joseph's treatment of his brothers and father "unavoidable." He justifies Joseph's withholding his identity from his brothers, his accusing them of being spies, his forcing them to bring Benjamin to Egypt against their father's will, his planting of his goblet in Benjamin's sack and seizing him as hostage—as *necessary.* Joseph, Hirsch maintains, had to protect himself, his position, and his family. He had to be certain that his brothers could be trusted and that they were no longer out to destroy him. He had to test them. Joseph, says Hirsch, acted out of wisdom, not out of spite or revenge.

The differences of opinion remain about whether Joseph's behavior was justified or not. And so do the questions: Did he care about the feelings of his brothers or his aging father? Was he still angry about what his brothers had done to him? Was he determined to make them suffer as he had suffered? Did Joseph want revenge or reconciliation?

PEREK GIMEL: *Jacob's Choice—Risking Death for Survival*

Jacob's sons returned from Egypt with food but without Simeon. They explained to Jacob that "the lord of the land" spoke harshly to them, accused them of spying, and told them not to return unless they brought their youngest brother, Benjamin, with them.

Jacob responded with anger. "It is always me that you bereave: Joseph is no more and Simeon is no more, and now you would take away Benjamin." Hoping to win his father's trust, Reuben declared that if anything happened to Benjamin he would allow Jacob to put to death his own two sons. But Jacob refused. He would not allow them to take Benjamin to Egypt.

Months passed. Their food provisions began to run low, and famine threatened. So the brothers, once again, approached their father, hoping to convince him to send Benjamin with them back to Egypt. Judah spoke on their behalf, promising to care for Benjamin. This time, Jacob agreed. He sent them off with gifts and money. "As for me," he told them, "if I am to be bereaved, I shall be bereaved."

The incident is a dramatic illustration of family tension and parental love. And it raises important questions: What prompts Jacob's change of mind? Why is Judah able to convince Jacob to send Benjamin when Reuben's argument failed? Why is Jacob suddenly ready to risk Benjamin's life, with the potential of bringing great sorrow upon himself?

According to Rabbi Judah, Reuben demonstrated his moral insensitivity and stupidity when he tried to persuade Jacob to allow Benjamin to go down to Egypt with his brothers. His proposition to Jacob that, if anything were to happen to Benjamin, he could take the lives of his own sons was unacceptable. Jacob dismissed it by telling Reuben: "Fool! Do you not realize that your sons are my grandsons. How could I take their lives?" (*Genesis Rabbah* 91:8)

Rashi

On the other hand, Rashi believes that the real reason Jacob dismissed Reuben's argument but accepted Judah's was simply a matter of timing. Reuben approached Jacob just after returning from Egypt. Jacob was deeply upset that his sons had returned without Simeon and refused to place Benjamin's fate in their hands. Furthermore, because they had brought back plenty of food, he was not concerned with the danger of famine. He saw no reason, at that time, to risk losing another son.

Consequently, as Rashi points out, Judah waited until hunger finally threatened Jacob's entire family. Then, he came before his father and presented his argument. According to Rashi, Judah told Jacob: "You say that you fear for Benjamin. Well, none of us knows whether or not he will be seized by the Egyptian ruler. What we do know is that, if we do not return to Egypt with

Benjamin, all of us will die of starvation. Is it not better to let go what is doubtful and snatch what is certain?"

The worst decision
A story is told of two pious men who went on a sea journey. A huge wave threatened to sink their ship. One of them said: "This is the worst!" The other replied: "It could be much worse." "How is that possible?" asked the first. "We are at the gates of death. Can there be anything worse?" "Yes," explained the other. "We could be placed in the predicament of Jacob whose sons came to him seeking bread, and he had none to give them. Remember that choice. As long as he had food in the bin, he refused to allow Benjamin to go to Egypt. But, as soon as the bin was empty, he was forced to say: "Take your brother." (As related in Nehama Leibowitz, Studies in Bereshit, p. 474)

Can one life be sacrificed for many? *A group of people, walking along a road, are stopped by evil people who say to them: "Give us one of you, and we will kill him. If not, we will kill all of you." What shall be done? Rather than surrendering one person, let all of them be killed. But, if the evil people single out one person, as was the case with Sheba ben Bichri (who rebelled against King David), that person may be surrendered to them so that the others may be saved. Rabbi Simeon ben Lakish said: "Only someone who is under sentence of death, the way Sheba ben Bichri was, may be turned over."*

But Rabbi Yochanan disagreed. He argued that, if the evil people single out one person, then the others should save themselves by turning that person over to them. (Jerusalem Talmud, Terumot 8:12)

Nachmanides agrees with Rashi's view but extends it. He suggests that Judah wisely counseled his brothers to wait until there was no bread left in the house. Then Jacob would listen. He would make the difficult decision to risk one life in order to save many lives. (Nachmanides on Genesis 42:37)

Nehama Leibowitz wonders what it was that convinced Jacob to change his mind and agree to send Benjamin with his brothers. He does not seem to have been moved by either Simeon's imprisonment or by Reuben's appeal. Leibowitz believes that it was the hunger of his grandchildren that persuaded the patriarch. It was seeing the children wasting away, crying for food that moved him. "The hunger of the little ones finally broke his resistance. Judah meaningfully ended the first sentence of his appeal with the words: '. . . and also our little ones.' " (*Studies in Bereshit*, p. 474)

Jacob's refusal to go along with Reuben's suggestion that the brothers return immediately to Egypt with Benjamin in order to rescue Simeon raises several questions: Was it right for him to leave Simeon imprisoned and, perhaps, suffering for so long? Was he justified in delaying until they ran out of food, endangering the children?

Our commentators all suggest that the patriarch acted justly. He carefully weighed his options, waiting to see what events might bring. In the end, his difficult decision was based on compassion for all his children and upon what might guarantee their survival.

QUESTIONS FOR STUDY AND DISCUSSION

1. According to our commentators, what is the art of interpreting dreams? Are dreamers essential for human development?

2. Who has the better argument about Joseph's treatment of his brothers and father: Abravanel, Samuel, and Wiesel or Nachmanides and Hirsch? Was Joseph's motive innocent or deliberate revenge?

3. Should Jacob have rejected Reuben's plea to return immediately with Benjamin to Egypt? Was it just for him to wait until starvation threatened his grandchildren?

4. Are parents justified in taking any risk to prevent their children from starving?

PARASHAT VAYIGASH
Genesis 44:18–47:27

Vayigash, which means "and he approached him," begins with the confrontation between Judah and Joseph, whose identity is still unknown to his brothers. Judah tells Joseph that, if he refuses to allow Benjamin to return to his father, the old man will die. He pleads with Joseph to take him as a slave in place of Benjamin. Joseph hears Judah and then dramatically reveals his identity to his brothers. He instructs them to bring Jacob to Egypt and to settle there in Goshen. Pharaoh also invites Joseph's family "to live off the fat of the land." Jacob arrives in Egypt for an emotional reunion with Joseph and is welcomed as well by Pharaoh. The famine continues, and Joseph arranges for people to exchange livestock for food and, then, land for food. Controlling the land for Pharaoh, Joseph distributes seed for planting with the agreement that the people will give one-fifth to Pharaoh and keep four-fifths for themselves. Meanwhile, Jacob and his family increase in numbers and wealth in the area of Goshen.

OUR TARGUM

·1·

Joseph arranges to have his goblet placed in Benjamin's sack and then arrests his brothers for stealing. His identity is still unknown to them. Now they appear before him falsely accused of a crime, fearful that he will enslave Benjamin. They know that, if they return without their youngest brother, the loss will kill their father, Jacob.

Judah approaches Joseph, reminding him of a previous conversation in which Judah told Joseph that, if the brothers returned without Benjamin, their father would die of sorrow. He pleads with Joseph to enslave him rather than Benjamin. "For how can I go back to my father unless the boy is with me? Let me not be witness to the sorrow that would overtake my father."

Joseph is moved and tells his attendants to leave the room. He then reveals his identity. "I am Joseph," he tells his brothers. "Is my father still well [alive]?" His weeping is so loud that the Egyptians in his house hear him and pass the news about his brothers to Pharaoh's court.

The brothers are stunned and afraid. Joseph assures them that, although they sold him into slavery, all has turned out well. "God," he explains, "has sent me ahead of you to insure your survival on earth and to save your lives in an extraordinary deliverance."

He tells them to hurry back to their father and to bring the entire family to Egypt. He promises to provide for them in the fertile region of Goshen, which is located today in the area between Port Said and the Suez. "You must tell my father everything about my high station in Egypt and all that you have seen; and bring my father here with all speed."

When Pharaoh and his court hear about Joseph's brothers, they are pleased. Pharaoh offers the brothers wagons with which to bring their households to Egypt and promises to give them "the best of the land of Egypt" as a place to dwell. They return to Canaan with bread, grain, and the fruits of Egypt, and they report to their father: "Joseph is still alive; yes, he is ruler over the whole land of Egypt."

Jacob is overjoyed with the news. He declares: "My son Joseph is still alive. I must go and see him before I die."

· 2 ·

Soon afterwards, they all set out for Egypt. Jacob travels to Beer-sheba where he encounters God in a night vision. God promises to be with him in Egypt—and that his people will become "a great nation."

Joseph and Jacob meet in Goshen. The old man embraces his long lost son. "Now I can die," he says, "having seen for myself that you are still alive."

·3·

Joseph explains to his brothers that the Egyptians hate shepherds but that he has arranged for them to dwell in the area of Goshen where they can care for their livestock. Preparing them for a meeting with Pharaoh, Joseph counsels them that the Egyptian ruler will ask them, "What is your occupation?" He tells them to answer that they have been shepherds as their fathers before them were shepherds.

When Pharaoh meets with them and hears their response, he assures them of their safety. Pharaoh tells Joseph: "The land of Egypt is open before you . . . let them stay in the region of Goshen. And, if you know any capable men among them, put them in charge of my livestock."

After a conversation between Pharaoh and Jacob, the family settles in Goshen. Joseph cares for them, providing food for all. Through the years the family increases greatly in both numbers and wealth.

·4·

With the famine increasing and the people without money to buy food, Joseph designs a plan, enabling the population of Egypt to purchase provisions in exchange for livestock. After the people have sold all their livestock, Joseph allows the people to trade their land for food.

Having gained control of all the land for Pharaoh, Joseph then offers the people a plan for production and taxation. At harvest time, they will pay Pharaoh with one-fifth of their produce and keep the remainder to feed themselves and their families. Only Pharaoh's priests are excluded from this arrangement since they already receive special payment from the Egyptian ruler.

THEMES

Parashat Vayigash contains four important themes:

1. The importance of speaking out for justice.
2. The difficulty and importance of achieving reconciliation.
3. Fear of the stranger.
4. Economic planning and justice.

PEREK ALEF: *Judah's Speech—A Plea for Justice*

Parashat Vayigash begins with Judah's plea for justice before the Egyptian head of state who has announced his intention to make a slave of Benjamin. The brothers are still unaware that it is Joseph with whom they are dealing, but they know that, if they return to Canaan without Benjamin, the loss will kill their father. As Judah steps forward, he realizes that everything now depends upon what he will say.

Interpreters of Judah's speech to Joseph call attention not only to the fact that it is the longest oration in Genesis but that Judah carefully calculates his arguments and even his tone of voice. His is not a spontaneous presentation. He is pleading for the life of his brother and father. Therefore, he measures every word, every gesture, every inflection.

Imagining Judah standing in Joseph's lavish court, the commentators provide us with a colorful portrait of their confrontation. Rabbi Onkelos, known as "the convert," who taught during the end of the first and the beginning of the second century, suggests that "Judah spoke with a pure, clear logic." Every point he made to Joseph was supported by facts and was impossible to refute. Another rabbi, perhaps a colleague of Onkelos, says that Judah diplomatically emphasized his concerns, arguing with Joseph until he was certain that he had penetrated his heart and turned his anger into compassion. (*Genesis Rabbah* 93:3–4)

What were the arguments Judah might have used in his plea for justice? How did he compel Joseph to reveal his identity and release Benjamin?

Hirsch

Rabbi Samson Raphael Hirsch believes that Judah decided to defend himself against Joseph's anger by flattering him. So he told him: "May that which I want to say not excite your sensitiveness for, see, you are as Pharaoh. I honor you as a pharaoh so, if anything that I say does not please you, do not think that I do it from lack of honor. What I say to you I would also say to Pharaoh." (On Genesis 44:18)

Rashi

Rashi speculates that Judah used a different approach. Rather than flattering Joseph, Judah attacked him. He told him: "You are as unreliable as Pharaoh. Just as he issues promises and does not carry them out, so do you. You promised that you only wanted 'to see' our youngest brother. Now you are making him your slave." In Rashi's view, Judah exposes Joseph's callousness. He tells him that he cannot be trusted, that he is a liar. (On Genesis 44:18)

Other interpreters say that Judah accused Joseph, not only of lying to them, but also of breaking Egyptian law. They explain that Judah confronted him with the fact that Egyptian law allows you to take from a thief everything he owns but does not permit you to make him your slave. "You are breaking your own laws," Judah complained to him. (*Midrash Tanchuma, Vayigash;* also Ba'al Ha-Turim on Genesis 44:18)

Abravanel

What Judah did not say
Abravanel asks: "Why is it that Judah did not criticize Joseph for falsely accusing him and his brothers of being spies?" Answering the question, Abravanel writes: "He did not mention it because he did not wish to give Joseph an opportunity to return, once again, to that subject."

Ramban (Nachmanides)

What really moved Joseph
Nachmanides suggests that it was not just Judah's speech that moved Joseph. "There were many people present in Pharaoh's house and other Egyptians pleading with Joseph to pardon Benjamin. Their compassion had been deeply stirred by Judah's plea, and Joseph could not overcome them all." (Nachmanides on Genesis 45:1)

Judah's offer
With Judah's selfless offer of himself as a substitute for Benjamin, Joseph finally had irrefutable proof of change in his brothers' old attitudes. Judah exemplified their devotion to Jacob, their love for Benjamin, and their sincere repentance for their crime against Joseph himself." Convinced of their love, Joseph reveals himself to them. (Meir Zlotowitz, trans., Bereishis, Vol. VI, Art Scroll Tanach Series, New Mesorah Publications Ltd., 1981, p. 1958)

Rabbi Judah comments that "Judah approached Joseph to do battle with him." Other interpreters agree, pointing out that Judah criticized Joseph for wrongly accusing him and his brothers of being spies. He also complained that Joseph had singled them out at the border for special questioning and harassment. "Thousands of others have come here seeking grain," Judah told Joseph. "Not once have you cross-examined any of them. So why did you treat us so meanly?"

Some commentators say that Judah became enraged as he spoke to Joseph. Shaking a finger at him, Judah declared: "If you do not release Benjamin, we will paint Egypt in blood. We will destroy its markets and cities."

Others say that Judah tried another tactic. Because he wanted to frighten Joseph, he told him that his father, Jacob, possessed the deadly power of cursing others. "If I return to him without Benjamin, he will lay a curse of destruction not only upon Egypt but also upon you." Joseph became terrified and immediately revealed himself to his brothers. (*Tze'enah u-Re'enah, Vayigash,* Genesis 44:19)

Other interpreters disagree. It was neither Judah's threat of violence against Egypt nor a curse by Jacob that persuaded Joseph to reveal himself to his brothers. Instead, it was Judah's willingness to offer himself as a slave in place of Benjamin, together with his plea for consideration of their father's feelings.

Jacob ben Isaac Ashkenazi of Yanof, the author of *Tze'enah u-Re'enah,* explains that Judah approached Joseph and said to him: "Take me instead of Benjamin. For I have guaranteed his life to my father. I have promised to bring him back home." Judah hoped to appeal to the Egyptian leader's sense of compassion. He wished to convince Joseph of his genuine concern for his brother and father.

Modern commentator Nehama Leibowitz points out that Judah uses the word "father" fourteen times in his speech to Joseph. The repetition, Leibowitz believes, is not accidental. It "is calculated to arouse compassion in the hardest of hearts, appealing to the most elemental of affections—parental love." Judah, Leibowitz argues, hoped that, by repeating the word "father," his plea for justice might touch the heart of the Egyptian leader with a sense of the pain that a loss of a child might bring to a parent.

The interpreters of Judah's plea for justice suggest a wide range of reasons that may account for Joseph finally revealing himself to his brothers: Judah's flattery of him, his attack upon him, his threat of Jacob's curse upon him, or his willingness to sacrifice his own life for Benjamin's. As with many interpretations of Torah, the challenge to uncover the reason—or combination of reasons—remains.

PEREK BET: *The Hard Way of Reconciliation*

The scene in which Joseph reveals himself to his brothers is a memorable and emotional one. Over-

come with tears, he tells his brothers, "I am Joseph. Is my father still well?" His brothers are astonished; they are speechless. So he says to them: "Come forward to me. I am your brother Joseph, he whom you sold into Egypt." He then explains to them that God sent him to Egypt to save them, and he instructs them to return to Canaan to bring their father, Jacob, and the rest of the family down to Egypt to settle in Goshen.

For many centuries, Torah interpreters have wondered about how these brothers who hated one another could undergo such "dramatic" reconciliation. They had a long history of bitterness and suspicion to repair. Suddenly the man who treated them like spies, arrested them, and jailed them reveals that he is the brother they sold into slavery. How could they build trust and faith in one another? How would they be able to overcome the hostility between them?

Peli

Modern commentator Pinchas Peli believes that Joseph acted wisely in asking everyone to leave the court so that he and his brothers could be alone when he revealed his identity to them. Peli explains: "It was one of those moments when no outsider should be present, when deep feelings should be confined to the inner circle of the close family. Only there may one voice the grievances that demand expression."

Peli may be correct. The fact that Joseph chose to be alone with his brothers so that they could privately voice their accusations and hostility may have helped to speed their reconciliation. But was it enough? Might it even have been dangerous?

Two of the ancient commentators have a serious disagreement about how wise it was for Joseph to tell all of his servants to leave the court so that he could be alone with his brothers. Rabbi Hama ben Hanina believed that it was a serious mistake. "Joseph did not act carefully," he argues. "After all, the brothers could have attacked and killed him."

Rabbi Samuel Nachmani claims that Joseph acted with great sensitivity and wisdom. He did not fear his brothers. After overhearing them speaking to one another, he knew that they felt very guilty for selling him into slavery. Seeing how much they regretted what they had done to him, and how they feared now for the welfare of both Benjamin and their father, he was right to trust them. (*Genesis Rabbah* 93:9)

A later interpreter adds to Rabbi Samuel's argument. He explains that Joseph insisted on being alone with his brothers for two other reasons. First, he did not want them publicly humiliated at the moment when he revealed that he was the brother they had sold into slavery. It was now a private matter between them. Second, he was afraid that, if the Egyptians found out that his brothers had sold him into slavery, the Egyptians might never trust them or allow Joseph to settle them in Egypt. (*Tze'enah u-Re'enah, Vayigash*)

Other commentators speculate on additional factors that helped the brothers reconcile after years of hostility and separation. Some claim that, when Joseph asked his brothers to approach him, he opened his garment and showed them that he was circumcised. Seeking to prove that he was one of them, he also addressed them in Hebrew. Others add that he spoke to each of them, showing no preference between them and thus convincing them that he bore no grudge toward any one of them. (*Genesis Rabbah* 93:10; *Tze'enah u Re'enah* on Genesis 45:12)

Be forgiving
Rabbi Asher ben Yechiel taught: "Each night before going to sleep, forgive whomever wronged you." (Hanhaga, c. 1320)

Raba taught: "He who forgives . . . will himself be forgiven." (Yoma 23a)

The poet Heinrich Heine (1797–1856) commented: "Since I myself stand in need of God's forgiveness, I grant forgiveness to all who have wronged me."

Austrian psychiatrist William Stekel (1868–1950) once said: "To be able to forget and forgive is the prerogative of noble souls."

Basing herself on many traditional commentaries, Nehama Leibowitz claims that Joseph smoothed the way to reconciliation between himself and his brothers by offering an explanation for what they

had done and what had happened to him. He told them to think of the "large picture" and to focus on the positive results of selling him into Egyptian slavery. On the surface it might appear as an evil act. Yet, considering the whole picture, their actions led to his becoming second in command in Egypt, a position from which he could save his entire family. Joseph told them: "Now, do not feel bad or guilty because you sold me into slavery. It was actually to save life that God sent me ahead of you."

Leibowitz's argument is that Joseph made the reconciliation possible by offering a new explanation for what had happened between the brothers. It was not the brothers, but rather God, who had directed all the events. Good had resulted from evil. Viewing events on a broader scale helped them heal their hostilities, overcome their guilt, and move on to saving their lives.

Good out of evil
Rabbi Samson Raphael Hirsch comments: "Joseph repeatedly points out to his brothers how this whole chain of events clearly stands out as Divine Management. . . . The great Master of the world achieves everything from the smallest beginnings. . . . God it is who brings everything to service. Without knowing it and without wishing it, folly and sin also are used to serve God's ends." (On Genesis 45:11)

Don Isaac Abravanel strongly disagrees with those who argue that "evil leads to good" or that evil should ever be excused because it led to a positive outcome. He condemns Joseph's brothers. He writes: "The fact that by a fluke the sale turned out well did not lessen their offense. A person is not judged by the accidental results of his deeds but by his intent. The accidental results are irrelevant to the moral dimension."

So far as Abravanel is concerned, offering excuses for the evil the brothers had intended to do—and actually did in selling Joseph into slavery—would not have led to their reconciliation. Instead, it might have brought about more suspicion and fear. They might have wondered: When will he turn the tables on us and pay us back for the suffering we inflicted upon him? In this regard, it is interesting to note that later, after Jacob dies, the brothers express their fear that Joseph will finally punish them for what they had done to him. (See Genesis 50:15ff.)

Other interpreters, agreeing with Abravanel, hold that Joseph insisted that he be left alone with his brothers because he realized that making peace required honesty. Neither he nor they could pretend that what they had done to him was "good." They had to face one another in the privacy of their family and talk out their differences and their hostility. They had to get rid of their anger and suspicions in order to reach new levels of understanding and commitment.

So, according to one interpreter, when Joseph saw that his brothers were terrified after he told them who he was, he calmed them by saying, "I am *your brother* Joseph." He emphasized the words *"your brother,"* making certain that they understood that their family bond made it possible for him to be honest with them and to forgive them.

Other commentators say that Joseph kissed each of the brothers, showing them genuine affection. Then he assured them that they were safe in his house and that he would make sure that they returned unharmed to their father. He comforted them by promising to save them from famine by settling them safely in Goshen. Joseph even pledged to them that he would never tell Jacob that they had sold him into slavery. It was to be their secret, not something he used against them. (*Tze'enah u Re'enah* on Genesis 45:3 and 11)

Jewish commentators through the centuries have tried to figure out Joseph's strategy for reconciling with his brothers. Some of their explanations excuse the evil intentions of the brothers; others describe Joseph as a kind, thoughtful, and caring brother and son. They claim he was a devoted Jew, anxious to forgive his brothers and forget the pain they had caused him. From the varying descriptions and disagreements among those who have studied Joseph's treatment of his brothers, we learn much about the difficulties of forgiveness and reconciliation.

PEREK GIMEL: *Strangers in the Land*

The Torah informs us that, after the brothers reconciled, Pharaoh invited Joseph's family to settle in Egypt. He sent wagons to Jacob to ease his journey, and he and his heads of state festively greeted Jacob and Joseph's brothers and families upon their arrival. The welcome appears to have been a very warm one. Pharaoh invited them all to settle in Goshen.

Interpreters of this part of the Joseph story are not satisfied with the Torah's "happy ending." They raise some significant questions: What was it like to be immigrants and strangers in a foreign land? Were Pharaoh and other Egyptians happy about welcoming Jews into their land? What about Jacob and his family? Did they fear being overwhelmed by Egyptian culture?

According to one interpretation, Pharaoh and the other leaders of Egypt were delighted to learn that Joseph—to whom they had given such high office and vast responsibilities—was not a common slave but the son of noble parents. They had been embarrassed by what they believed were his slave origins. In Egypt human beings were not judged by their talents and character but by their place in the social and economic order. Slaves were at the bottom of the society. The knowledge that Joseph was from distinguished parentage actually boosted his status and reputation among the Egyptians. (*Tze'enah u-Re'enah* on Genesis 45:14)

For some commentators that explains why Pharaoh welcomed Jacob so warmly. He considered him a "prince," a leader of another people. So he honored him with transportation, food, hospitality, and the generous offer of settlement in Goshen.

Other interpreters speculate that Pharaoh rushed out to greet Jacob and his family and offered them Goshen because he was afraid of losing Joseph as an advisor. He required Joseph's skills at administering Egypt's successful famine relief program. Joseph's leadership and knowledge were very valuable to the Egyptian ruler. Pharaoh reasoned that, if Joseph's father and brothers settled in Goshen, then Joseph would remain in Egypt. So he offered them the best of his land and assured them his protection. (*Midrash Tanchuma* to *Vayigash*)

Some commentators, however, do not agree that Pharaoh's welcome of Jacob and his sons was so enthusiastic. They say that many of Pharaoh's ministers complained that Jews, like Joseph, would compete with them for positions of leadership. "When Joseph came to power," they said, "we lost our positions. Now he will give positions to his brothers and make them lords over us." (*Midrash ha-Gadol* on Genesis 45:17)

Abravanel believes that Joseph was also concerned about the negative feelings of Egyptians toward Jews. He wanted it clearly understood that they were not arriving to take other people's positions or to be a burden upon Egyptian society. Abravanel says that Joseph told Pharaoh that his people would never require special support. They would always take care of their own needs.

Abravanel also explains why Joseph deliberately counseled his brothers to say that they were "shepherds." He knew that Pharaoh had a great need for shepherds because most Egyptians were farmers. So he reasoned that other Egyptians would accept them more easily if they seemed unlikely to compete for jobs with them.

Clearly, Abravanel believes that Joseph worried about the Egyptians accepting his family. He feared jealousy or an outbreak of suspicion and prejudice. Joseph sensed that as a minority their situation was precarious, even dangerous.

His family would be strangers in a new land. They would speak Egyptian with an accent; their names would be different. Their clothing and their preference of foods and styles might also be different from the Egyptian lifestyle. Joseph realized that their safety and success would depend upon how the majority population treated them.

Modern commentator Pinchas Peli raises another issue that he believes concerned Joseph. Peli explains that, just before Joseph sent his brothers back to the Land of Israel, he warned them to be very careful about how they treated any Egyptians they might meet on their journey. Joseph told his brothers to avoid all quarrels with the Egyptians and not to act superior because of their special relationship to him.

What Peli seems to be suggesting is that Joseph was worried that his brothers would call attention to themselves, embarrass him, or endanger themselves by arousing resentment. So Peli suggests that Joseph advised them that as strangers they should assume a "low profile." They should call as little attention to themselves as possible by always acting quietly and humbly. (*Torah Today*, pp. 47–48)

At least one commentator stretches this concern

of Joseph for the safety of his family to his land reforms. The author of *Lekach Tov* suggests that, because Joseph worried about the status of his family, he decided to relocate all the Egyptians from one city to another throughout Egypt. In this way, so the argument goes, he made every Egyptian a "stranger." He thought that, if the Egyptians experienced some of the problems and difficulties of starting all over again in a new place with new people, they might have a greater sensitivity to his family who were new settlers in Goshen.

Separate occupations

Joseph chose for his brothers a good, upright—but hated—public occupation. Had he wished, he could have appointed them to high positions but, instead, he had them say that they were shepherds. . . . The idea was to segregate them from the Egyptians . . . and to have Pharaoh settle them in Goshen. (Rabbi Isaac Arama)

Separate place

Joseph arranged matters to achieve the goal that they would live separately from the Egyptians in the area of Goshen. While this was contrary to what Pharaoh had wished, it was worth the sacrifice since it meant guaranteeing Israel's identity and traditions. (Rabbi Naphtali Zvi Judah Berlin, Ha-Emek Davar)

Assimilation

Rabbi Bechaye notes that Jacob wanted his sons to stay away from the royal court so that they would not be in danger of achieving high positions. He feared assimilation—that they might trade their loyalty to their people and traditions for the glory of high office.

Both Rabbi Isaac Arama and the modern Zionist writer Rabbi Naphtali Zvi Judah Berlin argue that Joseph was also very concerned with the difficulties of preserving Jewish tradition and culture. He feared that all the temptations of Egyptian life—riches, entertainments, sports, politics, and various religions—would eventually lead to assimilation and the end of Jewish family loyalties. So he convinced Pharaoh to segregate his people and to restrict them to the region of Goshen.

Rabbi Hizkiyahu ben Manoah, a thirteenth-century commentator who lived in France, also follows this line of reasoning. He explains that it was not only Joseph who worried about preserving Jewish identity. Jacob, he says, was also concerned that life in Egypt would become so comfortable and prosperous that Jews would forget their own history, language, land, and traditions. Therefore he told his son not to appoint his brothers to any high positions of government. He did not want them tempted by honors or by power. Instead, according to Hizkiyahu ben Manoah, Jacob told Joseph to send them off to Goshen where they might live separately and safely within Egyptian culture.

As the commentators point out, living as "strangers" or "immigrants" in a new land presents a number of difficult problems. While often newcomers are welcomed warmly, as Pharaoh greeted Jacob and his family, others in the settled population remain suspicious and hostile to aliens. They fear that their jobs will be taken, their neighborhoods changed, their schools invaded, and their economic situation endangered.

One of the most serious problems facing all immigrant groups is how to hold on to their traditions, language, and group identity. Interpreters of the Joseph story are correct when they point out two responses to the challenge of assimilation. One is to segregate into ghettos, to seal yourself off from the rest of society around you; the other is to participate fully in the society but also to work at retaining your historic traditions.

For centuries, Jews have struggled with the stress and strains of assimilation. In some places, they have flourished, contributing richly to the greater society while also preserving and advancing Jewish culture and faith. At other times, they have suffered the brutality of anti-Semitism or even the rejection and abandonment by some Jews of their own community.

The status of "stranger," "alien," or "newcomer" is a difficult one. Perhaps that is why the Torah constantly emphasizes sensitivity and compassion in our treatment of the stranger. Repeatedly we find the commandment: "You shall not wrong a stranger or oppress him, for you were strangers in the land of Egypt."

PEREK DALET: *Joseph's Economic Success*

Our Torah portion claims that Joseph not only saved his own family from famine but also brilliantly rescued Egypt from economic ruin. He designed and managed a series of strategies that guided the people through seven years of plenty and sustained them through seven years of famine.

What were these "strategies"? How did Joseph save Egypt and, some say, the entire world from the ravages of famine?

Nachmanides explains that Joseph did not allow individuals to build and operate private silos for food storage. Instead, he created public granaries. "He stored everything," Nachmanides writes, "and divided it out to the people in annual rations." By controlling the supplies, Joseph prevented private profiteering and selfish hoarding. By rationing and distributing foods fairly, he gained the confidence and support of the people.

Furthermore, Nachmanides claims that Joseph gave his own family the same rations as others received. Refusing to take advantage of his position or to grant special favors, he treated everyone equally. Joseph realized that only such fairness would guarantee the trust of those who depended upon him. In the absence of such trust people would begin to cheat and hoard supplies for themselves, and the cooperative effort for saving Egypt would collapse.

The Midrash comments on Joseph's wise policy of locating silos. Rather than putting them in one place, he built them in different cities throughout Egypt. With the distribution centers so near to to the population, the people felt secure. They did not have to travel long distances to find food for their families. Nor did they need to stand on long lines to receive their supplies. Joseph's plan was efficient. It promoted confidence in a time of potential panic.

According to the rabbis of the Midrash, Joseph also adopted special laws regulating the way in which aid was distributed to foreigners who entered Egypt for help. They were prohibited from entering without registering their family names. In this way the government could control how many times a foreigner visited the country and requested help. Visitors were also prohibited from entering with more than one donkey. This made certain that no food was later sold for profit and that each visitor received only that which his family required for survival. (*Genesis Rabbah* 91:4)

I'll take care of myself
When the public experiences a disaster, let no person say: "I shall take food and drink for myself. I can't be bothered about others." (Ta'anit 11a)

Joseph could have given the members of his family more than everyone else in Egypt, but he did not. He supplied them with what they needed just as he supplied everyone else. (Sforno on Va-yigash)

The most complex aspect of Joseph's economic plan unfolded in the midst of the years of famine. As the people ran out of money with which to purchase their rations, they began to sell off their land and themselves as slaves to Pharaoh. Again, Joseph responded with creative solutions. He moved whole towns of people from one place to another, and he promised the people that they would receive four-fifths of the harvest and Pharaoh would take only one-fifth.

Luzzatto

Commentator Samuel David Luzzatto explains the brilliance of Joseph's tactic. He points out that Joseph did not split the Egyptians into small groups and scatter them among many different cities and populations. Instead, he resettled them "city by city," preserving their bonds of trust, cul-ture, family, and friendship. They were settled in a new environment, but they were not separated from their families, friends, old neighbors, and important sources of support. In this way, Joseph insured the high morale and positive feelings of the people for him, for Pharaoh, and for the stability of Egypt during difficult times of crisis.

Rabbi Samson Raphael Hirsch writes that Joseph also demonstrated strong leadership when the people became desperate and began offering to sell their lands and themselves as slaves to Pharaoh for continuing rations. Instead of accepting their offer, Joseph rejected it. Hirsch comments that Joseph opposed slavery. Rather than allow the people to sell themselves into bondage, he adopted a policy of purchasing the land for the central government. Then, he leased it back to the people.

The result, as Hirsch explains, was that "the ground belonged to Pharaoh for a fifth of the produce" while the farmer lived on four-fifths of the produce. The one-fifth, or 20 percent, was the citizen's tax to the state. The result of Joseph's plan, as Hirsch interprets it, was that, rather than making the people slaves, they became "tenant farmers." (Commentary on Genesis 47:26)

Hirsch's interpretation is close to an earlier view developed by Nachmanides who believed that Joseph's offer was exceedingly generous. Nachmanides speculates that Joseph told the people: "By rights Pharaoh, as lord of the land, is entitled to four-fifths and you as tenants to one-fifth. But I will treat you generously and give you the land-owner's share, and Pharaoh will take the tenant's share." In Nachmanides' view, Joseph's act was a demonstration of generosity, not simply clever economics. (Commentary on Genesis 47:26)

From the viewpoint of most interpreters, Joseph's economic revolution demonstrates sound planning, good management, and justice. At a time when it might have been easy for the rich to look out only for themselves and to profit from the poor, the commentators make clear that Joseph legislated laws guaranteeing equal distribution to all people. He even favored the poor when they lost their land and were about to declare themselves slaves.

Joseph also demonstrates a high level of moral leadership. He refuses to take profits for himself or offer preferential treatment to his own family.

For all these reasons, Joseph is known in Jewish tradition as a *tzadik,* a "righteous person."

QUESTIONS FOR STUDY AND DISCUSSION

1. The debate about the best way to achieve justice from individuals or from leaders in political power still remains. What approach should minority groups, such as Jews, take to confront government? Which of Judah's appeals or arguments might work best?

2. Does good result from evil? Could God have meant to have Joseph's brothers sell him into slavery so that he might later save them from famine?

3. Should there be such things as unforgivable offenses in a family? What might we learn from the story of Joseph and his brothers about reconciliation?

4. Must Jews maintain a "low profile" in order to succeed in societies where they are a minority? Would such a posture have been helpful during the rise of the Nazis in Germany?

5. The ancient rabbis suggest that the Israelites in Egypt prevented assimilation by four means: (1) They avoided sexual promiscuity with Egyptians. (2) They did not gossip about one another. (3) They did not change their names. (4) They did not change their language. Would such remedies work today? What other remedies might you suggest for stopping assimilation and guaranteeing Jewish survival?

6. What solutions for famine relief developed by Joseph might solve some of our modern problems today?

PARASHAT VAYECHI
Genesis 47:28–50:26

Vayechi may be translated "and he lived" and records the last years and death of Jacob. After living in Egypt for seventeen years, Jacob calls his son Joseph and his grandsons, Manasseh and Ephraim, to his bedside for a blessing. He asks Joseph to bury him with Abraham and Isaac at the cave of Machpelah. Afterwards he calls all of his sons to his side and blesses each one. When Jacob dies, Joseph and his brothers bury him in Hebron. After their father's death, Joseph's brothers begin to fear that Joseph will now punish them for selling him into slavery. He reassures them that they are safe and promises to care for them and their families. Joseph lives to the age of one hundred and ten. Just before he dies he tells his family that God will return them to the Land of Israel and instructs them to carry his bones up from Egypt at that time.

OUR TARGUM

·1·

When Jacob is one hundred and forty-seven years old and has lived in Egypt for seventeen years, he calls Joseph to him and makes Joseph take a vow. "Promise that when I die you will bury me with my fathers, Abraham and Isaac, in the cave of Machpelah." Joseph assures his father that he will carry out his wish.

Afterwards, when Jacob is ill, Joseph brings his sons, Manasseh and Ephraim, to him for a special blessing. Jacob reminds Joseph of God's promise to give the Land of Israel to his children and tells Joseph that Manasseh and Ephraim shall be counted as his own sons. He then blesses his grandchildren, placing his right hand upon Ephraim's head and his left hand upon Manasseh's head. Joseph notices that his father is blessing the younger with his right hand and the older with his left hand and tries to move his father's hands. Jacob, however, indicates that he knows what he is doing by putting Ephraim before Manasseh.

· 2 ·

Jacob calls his twelve sons to gather about his bed. He presents each of them with an evaluation of and a prediction for the future. He reminds them that they are to bury him in Hebron, and then he dies.

· 3 ·

Joseph weeps for his father and orders that he be embalmed. After a mourning period of seventy days, he requests permission from Pharaoh to take Jacob's body to the Land of Israel for burial. Pharaoh grants his wish, and Joseph, his brothers, and many Egyptians travel to Hebron for the burial. Once there, they observe a mourning period of seven days. Then they bury their father and return to Egypt.

· 4 ·

Upon their return, Joseph's brothers fear that he will now punish them for having sold him into slavery. So they send him a message indicating that, before he died, their father asked Joseph to forgive them. They tell Joseph: "We are prepared to be your slaves."

Joseph assures them that, while they might have intended harm for him, God intended what they had done for good. He promises to care for them and their families.

· 5 ·

After living to one hundred and ten years, Joseph is about to die. He gathers his family about him and tells them that God will one day return them to the Land of Israel. "When that day comes, carry up my bones from here." Upon his death, Joseph is embalmed and placed in a coffin in Egypt.

THEMES

Parashat Vayechi contains three important themes:

1. Burial and mourning traditions.
2. Making honest evaluations; defining "leadership."
3. Lying in the cause of peace.

PEREK ALEF: *Jacob's Death—Burial and Mourning Traditions*

Our Torah portion provides an important description of burial and mourning practices. Jacob requests that he not be buried in Egypt but rather in Hebron with Abraham and Sarah, Isaac, Rebekah, and Leah. At his death, we learn that Joseph orders Egyptian physicians to embalm Jacob, a process that takes forty days. The Torah also tells us that the Egyptians mourned for Jacob's loss for seventy days and that Joseph and his brothers mourned him for seven days before his burial in the cave of Machpelah.

Jewish burial and mourning customs have changed and evolved since biblical times. For instance, although embalming a dead body in order to prevent its decay was accepted during the time of Jacob and Joseph, later Jewish authorities opposed the practice.

Several reasons were given: First, embalming delays burial. Jewish tradition favored immediate burial most likely out of consideration for the health of the community. Some commentators also suggest that the rule of immediate burial may have been derived from God's statement to Adam: "Dust you are and to dust you shall return." (Genesis 3:19)

Second, embalming prevents the natural decay of the body and is actually a desecration of the body. Within Jewish tradition the human body is considered the sacred container for the soul. It should be buried with honor and without any mutilation or unnatural interference with its decomposition.

Third, embalming was opposed because it interfered with the mourner's necessary acceptance of the reality of death. Rabbi Maurice Lamm comments that "the art of the embalmer is the art of complete denial. Embalming seeks to create an illusion, and, to the extent that it succeeds, it only hinders the mourner from recovering from . . . grief." In other words, because the embalmer's job is to make the dead person appear "alive" and "beautiful," the result may be that mourners are actually prevented from accepting the finality of death. When that happens, a mourner often has difficulty getting on with all the responsibilities of life. (*The Jewish Way in Death and Mourning*, Jonathan David Publishers, New York, 1975, pp. 12–15)

Reform Judaism on burial
Since Judaism prescribes that the body should be returned to the dust from which it came, embalming *is discouraged except when required by law or circumstances.*

Burial *is the most widely practiced method of disposition of the body among Jews and is, in fact, the only method allowed by tradition. However, it is clear that other methods (interment in caves) were practiced among Jews in ancient times. And so, while both* cremation *and* entombment in mausoleums *are acceptable in Reform Judaism, burial is the normative Jewish practice.* (*Simeon J. Maslin, editor,* Gates of Mitzvah, *Central Conference of American Rabbis, New York, 1979, pp. 52–57*)

Among the ancient commentators a serious disagreement developed over whether or not Joseph should have embalmed his father, Jacob. Rabbi Judah Ha-Nasi believed that Joseph had made a serious mistake and that his life ended early because he did not honor his father in death.

Other rabbis argue that Joseph honored his father by following his instructions to bury him in the Land of Israel with his family. By embalming him they prepared his body so that it could be taken on the long journey from Goshen to Hebron. (*Genesis Rabbah* 100:3)

Although Jewish tradition opposes embalming, or any delays in burial, it did allow room for special circumstances. Embalming was permitted in cases where public health was endangered. It was also permitted when it was necessary to send the body long distances for burial (as in the case of Jacob) or when there was a necessary delay in the burial because close relatives needed to travel to the funeral.

Reform Judaism on mourning
Jewish tradition prescribes several periods of mourning, differing in intensity and obligation, following the death of a loved one. These are:

Avelut: *The name applied generally to the entire mourning period.*

Aninut: *The period between death and burial.*

Shivah: *The seven days of mourning following the funeral. Mourners are encouraged to remain at home during these days (except on Shabbat or festivals, when they should join the congregation in prayer), to refrain from their ordinary pursuits and occupations, and to participate in daily services in the home. . . . The first three days of the* shivah *period are considered the most intense and in Reform congregations are considered the minimum mourning period.*

Sheloshim: *The thirty-day period (including* shivah) *when normal life gradually resumes, and the mourners return to their daily activities while yet observing certain aspects of mourning. One should avoid joyful social events and entertainment during this period.*

The First Year: *The period during which a mourner recites* Kaddish *for a parent.* (Gates of Mitzvah, *pp. 59–60*)

Our Torah portion makes it clear that it took forty days to embalm Jacob but that the Egyptians mourned him for seventy days. Afterwards, Joseph and his brothers took their father's body to Hebron. Once there, they mourned for seven days and then buried him in the cave of Machpelah.

The mourning period observed by Joseph and his brothers does not conform with what has evolved into accepted Jewish practice. The seven days (*shivah*) are observed after burial, not before it. However, if the burial is at a great distance, then it is permitted to begin the *shivah* period at the time the vehicle carrying the body sets out on the journey. (I. Klein, *A Guide to Jewish Religious Practice,* Jewish Theological Seminary, distributed by Ktav, New York, 1979, p. 286)

The *shivah* period of mourning and the other designated times for grief (*sheloshim* and the saying of *Kaddish* during the first year after the death of a loved one) are all meant to ease the pain of losing someone we loved. Visits from friends provide comfort at a time when loneliness and loss are felt most deeply. Prayers recited with others, especially the *Kaddish,* affirm that we are not alone. They remind us that death is a part of the pattern of life and that God is to be thanked for the gift of the loved one we have lost and whose memory we cherish.

Commenting on the Jewish periods of mourning, Rabbi Jack D. Spiro writes: "Judaism . . . recognizes that the difficult work of mourning takes time; there is no shortcut on the road to recovery." (*A Time to Mourn,* Bloch, New York, 1968, p. 138)

Through the centuries, Jewish tradition has developed a process for confronting death and mourning. The procedures for burial are ones that honor the body and spirit of the dead. The designated periods and rituals of mourning allow for a healthy—and necessary—expression of grief. Jacob's death and his children's mourning teach us that losing a loved one is a deep wound. It requires time, support, and care from others to heal.

PEREK BET: *Jacob and His Sons— Honest Evaluations*

Just before he is about to die, Jacob calls his twelve sons to gather about his bed. His words to them are a combination of blessing, criticism, and prediction.

The dying patriarch is bluntly honest in his evaluation of his sons. He tells Reuben that he is "unstable as water," accuses Simeon and Levi of "lawlessness" and "fierce anger," and assesses Issachar as a "strong-boned ass." He calls Dan a "serpent"; he tells Joseph that he is "a wild ass" and Benjamin that he is "a ravenous wolf."

Why, we might ask, was Jacob so harshly critical of his sons?

Peli

Modern interpreter Pinchas Peli believes that Jacob's evaluation was meant to be helpful to them. His honesty taught them important lessons about their strengths and weaknesses. As their father, he could say things that no one else would tell them. Peli argues that "our lives often become confused and entangled for lack of a precise definition of who and what we really are." He claims that Jacob's evaluation of his sons "was meant to help his children find their proper identity. Such a criticism of them," Peli comments, "would help them find their way towards the future, in which they were destined to assume the roles as heads of the tribes of Israel."

Peli's psychological approach has special appeal. A parent's role is to help children understand their strengths and weaknesses. Constructive criticism builds character. It can deepen sensitivity to one's self and to others and improve one's social skills.

But parental criticism can also undermine confidence or mislead children about their real talents. Perhaps, instead of being helpful, Jacob's last words to his sons were harmful. How were they to feel about themselves when their father on his deathbed characterized them with such negative descriptions?

Not all commentaries, however, agree that "improving character" was the reason for Jacob's critical evaluation of existence.

Abravanel

Don Isaac Abravanel offers a different answer. It is the one most accepted by Jewish interpreters.

Abravanel's theory is that, when it came time for Jacob to die, he decided to pass on the leadership (or rule) of his family to the son who was most qualified. He struggled with his decision because he realized that the future of the Jewish people depended upon his choice.

For that reason, he assessed carefully the strengths and weaknesses of each son. When he reached his conclusion about who was the most qualified leader, he then gathered his sons together and announced it to them. Because he wanted them to appreciate his conclusions, he honestly shared his evaluation with them. Jacob wanted each of them to understand why he had disqualified him for leadership of the Jewish people.

Whether or not Abravanel's view of what motivated Jacob is correct, his discussion of what qualifies or disqualifies someone for leadership is very valuable. The following summary presents what Abravanel believes Jacob was saying about his sons and the important qualities he took into consideration when he thought about each of them.

Jacob's Sons and Leadership

Qualities for leadership
Judah: Trusted and accepted by his brothers.
   Brave and successful in battle.
   Steady, thoughtful, and dependable.
   Clear about his goals and determined
      to fulfill them.

Qualities that disqualified for leadership
Reuben: Unstable as water.
Simeon, Levi: Use of violence and force.
Zebulun: Always looking for profit.

Issachar: Use of others to fight his battles.
Dan: Snipes at others behind their backs.
Gad: Weakly gives in to his opponents.
Asher, Naphtali: Serve others but do not
      command respect.
Joseph: Hated and distrusted by his brothers.
Benjamin: Lacks balance of judgment and
      concern for others.

Abravanel's emphasis here is upon the important qualities that define leadership. Jacob, he argues, did not speak to his sons in order to hurt their feelings or to cause bitterness between them. His purpose was to clarify for them why Judah, above them all, qualified as the leader of the tribe that would produce King David and future rulers of Israel.

What makes a leader?
No fanatic can be a leader of the people of Israel.
(Rabbi Mendel of Kotzk)

A gentle leader here on earth will also be a leader in the world to come. (Rabbi Eleazar ben Pedat)

A leader must always show respect for the community. (Rabbi Nachman ben Jacob)

God weeps over a community leader who is domineering. (Hagigah 5b)

Jacob's last words to his sons were neither a blessing nor a promise for a peaceful future. Instead, Jacob presented them with a blunt and honest evaluation of their behavior and personalities. Our interpreters believe that his purpose was to provide his sons with some critical insights into themselves and their motivations. In doing so, Jacob also created some valuable standards for defining the difference between good and bad leadership qualities.

PEREK GIMEL: *Are We Permitted to Lie in the Cause of Peace?*

The Torah reports that, after Jacob's death and burial in Hebron, Joseph and his brothers return to Egypt. The brothers, however, fear that they are in danger. They say to one another: "What if Joseph seeks to pay us back for all the wrong that we did to him?"

So they decide to send a message to Joseph. They tell him: "Before his death your father left this instruction: So shall you say to Joseph, 'Forgive, I urge you, the offense and guilt of your brothers who treated you so harshly.'" (Genesis 50:15–17)

The message is a strange one and raises many important questions. A bit of research reveals three important facts: First, Joseph never told Jacob that his brothers had thought to kill him and then sold him into slavery. Second, none of the brothers is reported to have told Jacob what they did to Joseph. Third, Jacob never indicates that he knew what the brothers had done to Joseph or gives any instruction about what they should say to Joseph after his death.

So why do the brothers make up such a story? Why do they lie to Joseph?

Many biblical interpreters have explored these questions. One of the first was Rabbi Levi, who lived in the Land of Israel during the third century. Rabbi Levi explains that, prior to Jacob's death, Joseph invited his brothers to dinner with him every evening. Suddenly, they were not invited, and they began to suspect that his attitude toward them had changed and that they were in danger.

Rabbi Isaac, who taught at the same time as Rabbi Levi, disagrees with his interpretation. The brothers, he suggested, suspected that Joseph was plotting to harm them because, on their way back to Egypt from Hebron, they watched Joseph stop at the pit into which they had thrown him before selling him into slavery. Rabbi Levi explains that, when the brothers saw him standing by the pit, they feared that he remembered how badly they

had treated him and that he would soon seek revenge. (*Genesis Rabbah* 100:8)

The modern Torah commentator Nehama Leibowitz explains Joseph's behavior and his brothers' reaction to it in a slightly different way. She points out that, after Jacob's death, Joseph, who was still in mourning, was overwhelmed by the responsibilities of governing Egypt. His schedule did not permit him to see his brothers and family each day as he had when his father was sick. Jacob's illness and all the responsibilities of his burial no longer held the family together. As a result, the brothers may have suspected that Joseph's attitude toward them had changed and that he was about to harm them. Perhaps, that is why they decided to lie to him about what Jacob had said before his death. (*Studies in Bereshit,* pp. 556–558)

Nearly all commentators agree that the brothers lied to Joseph about Jacob's instructions to them. While commentators may cite different reasons for the behavior of the brothers, all conclude that the brothers were deliberately dishonest. That, however, is not the only instance of deception in our Torah portion. Joseph and his brothers also kept the truth from their father about how they had sold Joseph into slavery.

Some interpreters point out that the brothers said nothing because they feared their father would curse them. Other commentators claim that Joseph said nothing because he did not want to make trouble for his family. In other words, for the sake of peace, Joseph and his brothers did not reveal to Jacob what had happened between them in the distant past.

Others paint a slightly different picture. They maintain that Joseph visited his father only a few times after his arrival in Egypt. Joseph feared that, if he visited him often, Jacob would ask him embarrassing questions about how he had reached Egypt. Joseph preferred avoiding such discussions. He did not want to be forced into explaining to his father that his brothers had lied about what they had done to him. Joseph realized that his father might never forgive his brothers if he knew that they had plotted to kill him and then decided to sell him into slavery. So, for the sake of peace in the family, Joseph seldom visited his father and refused to speak with him about the past. (*Pesikta Rabbati* on Genesis 48:1)

If this explanation is correct, then another question should be asked. Does Jewish tradition justify lying—or avoiding the truth—for the sake of peace?

Peace and truth
Peace without truth is a false peace. (*Rabbi Mendel of Kotzk*)

Seek peace
"Seek peace and pursue it." That means, seek it in your own place and pursue it in all other places. (*Jerusalem Talmud*, Peah *1:1*)

Peace is more important than anything else. (Sifra Bechukotai)

Great is peace. Quarreling is hateful. (Sifre *to* Naso *2*)

According to most interpreters of our Torah portion the answer is yes. For example, the respected president of the Sanhedrin in Jerusalem during the first century, Rabbi Shimon ben Gamaliel, taught that peace was so important that it was permissible to lie for the purpose of promoting it. This great leader of the Jewish people justified his argument by using Joseph and his brothers as an example. "They lied about what their father had said to them in order to convince Joseph not to punish them but to accept them and live with them peacefully as his brothers." (*Genesis Rabbah* 100:9)

Other commentators not only agree with Rabbi Shimon ben Gamaliel's position, but they elaborate on it. Rabbi Ila'a, quoting Rabbi Eleazar ben Shimon, says that, when the brothers altered the facts for the sake of peace, they did the right thing.

Rabbi Ishmael notes that even God occasionally changes the facts for the sake of peace. He explains that, when God told Sarah that she would bear a child, she replied that it would be impossible because Abraham "is an old man." (Genesis 18:9–15) But, for the sake of peace, Rabbi Ishmael says that God lied to Abraham about Sarah's reaction. Instead of reporting that she had responded with the insult "Abraham is an old man," God reported that she had said, "I am old."

One of Ishmael's students summarized his teacher's attitude when he concluded: "For the sake of family peace, even the Torah allows for misquotes or a shaving of the truth." (*Yevamot* 65b)

In the same commentary, Rabbi Nathan holds that it is a mitzvah, "an obligation," to lie or to change the facts if it will bring about peace. Illustrating his position, he recalls the story of God's asking Samuel to appoint David in place of Saul as king of Israel. Samuel is frightened that Saul will kill him. So God tells him to make it look as if he were going to offer a sacrifice. Then Saul will be fooled, and Samuel will be saved and able to appoint the new king. Samuel lies and lives, and Rabbi Nathan concludes by teaching, "For the sake of peace, you can lie." (*Yevamot* 65b)

But this is not always so. The modern interpreter Rabbi Elie Munk reports an important exception that appears in *Sefer Hassidim* (426): "If a person comes to you for a loan, and you do not want to give the money to him for fear that he will not repay it, you *do not* have the right to lie and say that you *do not* have the money to give him for a loan. You must tell him the truth. For the permission to tell a 'white lie' in the interest of peace applies *only* to cases that have already happened, and which cannot be changed, but not to events that are in the future."

In summary, the rule of lying for the sake of truth is as follows: If you are faced with a situation that has already happened, then, for the sake of peace, you can alter the memory of it, as the brothers did about what their father had instructed them to say to Joseph. Creating trust and caring among family members is more important than recalling accurately all the facts of the past, especially when we know those facts will only hurt others and divide the family into angry factions. But, when dealing with others in business or in other negotiations, you must not lie or deal in falsehoods.

The present and future must be built on honesty. Jewish tradition teaches: "Every person shall speak the truth with his neighbor." (Zechariah 8:16)

QUESTIONS FOR STUDY AND DISCUSSION

1. If the body is merely a repository for the soul, why does Jacob request that his bones be brought back to the Land of Israel? What does it say about Jacob's view of Egypt? What might the biblical authors have intended by his request?

2. Should parents present their children with critical evaluations? What are the dangers of such evaluations? What are the dangers if they are not offered? What do we learn from Jacob's critique of his sons?

3. Is there a difference between lying about the past to foster family peace and rewriting, distorting, or avoiding history in order to further better relations between nations? Examples might include avoiding such subjects as the Holocaust with Germans, civil rights for Indians or Blacks with Americans, or terrorism with Palestinians.

4. Can you think of an example when, for the sake of family unity and peace, it would be better to lie?

Glossary of Commentaries and Interpreters

(*For further information on those entries followed by an asterisk, see Introduction II in this book.*)

Abravanel, Don Isaac.*

Adani, David ben Amram (13th century). (See *Midrash ha-Gadol.*)

Akedat Yitzhak. A commentary to the Torah by Isaac ben Moses Arama. (See Arama, Isaac ben Moses.)

Alshikh, Moshe ben Adrianopolis (1508–1600). Lived and taught in Safed in the Land of Israel. His commentary to the Torah contains his Sabbath sermons.

Arama, Isaac ben Moses (1420–1494). Author of the Torah commentary *Akedat Yitzhak.* Spanish rabbi. Known for his sermons and allegorical interpretations of Torah. Defended Judaism in many public disputes with Christians and settled in Italy after the expulsion of Jews from Spain in 1492.

Ashkenazi, Eliezer ben Elijah (1513–1586). Lived in Egypt, Cyprus, Venice, Prague, and Posen. Died in Cracow. Emphasized the gift of reason and in his commentary, *Ma'aseh ha-Shem* (see below), urged students to approach the Torah with care and independence. Worked as a rabbi, Torah interpreter, and physician. (See *Ma'aseh ha-Shem.*)

Ashkenazi, Shimon (12th century). (See *Yalkut Shimoni.*)

Ashkenazi of Yanof, Jacob ben Isaac (13th century). Author of *Tze'enah u-Re'enah.* (See *Tze'enah u-Re'enah.*)

Astruc, Anselm Solomon. (See *Midrashei Torah.*)

Attar, Chaim ibn (1696–1743). Born in Morocco and settled in Jerusalem where he opened a school. His Torah commentary, *Or ha-Chaim* (see below), combines talmudic and mystical interpretations.

Avot or *Pirke Avot,* "Sayings of the Fathers." A book of the *Mishnah,* comprising a collection of statements by famous rabbis.

Avot de-Rabbi Natan (2nd century). Compiled by Rabbi Nathan, sometimes called "Nathan the Babylonian." Based on *Pirke Avot.*

Ba'al Ha-Turim, Yaakov (1275–1340). Born in Germany. Fled persecutions there in 1303 and settled in Spain. Author of the very important collection of Jewish law *Arba'ah Turim,* "Four Rows," the basis for the later *Shulchan Aruch,* "Set Table," by Joseph Karo. His Torah commentary known as *Ba'al ha-Turim* often includes interpretations based on the mathematical meanings of Hebrew words.

Bachya ben Asher (14th century). Lived in Saragossa, and Aragon. Known for his Torah commentary.

Bachya ben Joseph ibn Pakuda (11th century). Lived in Spain as poet and author of the classic study of Jewish ethics *Hovot ha-Levavot,* "Duties of the Heart." (See *Hovot ha-Levavot.*)

Bamberger, Bernard J.*

Berlin, Naphtali Zvi Judah (1817–1893). Head of the famous yeshivah at Volozhin. Supporter of early Zionism, his Torah commentary, *Ha-Emek Davar* (see below), is a record of his lectures on the weekly portions.

Bin Gorion, Micha Joseph (Berdyczewski) (1865–1921). Though a Russian citizen, spent most of his years in Germany. A Hebrew writer, his collection of Jewish folktales, *Mimekor Yisrael* (see below), is considered a classic.

Biur.*

Buber, Martin Mordecai (1878–1965). Born in Vienna. Became renowned as a twentieth-century philosopher. With Franz Rosenzweig, translated the Bible into German. His *Moses* is a commentary on Exodus.

Caspi, Joseph ben Abba Mari (1280–1340). A philosopher and commentator who lived in France. His commentary seeks to blend reason with religious faith.

Da'at Zekenim mi-Ba'alei ha-Tosafot. A thirteenth-century collection of Torah commentaries by students of Rashi who sought to resolve contradictions found within the talmudic discussions of the rabbis.

De Leon, Moses. (See *Zohar.*)*

Deuteronomy Rabbah. One of the early collections of *midrashim.**

Dubno, Solomon. (See *Biur.*)*

Ecclesiastes Rabbah. One of the early collections of *midrashim.**

Edels, Shemuel Eliezer ben Yehudah Halevi (1555–1631). One of the best known and respected interpreters of Talmud. Born in Cracow. Also known as the *Maharsha.*

Epstein, Baruch (1860–1942). Murdered by the Nazis in the Pinsk ghetto. (See *Torah Temimah.*)

Genesis Rabbah. One of the early collections of *midrashim.**

Gittin. A tractate of Talmud that discusses the laws of divorce.

Guide for the Perplexed. A philosophical discussion of the meanings of Jewish belief written by Moses Maimonides. (See Maimonides, Moses.)

Ha-Cohen, Meir Simcha (1843–1926). (See *Meshekh Hochmah.*)

Ha-Emek Davar. A Torah commentary written by Naphtali Zvi Judah Berlin. (See Berlin, Naphtali Zvi Judah.)

Ha-Ketav ve-ha-Kabbalah. A Torah commentary written by Joseph Zvi Mecklenburg.*

Halevi, Aharon (1230–1300). Born in Gerona, Spain. Served as rabbi and judge in Barcelona, Saragossa, and Toledo. Lecturer in Montpellier, Provençe, France, where he died. While *Sefer ha-Hinuch* (see below) is said to have been written by him, many doubt the claim.

Halevi, Isaac ben Yehudah (13th century). (See *Paneah Raza.*)

Halevi, Yehudah (1080–1142?). Born in Spain. Poet, philosopher, and physician. His book, *The Kuzari,* contains his philosophy of Judaism. It is a dialogue between the king of the Kazars and a rabbi who convinces the king of the superiority of Judaism.

Hallo, William W.*

Ha-Midrash ve-ha-Ma'aseh. A commentary to Genesis and Exodus by Yehezkel ben Hillel Aryeh Leib Lipschuetz. (See Lipschuetz, Yehezkel ben Hillel Aryeh Leib.)

Heinemann, Yitzhak (1876–1957). Born in Germany. Israeli scholar and philosopher. His *Ta'amei ha-Mitzvot,* "Reasons for the Commandments," is a study of the meaning of the commandments of Jewish tradition.

Hertz, Joseph Herman.*

Hirsch, Samson Raphael.*

Hirschensohn, Chaim (1857–1935). Born in Safed. Lived most of his life in Jerusalem. Supported the work of Eliezer ben Yehuda's revival of Hebrew. (See *Nimmukei Rashi.*)

Hizkuni. A Torah commentary by Hizkiyahu (Hezekiah) ben Manoah (13th century) of France.

Hoffman, David Zvi (1843–1921). A leading German rabbi. His commentary on Leviticus and Deuteronomy is based on lectures given in the 1870s, seeking to refute biblical critics who argued that the

Christian New Testament was superior to the Hebrew Bible.

Hovot ha-Levavot, "Duties of the Heart." A classic study of Jewish ethics by Bachya ben Joseph ibn Pakuda (see above). Concerned with the emphasis on ritual among the Jews of his times, Bachya argues that a Jew's highest responsibility is to carry out the ethical commandments of Torah.

Hullin. A tractate of Talmud that discusses laws dealing with killing animals for food.

Ibn Ezra, Abraham.*

Jacob, Benno.*

Kasher, Menachem. (See *Torah Shelemah*.)

Keley Yakar. A Torah commentary written by Solomon Ephraim ben Chaim Lunchitz (1550–1619) of Lvov (Lemberg) Poland.

Kiddushin. A tractate of Talmud that discusses laws of marriage.

Kimchi, David (RaDaK).*

Leibowitz, Nehama.*

Lekach Tov. A collection of *midrashim* on the Torah and the Five Scrolls (Song of Songs, Ruth, Lamentations, Ecclesiastes, and Esther), by Tobias ben Eliezer (11th century C.E.).

Lipschuetz, Yehezkel ben Hillel Aryeh Leib (1862–1932). Lithuanian interpreter of Torah and author of *Ha-Midrash ve-ha-Ma'aseh*. (See *Ha-Midrash ve-ha-Ma'aseh*.)

Luzzatto, Moshe Chaim (1707–1746). Known also as *Ramhal*. Italian dramatist and mystic whose commentaries were popular among chasidic Jews. His textbook on how to become a righteous person, *Mesillat Yesharim* became one of the most popular books on the subject of Jewish ethics. (See *Mesillat Yesharim*.)

Luzzatto, Samuel David.*

Ma'aseh ha-Shem. A commentary by Eliezer ben Elijah Ashkenazi published in 1583. (See Ashkenazi, Eliezer ben Elijah.)

Maimonides, Moses, Rabbi Moses ben Maimon (1135–1204). Known by the initials RaMBaM. Born in Cordova, Spain. Physician and philosopher. Wrote the *Mishneh Torah*, a code of Jewish law; *Guide for the Perplexed*, a philosophy of Judaism; *Sefer ha-Mitzvot*, an outline of the 613 commandments of Torah; and many other interpretations of Jewish tradition. Famous as a physician. Served the leaders in the court of Egypt.

MaLBIM, Meir Lev ben Yechiel Michael.*

Mechilta.*

Mecklenburg, Joseph Zvi. (See *Ha-Ketav ve-ha-Kabbalah*.)*

Megillah. A tractate of Talmud that discusses the biblical Book of Esther.

Mendelssohn, Moses.*

Meshekh Hochmah. A Torah commentary published in 1927. Written by Meir Simcha Ha-Cohen, rabbi of Dvinsk. Combines insights from the Talmud with a discussion of the philosophy of Judaism. (See Ha-Cohen, Meir Simcha.)

Mesillat Yesharim, "Pathway of the Righteous." A discussion of how one should pursue an ethical life. Written by Moshe Chaim Luzzatto (see above).

Messengers of God. A study of several important biblical personalities, by Elie Wiesel. (See Wiesel, Elie; also Bibliography in this book.)

Midrash Agadah. A collection of rabbinic interpretations. (See discussion of *midrashim*.)*

Midrash ha-Gadol. A collection of rabbinic interpretations dating to the first and second centuries, by David ben Amram Adani, a scholar living in Yemen. (See Adani, David ben Amram.)

Midrash Sechel Tov. Compiled by Menachem ben Solomon in 1139. Combines selections of *midrash* and *halachah* on every Torah portion.

Midrash Tanchuma. Known also as *Tanchuma Midrash Yelamedenu*. A collection said to have been collected by Rabbi Tanchuma (427–465 C.E.). Many of the *midrashim* begin with the words *Yelamedenu rabbenu*, "Let our teacher instruct us. . . ."*

Midrashei Torah. A Torah commentary by Anselm Solomon Astruc who was murdered in an attack on the Jewish community of Barcelona in 1391.

Mimekor Yisrael. A collection of folktales from Jewish tradition by Micha Joseph Bin Gorion (Berdyczewski). (See Bin Gorion.)

Mishnah.*

Mizrachi, Eliyahu (1440–1525). A Chief Rabbi of Turkey during the expulsion of Jews from Spain.

Helped many immigrants. Wrote a commentary to Rashi's Torah interpretation.

Morgenstern, Julian.*

Nachmanides.* (See RaMBaN.)

Nedarim. A tractate of Talmud that discusses vows or promises.

Nimmukei Rashi. A commentary on Rashi's Torah interpretation by Chaim Hirschensohn. (See Hirschensohn, Chaim.)

Numbers Rabbah. An early collection of *midrashim.**

Or ha-Chaim. A Torah commentary by Chaim ibn Attar. Combines talmudic observations with mystical interpretations. (See Attar, Chaim ibn.)

Paneah Raza. A Torah commentary by Isaac ben Yehudah Halevi who lived in Sens. (See Halevi, Issac ben Yehudah.)

Peli, Pinchas Hacohen (20th century). Jerusalem-born scholar, poet, and rabbi. His "Torah Today" column in the *Jerusalem Post* seeks to present a contemporary view of the meaning of Torah.

*Pesikta de-Rav Kahana.** A collection of *midrashim* or early rabbinic sermons based on Torah portions for holidays of the Jewish year. *Pesikta Rabbati* is similiar in both content and organization.

*Pesikta Rabbati.** (See *Pesikta de-Rav Kahana.*)

*Pirke de-Rabbi Eliezer.** A collection of *midrashim* said to have been written by the first-century C.E. teacher Rabbi Eliezer ben Hyrkanos. Contents include mystic interpretations of creation, early human life, the giving of the Torah at Mount Sinai, comments about the Book of Esther, and the Israelite experience in the Sinai.

Plaut, W. Gunther.*

RaDaK, Rabbi David Kimchi.*

RaMBaM, Rabbi Moses ben Maimon. (See Maimonides.)

RaMBaN, Rabbi Moses ben Nachman.* (See Nachmanides.)

RaSHBaM, Rabbi Shemuel (Samuel) ben Meir.*

RaSHI, Rabbi Shelomoh (Solomon) Itzhaki.*

Reggio, Yitzhak Shemuel (1784–1855). Known also as YaSHaR. Lived in Italy. Translated the Bible into Italian. Created a Hebrew commentary that sought to harmonize science and religion.

Rosenzweig, Franz (1886–1929). German philosopher. Worked with Martin Buber in translating the Bible into German. Best known for book *The Star of Redemption,* which seeks to explore the meanings of Jewish tradition.

Sa'adia ben Joseph Ha-Gaon.* (See also Introduction I of this book.)

Sanhedrin. A tractate of Talmud that discusses laws regulating the courts.

Sarna, Nahum M.*

Sefer ha-Hinuch. Presents the 613 *mitzvot,* "commandments," found within the Torah. Divided according to weekly Torah portions. Said by some to have been written by Aharon Halevi of Barcelona. (See Halevi, Aharon.)

Sforno, Obadiah.*

Shabbat. A tractate of the Talmud that discusses the laws of the Sabbath.

*Sifra.** A *midrash* on Leviticus. Believed by scholars to have been written during the fourth century C.E.

*Sifre.** A *midrash* on Numbers and Deuteronomy. Believed to have been composed during the fifth century C.E.

Simeon (Shimon) ben Yochai.* (See *Zohar.*)*

Solomon, Menachem ben. (See *Midrash Sechel Tov.*)

Sotah. A tractate of the Talmud that discusses laws concerning a woman suspected of adultery.

Speiser, Ephraim Avigdor.*

Steinsaltz, Adin (20th Century). An Israeli Talmud scholar. His book *Biblical Images* contains studies of various biblical characters.

Ta'amei ha-Mitzvot. (See Yitzhak Heinemann.)

Ta'anit. A tractate of the Talmud that deals with the laws concerning fast days.

*Talmud.** Combines the *Mishnah* and *Gemara.* Appears in two versions: the more extensive *Talmud Bavli,* "Babylonian Talmud," a collection of discussions by the rabbis of Babylonia from the second to the fifth centuries C.E., and *Talmud Yerushalmi,* "Jerusalem Talmud," a smaller collection of discussions from the second to the fourth centuries C.E.

Tanna Debe Eliyahu. A *midrash* and book of Jewish philosophy and commentary believed by scholars to have been composed during the third to tenth centuries. Author unknown.

Targum Onkelos.*

Targum Yerushalmi.*

Toledot Yitzhak.

Torah Shelemah. A study of each Torah portion, which includes a collection of early rabbinic interpretations along with a commentary by Rabbi Menachem Kasher of Jerusalem, Israel.

Torah Temimah. A Torah commentary by Baruch Epstein. Includes a collection of teachings from the Talmud on each Torah portion. (See Epstein, Baruch.)

Tosafot. "Supplementary Discussions" of the Talmud. Collected during the twelfth and thirteenth centuries in France and Germany and added to nearly every printing of the Talmud since.

Tzedeh Laderech. An interpretation of Rashi's Torah commentary by Issachar Ber ben Israel-Lazar Parnas Eilenberg (1550–1623), who lived in Italy.

Tze'enah u-Re'enah. A well-known Yiddish paraphrase and interpretation of the Torah. First published in 1618. Written for women by Jacob ben Isaac Ashkenazi of Yanof. Divided by weekly Torah portions. One of the first texts developed to educate women. (See Ashkenazi of Yanof, Jacob ben Isaac.)

Wessely, Naftali Herz. (See *Biur.*)*

Wiesel, Elie (1928–   ). Nobel Prize-winning novelist. Author of *Messengers of God,* among other books. (See *Messengers of God.*)

Yalkut Shimoni. A collection of *midrashim.* Believed to be the work of Shimon Ashkenazi. (See Ashkenazi, Shimon.)

Yevamot. A tractate of Talmud that deals with laws concerning sisters-in-law.

Yoma. A tractate of Talmud that deals with laws concerning Yom Kippur.

Zohar.*

Bibliography

Abbott, Walter M.; Gilbert, Arthur; Hunt, Rolfe Lanier; and Swain, J. Carter. *The Bible Reader: An Interfaith Interpretation.* New York: Bruce Publishing Co., 1969.

Adar, Zvi. *Humanistic Values in the Bible.* New York: Reconstructionist Press, 1967.

Adler, Morris. *The Voice Still Speaks.* New York: Bloch Publishing Co., 1969.

Aharoni, Yohanan, and Avi-Yonah, Michael. *The Macmillan Bible Atlas.* New York: Macmillan, 1976.

Alter, Robert. *The Art of Biblical Narrative.* New York: Basic Books, 1981.

Asimov, Isaac. *Animals of the Bible.* Garden City, New York: Doubleday, 1978.

Avi-Yonah, Michael, and Malamat, Abraham, eds. *Views of the Biblical World.* Chicago and New York: Jordan Publications, Inc., 1959.

Baron, Joseph L., ed. *A Treasury of Jewish Quotations.* New York: Crown Publishers, Inc., 1956.

Blumenthal, David R. *God at the Center.* San Francisco: Harper and Row, 1987.

Braude, William G., and Kapstein, Israel J., trans. Author unknown. *Tanna Debe Eliyahu.* Philadelphia: Jewish Publication Society, 1981.

Buber, Martin. *Moses.* New York: Harper and Row Publishers, Inc., 1958.

Bulka, Reuven P. *Torah Therapy: Reflections on the Weekly Sedra and Special Occasions.* New York: Ktav, 1983.

Chavel, Charles B., trans. *Ramban (Nachmanides) Commentary on the Torah.* New York: Shilo Publishing House, Inc., 1974.

Chiel, Arthur. *Guide to Sidrot and Haftarot.* New York: Ktav, 1971.

Chill, Abraham. *The Minhagim: The Customs and Ceremonies of Judaism, Origins and Rationale.* New York: Sepher-Hermon Press, 1979.

Cohen, Philip. *Rambam on the Torah.* Jerusalem: Rubin Mass Ltd. Publishers, 1985.

Culi, Yaakov. *The Torah Anthology, Yalkut Me'am Lo'ez.* Translated by Aryeh Kaplan. New York and Jerusalem: Maznaim Publishing Corp., 1977.

Danby, Herbert, trans. *The Mishnah.* London: Oxford University Press, 1933.

Deen, Edith. *All of the Women of the Bible.* New York: Harper and Brothers, 1965.

Doria, Charles, and Lenowitz, Harris, trans. and eds. *Origins, Creation Texts from the Ancient Mediterranean.* New York: Anchor Press, 1976.

Dresner, Samuel H., and Siegel, Seymour. *The Jewish Dietary Laws.* New York: Burning Bush Press, 1959.

Efron, Benjamin. *The Message of the Torah.* New York: Ktav, 1963.

Epstein, I., trans. and ed. *The Babylonian Talmud.* London: Soncino Press, 1952.

Fields, Harvey J. *Bechol Levavcha: With All Your Heart.* New York: Union of American Hebrew Congregations, 1976.

Freedman, H., and Simon, Maurice, trans. *Midrash*

Rabbah: Genesis, Vols. I and II. London: Soncino Press, 1961.

Friedman, Alexander Zusia. *Wellsprings of Torah.* Compiled and edited by Nison Alpert. Translated by Gertrude Hirschler. New York: Judaica Press, 1986.

Friedman, Rikchard Elliott. *Who Wrote the Bible?* New York: Summit Books, 1987.

Fromm, Erich. *You Shall Be as Gods.* New York: Holt, Rinehart and Winston, 1966.

Frye, Northrop. *The Great Code: The Bible and Literature.* New York: Harcourt Brace Jovanovich Publishers, 1981.

Gaster, Theodor H. *Festivals of the Jewish Year.* New York: William Morrow and Co., Inc. 1953.

Gilbert, Martin. *Jewish History Atlas.* New York: Macmillan, 1976.

Ginzberg, Louis. *Legends of the Jews.* Philadelphia: Jewish Publication Society, 1968.

Glatzer, Nahum N., ed. *Hammer on the Rock: A Midrash Reader.* New York: Schocken Books, 1962.

————. *On the Bible: 18 Studies.* New York: Schocken Books, 1968.

Goldman, Solomon. *In the Beginning.* Philadelphia: Jewish Publication Society of America, 1949.

Graves, Robert, and Patai, Raphael. *Hebrew Myths: The Book of Genesis.* New York: Greenwich House, 1983.

Greenberg, Moshe. *Understanding Exodus.* New York: Behrman House, 1969.

Herford, R. Travers. *Pirke Aboth, The Ethics of the Talmud: Sayings of the Fathers.* New York: Schocken Books, 1971.

Hertz, J.H., ed. *The Pentateuch and Haftorahs.* London: Soncino Press, 1966.

Heschel, Abraham J. *The Prophets.* Philadelphia: Jewish Publication Society, 1962.

Hirsch, Samson Raphael, trans. *The Pentateuch.* London, England: L. Honig and Sons Ltd., 1959.

The Interpreter's Bible. 12 vols. Nashville: Abingdon, 1951–1957.

Jacobson, B.S. *Meditations on the Torah.* Tel Aviv: Sinai Publishing, 1956.

Katz, Mordechai. *Lilmod U'lamade: From the Teachings of Our Sages.* New York: Jewish Education Program Publications, 1978.

Lamm, Maurice. *The Jewish Way in Death and Mourning.* New York: Jonathan David Publishers, 1975.

Leibowitz, Nehama. *Studies in Bereshit.* Jerusalem: World Zionist Organization, 1980.

————. *Studies in Shemot.* Jerusalem: World Zionist Organization, 1980.

————. *Studies in Vayikra.* Jerusalem: World Zionist Organization, 1980.

————. *Studies in Bemidbar.* Jerusalem: World Zionist Organization, 1980.

————. *Studies in Devarim.* Jerusalem: World Zionist Organization, 1980.

Levine, Moshe. *The Tabernacle: Its Structure and Utensils.* London: Soncino Press Ltd., 1969.

Maimonides, Moses. *The Book of Knowledge: Mishneh Torah.* Translated by Moses Hyamson. Jerusalem and New York: Feldheim Publishers, 1974.

Matek, Ord. *The Bible through Stamps.* New York: Hebrew Publishing Company, 1967.

Miller, Madeline S., and Lane, J. *Harper's Encyclopedia of Bible Life.* New York: Harper and Row Publishers, 1978.

Morgenstern, Julian. *The Book of Genesis.* New York: Schocken Books, 1965.

Munk, Eli. *The Call of the Torah.* Vols. I and II. Jerusalem and New York: Feldheim Publishers, 1980.

Neusner, Jacob. *Meet Our Sages.* New York: Behrman House, 1980.

Orlinsky, Harry M., ed. *The Torah: The Five Books of Moses.* A New Translation. Philadelphia: Jewish Publication Society, 1962.

————. *Understanding the Bible through History and Archaeology.* New York: Ktav, 1972.

Peli, Pinchas H. *Torah Today.* Washington, D.C.: B'nai B'rith Books, 1987.

Phillips, Anthony. Exodus Commentary. *The Cambridge Bible Commentary: New English Bible.* Cambridge, England: Cambridge University Press, 1972.

Plaut, W. Gunther, ed. *The Torah: A Modern Commentary.* Commentaries by W. Gunther Plaut and Bernard J. Bamberger. Essays by William W. Halls. New York: Union of American Hebrew Congregations, 1981.

Pritchard, James B., ed. *Ancient Near Eastern Texts Relating to the Old Testament.* Princeton, New Jersey: Princeton University Press, 1955.

Rabbinowitz, J., trans. *Midrash Rabbah* (Genesis, Exodus, Leviticus, Numbers, Deuteronomy). London: Soncino Press, 1961.

Rabinowitz, Louis I. *Torah and Flora.* New York: Sanhedrin Press, 1977.

Rad, Gerhard von. *Deuteronomy.* Commentary and translation by Dorothea Barton. Philadelphia: Westminster Press, 1966.

Reed, Allison. *The Story of Creation.* New York: Schocken Books, 1981.

Rosenbaum, M., and Silbermann, A.M., trans. *Pentateuch with Targum Onkelos, Haphtaroth and Rashi's Commentary.* Jerusalem: Silbermann Family Publishers, 1973.

Samuel, Maurice. *Certain People of the Book*. New York: Alfred A. Knopf, Inc., 1955.

Sandmel, Samuel. *Alone Atop the Mountain: A Novel About Moses and the Exodus*. New York: Doubleday, 1973.

Sarna, Nahum M. *Understanding Genesis*. New York: Schocken Books, 1966.

Schneerson, Menachem M. *Torah Studies*. London: Lubavitch Foundation, 1986.

Silberman, A.M., ed. *Pentateuch with Rashi Commentary*. Jerusalem: Silbermann Family Publishers, 1933.

Silver, Abba Hillel. *Moses and the Original Torah*. New York: Macmillan, 1961.

Simon, Solomon, and Morrison, David Bial. *The Rabbis' Bible*. New York: Behrman House, 1966.

Speiser, E.A., trans. *The Anchor Bible: Genesis*. New York: Doubleday, 1964.

Van Doren, Mark, and Samuel, Maurice. *In the Beginning . . . Love*. Edited by Edith Samuel. New York: John Day Company, 1973.

Wiesel, Elie. *Messengers of God*. New York: Random House, 1976.

Zakon, Miriam Stark, trans. *Tz'enah Ur'enah: The Classic Anthology of Torah Lore and Midrashic Commentary*. Brooklyn, New York: Mesorah Publications Ltd./Hillel Press, 1983.

Zeligs, Dorothy F. *Psychoanalysis and the Bible*. New York: Bloch Publishing Company, 1974.

Zlotowitz, Meir, trans. *Bereishis*. Art Scroll Tanach Series. New York: Mesorah Publications Ltd., 1977–1981.